Hindu kingship and polity in precolonial India

Through the analysis of eighteenth- and early nineteenth-century texts on the Hindu Kingdom of Kota in Rajasthan, Norbert Peabody explores the ways in which historical consciousness, or memory, is culturally constructed and how this consciousness informs social experience. By building on the premise that no society receives the past in a transparent, universal and objective way, he unravels how the past in Kota has been fashioned. His analysis demonstrates how different styles of historical interpretation sustain different regimes, and how specific varieties of social and political activity are founded upon these different perceptions of the past. In this way, he suggests not only that different societies establish different coordinates of value in their constructions of the past, but also that the very processes of social and political transformation differ from society to society. This is a fascinating and challenging book which promises to become a classic in the field.

NORBERT PEABODY is the Graduate Officer in Research at the Centre of South Asian Studies, University of Cambridge.

Cambridge Studies in Indian History and Society publishes monographs on the history and anthropology of modern India. In addition to its primary scholarly focus, the series also includes work of an interdisciplinary nature which contributes to contemporary social and cultural debates about Indian history and society. In this way, the series furthers the general development of historical and anthropological knowledge to attract a wider readership than that concerned with India alone.

A list of titles which have been published in the series is featured at the end of the book

You see before you the wrath of the lord breaking forth... There is naught but towns emptied of their folk, monasteries razed to the ground or given to flames, fields desolated... . Everywhere the strong oppresseth the weak and men are like fish of the sea that blindly devour each other.

–The bishops of Rheims assembled at Trosly in A.D. 909
(cited in Marc Bloch, *Feudal Society*, p. 3.)

Hindu kingship and polity in precolonial India

Norbert Peabody
University of Cambridge

CAMBRIDGE
UNIVERSITY PRESS

Published in South Asia by

Foundation Books Pvt. Ltd.
CAMBRIDGE HOUSE
4381/4, Ansari Road
Daryaganj, New Delhi – 110002

First South Asian Edition 2006

ISBN 81-7596-366-2
This edition is for sale in South Asia only, not for export elsewhere.

This edition of *Norbert Peabody / Hindu kingship and polity in precolonial India* is published by arrangement with Cambridge University Press, The Edinburgh Building, Shaftesbury Road, Cambridge CB2 2RU, UK.

Published by Manas Saikia for Foundation Books Pvt. Ltd. and printed & bound at Raj Press, R-3 Inderpuri, New Delhi 110 012.

Contents

Sources

The material presented in this book draws, in part, on three of my previously published essays. These are:

'The King is Dead, Long Live the King!, or Karmic Kin(g)ship in Kotah', in *Gods, Kings, and Tigers: The Art of Kotah*, ed. Stuart Cary Welch (Munich: Prestel Verlag, 1997), pp. 73–82.

'In Whose Turban Does the Lord Reside?: The Objectification of Charisma and the Fetishism of Objects in the Hindu Kingdom of Kota', *Comparative Studies in Society and History* 33, 4 (October 1991): 726–754.

'*Kota Mahajagat*, or the Great Universe of Kota: Sovereignty and Territory in 18th Century Rajasthan', *Contributions to Indian Sociology* (N.S.) 25, 1 (January–June 1991): 29–56.

In some instances, the substance of these articles has been subtly reworked; in other instances, it has been massively transformed; and in yet other instances, it has not been altered at all. Whatever the case, I hope that, in bringing this material together in this way, I have managed to present in this book a picture of kingship in Kota that is greater than the sum of its constituent parts.

Illustrations

Plates

Figures

Maps

Conventions followed in the text

A well-known Hindi proverb, oft-repeated by British colonial officials, claims that in India 'the language changes every four *kos*,[1] the water every two' (*kos kos pai pani badle, char kos pai bani*).[2] Though this proverb, in British hands, naturalized Indian unintelligibility and irrationality, through the instrumentality of water, and moralized it, through the root metaphor of Babel, it does alert us to a linguistic complexity that characterizes many parts of India. The arguments presented in this book draw upon sources written in four interrelated languages: Hindi, Middle Marwari, Braj Bhasha, and Dingal.

In order to enhance the recognizability of Indian terms amidst this linguistic complexity, I have chosen to render all words in their standard Hindi form rather than their other avatars. There are two exceptions to this general rule. First, I employ Sanskritic spellings (with the word final and intersyllabic /a/) for terms that have already entered the academic lexicon through the tradition of Indology. I thus write *dharma* instead of *dharm*. By the same token, I retain the word final /a/ for words ending in conjunct consonants, such as *mantra* or *bhakta*, where they are commonly vocalized today. Second, when transliterating longer phrases or sentences, I retain the spellings of the original language.

I employ customary English spellings for proper names, place names, or personal titles. Finally, in pluralizing Indian words when used in the context of an English language sentence, I follow the English pattern by adding an /s/ at the end of the term. As non-specialist readers tend to find

[1] One *kos* equals approximately two miles or three kilometres.

[2] David Magier reports of a similar Marwari maxim from western Rajasthan: *baram kosam bhasa badle, tisam kosam mausim*, or 'language changes every twelve *kos*, weather every thirty'. See Magier, 'The Language of the Bard', in *A Carnival of Parting*, by A. Gold (Berkeley: University of California Press, 1992), p. 339. In the Hadauti language of southeastern Rajasthan there is a further related couplet, *boli boli ko antro, boli boli ko pharak/ap kaho pharista, mhan kahan jarakh*, or 'languages differ so much [from place to place] that [when] you say [the word for] angel, I understand [lit. 'say', the word for] hyena'.

diacritical marks off-putting (and specialist readers find them unnecessary), I have not employed them. Otherwise, I generally employ the transliteration scheme used by R. S. McGregor in *The Oxford Hindi–English Dictionary*. Indian words are only italicized the first time that I introduce them in the book.

1 Introduction: The logic of the fish

Classical Indian texts regularly depict a kingless age as an anathema. A country without a king is cursed with every holocaust from the merely despairing (barbarian invasion, drought, and pestilence) to the insufferable (an insecurity of personal property, a lapse in the teaching of the Vedas, and the inability to give daughters in marriage). Such an unfortunate realm is said to be governed by the 'logic of the fish' (Skt. *matsya-nyaya*), or the principle whereby big fish devour little fish.[1] This expression, however, is not a straightforward translation into a diluvian context of the more familiar law of the jungle. For one, in emphasizing the epistemological foundations of domination, as opposed to the more formal laws of command, 'logic of the fish' asserts an indigenous theory *avant la lettre* reminiscent of Michel Foucault's equation of knowledge with power insofar as specific discursive forms have the subtly prejudicial ability to institutionalize and naturalize attendant regimes of authority. Second, the Sanskrit expression also differs from its western counterpart in that some mediæval *sastri*s supplemented the preceding reading of *matsya–nyaya* – in which big fish eat little ones – with an even more fearful reading – in which little fish eat big ones![2] The unexpected subversion of the natural 'order of things' in this reading alerts us to the fact that all structures of domination, no matter how seemingly base or fundamental, are susceptible to reconfiguration.

Heeding these general precepts, this book explores the specific ways in which royal power was manifest, unsettled, and transformed in the Rajasthani kingdom of Kota during the eighteenth and early nineteenth centuries under late precolonial and early colonial rule. In undertaking this inquiry, this book has two principal aims. The first is to question a

1 The most well-known usage of the expression occurs in the *Mahabharata*, Santiparva 15.30 and 67.16 in two teachings to King Yudhishthira. The term also appears in the *Kautiliya Arthasastra* I.4.13, and it informs *Manu* VII.20, *Narada* XVIII.15, and *Visnudharmottara upapurana* II.2.1–16.

2 I am grateful to McKim Marriott (personal communication: 6 January 1993) for first alerting me to this interpretation.

pervasive ahistoricism that characterizes most ethnohistorical analyses of precolonial political relations in India. In the laudable attempt to reveal the cultural basis for political relations in 'traditional' India, many of these analyses have unwittingly presented visions of precolonial political culture as internally consistant, thoroughly integrated, and largely consensual. In their close attention to the cultural construction of politics, they have lost sight of the politics of culture. The data and analysis presented here will show that political relations in Kota were riven with tensions, paradoxes, and contradictions that were the grist for political contestation and cultural dynamism which led to significant historical transformations even prior to the substantial dislocations caused by the arrival of British colonial power. In other words, while retaining many of the lessons of ethnohistory, this book seeks to recoup a concern for processes of historical change provided, of course, that change is charted against cultural values and orientations that derive from the society under examination.

This book's second aim is a direct outcome from the first insofar as it explores how these tensions and politics then informed particular features of the early colonial encounter. Ever since the publication of Edward Said's *Orientalism*, western scholarship has derived considerable benefits from its attentions to how colonial ways of knowing the 'East' enabled many aspects of European domination over the 'East'.[3] Said's central insight – which initially focused on academic and literary representations – has since been expanded by other writers who have explored how colonial ways of 'knowing the country' were also instantiated through apparently benign colonial institutions and administrative structures such as the census, the geographic and archaeological surveys, public health regimes, and colonial architecture and town planning.[4] This body of research and argumentation has fostered at least one critical analytic distortion, namely a tendency to represent the colonized as largely inconsequential, passive onlookers of the colonial encounter or, when they

[3] Edward Said, *Orientalism* (New York: Routledge & Kegan Paul, 1978).

[4] Bernard Cohn, 'The Census, Social Structure and Objectification in South Asia', *Folk* 26 (1984): 25–49; Arjun Appadurai, 'Number in the Colonial Imagination', in *Orientalism and the Postcolonial Predicament: Perspectives on South Asia*, eds Carol A. Breckenridge and Peter van der Veer, pp. 314–339 (Philadelphia: University of Pennsylvania Press, 1993); Matthew H. Edney, *Mapping an Empire: The Geographical Construction of British India, 1765–1845* (Chicago: University of Chicago Press, 1990), David Arnold, 'Cholera and Colonialism', *Past and Present* 113 (1986): 118–151, and *Colonizing the Body: State Medicine and Epidemic Disease in Nineteenth-Century India* (Berkeley: University of California Press, 1993); Veena Talwar Oldenberg, *The Making of Colonial Lucknow, 1756–1877* (Princeton: Princeton University Press, 1984); Marriam Dossal, *Imperial Designs and Indian Realities: The Planning of Bombay City, 1845–1875* (Delhi: Oxford University Press, 1991).

occasionally did take to action, as unwitting imperial prætorians. However, in marginalizing indigenous agendas from the telling of colonialism's history, much 'post-Orientalist' scholarship ironically may come closer to success where colonialism itself tried and failed; that is, in suppressing native agency. This book will show that colonial power did not impose itself monolithically from outside, but arose much more dialogically from within the conditions that were manifest locally, with local agents often able to redirect the potentialities of colonial power to serve agendas at a tangent from, if not diametrically opposite to, the agendas of colonial power. This revelation is in no way meant to offer an apology for European colonialism. There is no excuse for the military conquest and economic exploitation of India during the colonial period. It is hoped, however, that it will stimulate more subtle understandings of the social, political, and epistemological dynamics involved in the colonial encounter.

State-formation in late precolonial India: history and ethnohistory

It has now been four decades since historians began to voice their unease with the application of models of the state deriving from European contexts (especially those associated with the unitary nation-state or one of its western precursors, such as feudalism) to the traditional royal polities of India.[5] During this time, there has been a concerted attempt to root academic analysis of traditional political relations in India within the constellation of meanings that Indians themselves applied to those relations. In taking this 'anthropological turn', western scholarship has grown increasingly sensitive to the manifold ways that power is culturally constructed and varies across space and time. For India, surely the pioneering, if no less controversial, work in this regard has been Burton Stein's study of the 'segmentary state' as he initially applied the concept to the Chola Empire. Here Stein offered a model of the traditional Indian polity that did not share with the modern unitary state its undivided sovereignty over a bounded territory, nor its centralized government supported by an integrated administrative bureaucracy, nor its monopoly

[5] Two early pieces that contrasted the decentralized character of precolonial state formations in India with models of the unitary state are Bernard Cohn's 'Political Systems in Eighteenth Century India: The Banares Region', *Journal of the American Oriental Society* 83 (1962): 312–320, and Robert Eric Frykenberg's 'Traditional Processes of Power in South India: An Historical Analysis of Local Influence', *Indian Economic and Social History Review* 1 (1963): 122–142. The best statement outlining the pitfalls in applying notions of European feudalism to the Indian context is Harbans Mukhia's 'Was There Feudalism in Indian History?', *Journal of Peasant Studies* 8 (1981): 273–310.

over the use of coercive force.[6] Stein proffered a more open-ended and largely decentralized conception of the state which was composed of a 'pyramidal' agglomeration of functionally autonomous political segments. Central to Stein's thesis was a conceptual distinction between 'political sovereignty', which he saw operating within each autonomous segment ranged around the royal centre, and 'ritual sovereignty', which was exercised by the 'anointed king' at the centre over his peripheral chiefs.

Although Stein's initial inspiration for his model derived from Aidan Southall's study of political organization among the Alur in southern Africa,[7] Stein was no slavish imitator. He reworked many aspects of Southall's thesis to provide a better fit with south Indian historical experience. For example, Stein identified the *nadus* (territorially based 'chieftainships'), which had no counterpart among the Alur, as the basic segments of the south Indian mediæval polity.[8] In this way, he did not root his version of the segmentary state in a 'segmentary lineage system' as had Southall and, later, Richard Fox.[9] He also noted some contradictions in Southall's original formulation (or at least differences with the

[6] The first full-blown statement of Stein's model appeared in his *Peasant State and Society in Medieval South India* (Delhi: Oxford University Press, 1980), especially pp. 264–285. Stein also previewed important facets of it in his article, 'The Segmentary State in South Indian History', in *Realm and Region in Traditional India*, ed. R. G. Fox (Durham: Duke University Program in Comparative Studies on Southern Asia, Monograph and Occasional Paper Series, No. 14, 1977), pp. 3–51. See also his essay, 'The Segmentary State: Interim Reflections', *Purusartha* 13 (1991): 217–238 as well as his application of this model to the Vijayanagar Empire in his *The New Cambridge History of India*, Volume I:2: *Vijayanagara* (Cambridge: Cambridge University Press, 1989).

[7] Aidan Southall, *Alur Society: A Study in Processes and Types of Domination* (Cambridge: W. Heffer, 1953).

[8] Stein, *Peasant State*, pp. 270–272.

[9] Stein was not the first South Asianist to look to Southall's segmentary state for inspiration. Several years earlier, Richard Fox had employed the model in his study of Rajput political structures in precolonial Uttar Pradesh. However, whereas Stein's interest in segmentation extended only insofar as it defined a set of structural relations among differentiated poltical units, Fox 'literalized' Southall's model by seeing a segmentary lineage system as the foundation underlying the segmentary state. This use of Southall's model left Fox open to several criticisms. Southall himself, for example, pointed out that, unlike Alur lineages, Rajput lineages did not ramify the entire length of the social hierarchy but were confined with a relatively small elite, dare I say, segment of society and therefore could not provide the foundation underlying all aspects of political segmentation in these polities. Similarly, Rajput polities were often nested within larger non-Rajput state formations – Mughal, Maratha, or British – with whom kinship links, at least in the conventional sense, did not extend. Moreover, as Muzzafar Alam noted the territorial spread of the Rajput lineages and their sub-divisions did not always map onto the relevent political units they were supposedly underlying. See Richard G. Fox, *Kin, Clan, Raja, Rule: State-Hinterland Relations in Preindustrial India* (Berkeley: University of California Press, 1971); Aidan Southall, 'The Segmentary State in Africa and Asia', *Comparative Studies in Society and History* 30 (1988): 52–82; Muzzaffar Alam, *The Crisis of Empire in Mughal North India: Awadh and the Punjab, 1707–1748* (Delhi: Oxford University Press, 1986), pp. 106–107.

Alur case), such as regarding his understanding of the distribution of coercive force between central and peripheral foci of power.[10] Most importantly, however (and this is Stein's enduring legacy), he took Southall's notion of 'ritual hegemony' and developed it with reference to the specific meanings attached to political relations in south India through his notion of 'ritually incorporative kingship' as constituted in important south Indian royal rites, such as the *mahabhiseka* or the *asvamedha*. This endeavour thus provided an important cultural basis for evaluating the nature of power in the south Indian polity, at least as exercised within the circumscribed domain of 'ritual sovereignty'.

More recently Stein's interest in the cultural construction of authority has been extended and deepened by Nicholas Dirks through his analysis of royal gift-giving in the south Indian 'little kingdom' of Pudukkottai in which he argued that the ritual, or symbolic, dimensions of authority permeated all political relations within the kingdom and not just those articulated by the 'anointed king' at the centre. Thus while heeding Stein's concerns about how power can be constituted differently in different cultures, Dirks simultaneously questioned the separability of 'political sovereignty' and 'ritual sovereignty' that was such a prominent feature of Stein's model. Instead Dirks aimed to fuse the two. In doing so, Dirks's analysis converged with Clifford Geertz's well-known formulation of the Balinese 'theatre-state' insofar as it reversed most conventional understandings of the relationship between ritual and power by suggesting that 'power served pomp, not pomp power' and 'ceremony was not form but substance'.[11]

Dirks's principal contribution, however, lay in his identification of a specific idiom – the royal gift – that articulated political hierarchies throughout the length and breadth of the kingdom. Building upon Marshall Sahlins's famous suggestion that chiefly pooling and redistribution of goods establishes a ranked centricity within groups,[12] Dirks argued that royal gift-giving – paradigmatically of honours, titles, and tax-free lands known as *inams* – was an essential royal activity whose performance *constituted* Hindu kingship and, hence, the polity. This view rested on a cultural logic that affirmed the king's divinity and in which the king's

[10] Stein, *Peasant State*, pp. 269–270.

[11] Clifford Geertz, *Negara: The Theatre-State in Nineteenth Century Bali* (Princeton: Princeton University Press, 1980), p. 13. Several critiques have noted, however, that at key moments in his analysis of the dynamic tensions animating Balinese politics, Geertz reverts to the Steinian type of separation between 'ritual' and 'political' power discussed above. See, for example, S. J. Tambiah, 'A Reformulation of Geertz's Conception of the Theatre-State', in *Culture, Thought and Social Action: An Anthropological Perspective* (Cambridge, MA: Harvard University Press, 1985), pp. 316–338.

[12] Marshall Sahlins, 'On the Sociology of Primitive Exchange', in *Stone Age Economics* (New York: Aldine de Gruyter, 1972 [1965]), pp. 185–275.

gift to his political clients represented the sharing of a portion of his munificent, celestial persona. In return, clients who accepted the royal gift established their graded incorporation into the whole polity embodied by the king at its centre. For Dirks:

> The substance of the gift – the land rights, the titles, emblems, honors, and privilege of service, usufruct and command – was the partial sovereign substance of the king. All those who were given (and who accepted) gifts became part of the whole king, and by implication the king's realm, the kingdom. Participation in the whole was not, however, unranked, for the differential nature and contingent character of all these entitlements provided the basis for the creation of a political hierarchy... Ultimately, entitlements by their very nature constituted hierarchy through a logic of variable proximity to the king, to sovereignty itself.[13]

According to Dirks, then, the alienation of land from the king to military clients was not a manifestation of royal weakness (an inability to maintain control over valuable material resources) but became, somewhat ironically, the basis of an alternative form of hierarchy and the very foundation of royal power. Indian kings were powerful insofar as they unstintingly gave honours, titles, and land to their clients. In this way, Dirks fashioned a conception of the precolonial polity that was not calibrated against its success or, more usually, its failure to live up to Eurocentric criteria of state-formation. Instead Dirks established a more sympathetic understanding of the Indian polity from coordinates established within the cultural tradition itself.

The problem with Dirks's analysis is that not all precolonial sources spoke with one voice on matters such as gift-giving, especially in tax-free land.[14] Thus consider, for instance, the admonitions of the early eighteenth-century *Ajnapatra*, or Royal Edict, composed for the Maratha king Shambaji of Kolhapur (r. 1712–60) by one of his ministers. This edict enjoined the king to raise and maintain a large salaried, standing army in preference to levies provided by estate-holders whose loyalties were regarded with circumspection.[15] Concerning these estate-holders, the minister warned:

[13] Nicholas Dirks, *The Hollow Crown: Ethnohistory of an Indian Kingdom* (Cambridge: Cambridge University Press, 1987), p. 129.

[14] In this regard, it is significant to note that Dirks relied on an extremely narrow range of texts, almost exclusively *vamcavalis*, in his analysis of the 'discourse on kingship'. Even within the Mackenzie Collection, which itself is a selective distillation of genres, *vamcavalis* comprise only a small proportion of the total range of available texts.

[15] Ramachandrapat Amatiya, 'The Ajnapatra or Royal Edict Relating to the Principles of Maratha State Policy', trans. S. V. Puntambekar, in *Journal of Indian History* 8 (1929): 83–105, 207–233.

They are not inclined to live on whatever watan [hereditary landed estate] they possess, or to always act loyally to the king... All the time they want to acquire new possessions bit by bit, and to become strong; and after becoming strong their ambition is to seize forcibly from some, and to create emnities and depredations against others... When a foreign invasion comes they make peace with the invader with a desire for gaining or protecting a watan, meet personally with the enemy, [and then] allow the enemy to enter the kingdom... For this reason the control of these people has to be very cleverly devised.[16]

Although the edict urged the king not to confiscate *pre-existing* landed estates from their hereditary holders, it warned the king of the dangers of granting *new* lands to his servants:

[It] is a great injustice to give lands as *inams* to servants or vritti-holders [hereditary office-holders] for the purpose of achieving a task. A king, if he be an enemy of his kingdom, should be generous in granting lands. A king is called the protector of the land for the sake of preserving the land, but if the land be given away, over what would he rule? whose protector will he be?... [A] king who wishes to rule a kingdom, to increase it and to acquire fame as one who is skilled in politics should not at all get infatuated and grant land to the extent of even a barley corn. To say that servants who have done service which is useful from generation to generation should be given something which would continue with them hereditarily is not proper.[17]

André Wink has called our attention precisely to the agonistic political environment underlying the *Ajnapatra*'s stern counsel with his discussion of *fitna* – the drawing away of allegiance or sedition – that quickened many eighteenth-century, north Indian polities. In characterizing the Indian state as 'a form of institutionalized dissidence',[18] Wink showed that sovereignty in India was shared with both subordinates *and* rivals in unbounded, overlapping domains. Attempts to woo the clients and local supporters of one's rival, to get them to switch allegiances (as well as attempts to prevent the foregoing), were crucial activities of Indian statecraft. As a result, political hierarchies of patrons and clients always remained open to contestation and negotiation, especially as they inflected the interests of rival, third parties.

In directing our attention to the discordant voice of sedition, it is not my intention to suggest, however, that the counterpoint to the incorporative dimensions of Dirks's 'redistributive polity' emerged out of some hard-nosed, extra-symbolic realpolitik. Dirks's mantra that the 'political' and the 'ritual' cannot be pried apart remains undiminished. What is no

[16] Ibid., pp. 214–215. [17] Ibid., pp. 217–218.

[18] André Wink, *Land and Sovereignty in India: Agrarian Society and Politics under the Eighteenth-Century Maratha Svarajya* (Cambridge: Cambridge University Press, 1986), p. 386.

longer tenable, on the other hand, is Dirks's assertion that in the precolonial polity 'the political world [was] a morally cohesive system'.[19] Rather we must recognize that there were various tensions and disjunctions in the meanings associated with political relations.[20] Moreover, each of these often overlapping, but not necessarily congruent, symbolic orientations had their own pragmatic entailments. We shall see that eighteenth-century north Indian society was dynamic and open to significant structural change as some of these faultlines became sites for linear, non-recurring socio-political transformations.[21]

One of the important outcomes of mapping these changes will be a deepening of the analytic potentialities of the discipline known as 'ethnohistory'. For many years now, it is has been a commonplace statement to suggest that no society receives the past in a transparent, universal, and objective way. Rather each society has its own manner of fashioning the past and the analyst must always be careful to assess exactly in what sense history exists for those who speak of it. This concern has led us to explore how different styles of historical reckoning instantiate different regimes of authority as well as the specific varieties of social and political action that may be built upon perceptions of the past. As Marshall Sahlins put it, 'different cultural orders have their own modes of historical action, consciousness, and determination – their own historical practice'.[22] However, what we have been less successful at showing is how these different ways of acting upon the past constituted different processes of

[19] Dirks, *The Hollow Crown*, p. 134.

[20] Despite Wink's marvellously 'thick' descriptions of many variant manifestations of *fitna*, the principal shortcoming of his book lies precisely in his failure to identify any of the conceptual paradoxes that ultimately motivated seditious behavior.

[21] It is in this interest in historical process that I part company with Stein's structural-functionalism. Even Dirks, who so carefully charted important transformations with the shift from Vedic sacrifice to the 'great gift' in early south Indian history, presented a largely static picture of the immediate precolonial era. Perhaps the most important attempt to break out of the structuralist straight-jacket of ethnohistory has been Tambiah's formulation of the 'galactic polity' in which he interprets the fluid and pulsating design of traditional Buddhist kingdoms of Southeast Asia against destabilizing contradictions and paradoxes within the over-all 'totality'. However, even the 'galactic polity' is a model of state-formation caught within a dynamic steady-state rather than a fully historicized one. See S. J. Tambiah, *World Conqueror and World Renouncer: A Study of Buddhism and Polity in Thailand against a Historical Background* (Cambridge: Cambridge University Press, 1976) and S. J. Tambiah, 'The Galactic Polity in Southeast Asia', in *Culture, Thought and Social Action: An Anthropological Perspective*, pp. 252–286 (Cambridge, MA: Harvard University Press, 1985 [1977]).

[22] Marshall Sahlins, *Islands of History* (Chicago: University of Chicago Press, 1985), p. 34. Among the important precursors of this position are Hayden White, *Metahistory: The Historical Imagination of Nineteenth Century Europe* (Baltimore: Johns Hopkins University Press, 1973); Shelly Errington, 'Some Comments on Style in the Meaning of the Past', *Journal of Asian Studies* 38: 231–244; S. J. Tambiah, *World Conqueror and World Renouncer*; and James T. Siegal, *Shadow and Sound: The Historical Thought of a Sumatran People* (Chicago: University of Chicago Press, 1979).

social change. It is no longer enough to suggest that different societies establish different coordinates of value in their constructions of the past. We must also consider the different processes of social and political transformation that are built upon those pasts.

Orientalism's legacy

This attention to historical process during the precolonial era should have profound implications for how we understand the operations, scope, and history of colonial power in India. While the Saidian tide has had a generally salutatory effect on the academy insofar as it called attention to the ways in which western academic practice must necessarily be included as part of the study of colonialism, it has not been without its own critical distortions and lacunæ. Detractors and followers alike have noted several shortcomings in Said's analysis.[23] At this point, let me mention three closely interrelated problems. The first pertains to the way in which Said baldly dichotomized Europe and the Orient into two radically opposed blocks each of which was internally homogeneous and fundamentally unified. In doing so, he did not give adequate consideration to how social difference established through colonial discourse inflected other sorts of social difference rooted in gender, religion, social class, or political faction. Said's unnuanced treatment of this matter blinded him from exploring how the interplay among these cross-cutting regimes of difference was refracted within the history of Orientalism itself. A second difficulty with Said's analysis is its treatment of Orientalism as a single discourse, undifferentiated across geographic space and over time. As such, Said represented colonial discourse as being internally consistent in its assumptions, propositions, and effects, with the result that it seamlessly reproduces itself in homeostatic fashion. This picture of consistency and stability entails a third problematic supposition, one which remains more implied than explicitly theorized in Said's analysis, but one that nonetheless exerts a powerful presence: namely that the colonized peoples whose lives came to be governed by these discourses were largely inconsequential to its formation and unfolding.

[23] Among the most trenchantly acerbic critiques of *Orientalism* are Sadik Jalal al-ᶜAzm, 'Orientalism and Orientalism in Reverse', *Khamsin: Journal of Revolutionary Socialists of the Middle East* 8 (1981): 5–26, and Aijaz Ahmad, 'Between Orientalism and Historicism: Anthropological Knowledge of India', *Studies in History* 7 (1991): 135–163. Equally important are two volumes of 'critical appreciations' of Said: Carol A. Breckenridge and Peter van der Veer, eds, *Orientalism and the Postcolonial Predicament: Perspectives on South Asia* (Philadelphia: University of Pennsylvania Press, 1993) and Gyan Prakash, ed., *After Colonialism: Imperial Histories and Postcolonial Displacements* (Princeton: Princeton University Press, 1995).

While the first two problems have received close attention in recent writings,[24] analyses of colonial power still routinely efface the presence of local peoples. Two principal lines of reasoning for this avowal can be discerned. The first, and arguably the weaker, is best represented by Gauri Vishwanathan in her well-known study of colonial policy on English education in India where she unequivocally states that:

> it is entirely possible to study the ideology of British education quite independently of an account of how Indians actually received, reacted to, imbibed, manipulated, reinterpreted, or resisted the ideological content of British literary education... If the colonial subject is a construct emanating from the colonizer's head, and therefore removed from history, the history to which the British responds, the impending 'event' to which his measures are so crucially attached, is real only to the extent that it provides the rationale for his actions. How the native *actually* responds is so removed from the colonizer's representational system, his understanding of the meaning of events, that it enters into the realm of another history of which the latter has no comprehension or even awareness.[25]

This proposition raises a troubling problematic for Vishwanathan, however, insofar as it establishes a profound – and surely unintended – ontological difference between colonizers and the colonized in terms of their ability to enter into and understand representational systems from outside their own cultural milieus. Although Vishwanathan denies the capacity of cultural translation to the colonizers, this capacity (or susceptibility) among the colonized is fundamental to how she understands their condition of subordination. Following Gramsci's suggestion that 'the supremacy of a social group manifests itself in two ways, as "domination" and as "intellectual and moral leadership"', Vishwanathan argues that colonial mastery was achieved in large measure through 'moral and intellectual suasion' that promoted 'voluntary cultural assimilation' among, at least, certain key Indian groups.[26] Indian commitment to British 'ways of being' could only have developed if Indians had some comprehension of the representational system of the colonizers, however partial that understanding may have been. If this were the case, then Vishwanathan must explain why it is the colonized were able to enter the British 'worldview' but not vice versa. If this were not the case and there were no comprehension on the part of Indians, then it is hard to imagine on what grounds the Indian commitment rested. Brute force? While this is certainly a

[24] Notable examples are Gauri Vishwanathan, *Masks of Conquest: Literary Study and British Rule in India* (London: Faber and Faber, 1990 [1989]); Ronald Inden, *Imagining India* (Oxford: Basil Blackwell, 1990); Thomas Metcalf, *The New Cambridge History of India*, Volume III.4: *Ideologies of the Raj* (Cambridge, UK: Cambridge University Press, 1994); Lata Mani, *Contentious Traditions: The Debate on* Sati *in Colonial India* (Berkeley: University of California Press, 1998).

[25] Viswanathan, *Masks of Conquest*, pp. 11–12.

[26] Ibid., pp. 1–2.

possibility, it is not the conclusion that Vishwanathan wants us to consider or aims to investigate.[27]

The more challenging case for asserting that the practices of the colonized had little net effect on the contours of colonial discourse has emerged from the contention that, far from altering or undermining the terms of that discourse, subaltern practices, even in dissent, have served, more often than not, to reinscribe and reinforce the dominant discourse's social validity. One of the most famous statements of this thesis has been Ashis Nandy's proposal that:

> the *ultimate* violence which colonialism does to its victims [is] that it creates a culture in which the ruled are constantly tempted to fight their rulers within the psychological limits set by the latter. It is not an accident that the specific variants of the concepts with which many anti-colonial movements in our time have worked have often been the product of the imperial culture itself and, even in opposition, these movements have paid homage to their respective cultural origins.[28]

This view then conceives resistance to be largely *isomorphic* with and reactive towards a 'totalizing' colonial discourse insofar as resistance is only able to exploit internal contradictions within the terms and conditions initially posited by the dominant discourse rather than ever being able to shift debate to new terrains. In ways that are somewhat reminiscent of Max Gluckman's use of the Aristotelian distinction between revolution and rebellion in his study of the Swazi *ncwala*, this view presents resistance as ultimately reinforcing the underlying structure of subaltern subordination rather than ever fundamentally transforming it.

Rosalind O'Hanlon in her review of the *Subaltern Studies* project, however, has noted that this position generally assumes 'that discourses have an existence which is prior to, and hence unsullied by, the interventions of those over whom they are to have jurisdiction'.[29] Colonial discourses are viewed as having their genesis entirely in western epistemologies and institutional constructs before the issue of native resistance to them or agency through them (for not all forms of native social action can be classified as 'resistance') is ever considered. But as O'Hanlon further remarks historically this is not the case.

[27] Indeed Vishwanathan claims, again following Gramsci, that 'cultural domination works by consent and can (and often does) *precede* conquest by force' (ibid., p. 1, emphasis added).

[28] Ashis Nandy, *The Intimate Enemy: Loss and Recovery of Self under Colonialism* (Delhi: Oxford University Press, 1983), p. 3.

[29] Rosalind O'Hanlon, 'Recovering the Subject: *Subaltern Studies* and Histories of Resistance in Colonial South Asia', *Modern Asian Studies* 22 (1988): 216. For similar concerns, see also Martha Kaplan and John D. Kelly, 'Rethinking Resistance: Dialogics of "Disaffection" in Colonial Fiji', *American Ethnologist* 21 (1994): 123–151, and Sherry B. Ortner, 'Resistance and the Problem of Ethnographic Refusal', *Comparative Studies in Society and History* 37 (1995): 173–193.

Rather, colonialism's discourses came into being as attempts at fields of knowledge precisely as a struggle between at least three parties: the Orientalist scholar, the native informant successful in convincing him of his authority to represent, and those others among the colonized unable to do so, but grievously aware of the potential disadvantages in which this would place them in any future political structure established under colonial power. The struggle was the site not only of contested understandings, but also of deliberate misrepresentations and manipulation, in which the seemingly omnipotent classifications of the Orientalist were vulnerable to purposeful misconstruction and appropriation to uses which he never intended, precisely because they had incorporated into them the readings and political concerns of his native informants.[30]

It is for this reason that the concluding part of this book will focus on the early colonial encounter for it is here that we can see a multiplicity of agendas and voices, not all of them of European origin, being inserted into Orientalist discourse from its very beginnings. In remaining alive to the 'dialogic' dimensions of Orientalism, the approach suggests that it was a more potentialist and open-ended set of practices than the reductionist and over-determined picture that heretofore has been typically tendered. Although beyond the scope of this book, this realization should allow us to see that Orientalism has a history too.

About the book

Given these theoretical interests, this book will focus on the century and a quarter encompassing the late precolonial and early colonial eras in Kota, roughly 1720 through 1840. Kota's initial political formation, however, dates to the early seventeenth century when Madho Singh Hada split Kota from its 'parent-state' of Bundi. Madho Singh, a younger son of Rao Ratan Singh Hada of Bundi, had originally held Kota in *jagir* (prebendal estate) from his father to whom he remained loyal throughout his life. But when Madho Singh's nephew (elder brother's son) suceeded Ratan Singh in 1631, Madho Singh used his influence at the Mughal court where he had served for many years to have his grant made permanent and direct from the Mughal Emperor and he performed his own *rajyabhisekha* (royal consecration rite) to signal his independence from Bundi. Despite these earlier origins, the early eighteenth century suggests itself as suitable beginning for this study on two grounds. First, the eighteenth century coincides with the precipitous decline of Muslim power in western India after the death in 1707 of the last great Mughal Emperor, Aurangzeb. As Mughal power waned, Kota emerged as a thriving 'successor state' that dominated much of southeastern Rajasthan and northern Malwa. Coincidentally, Aurangzeb's death occurred the

30 O'Hanlon, 'Recovering the Subject', pp. 216–217.

same year that Kota's most illustrious ruler, Maharao Bhim Singh, ascended the royal *gaddi* (Kota's low cushion-like throne). During his energetic thirteen-year reign (1707–20), Bhim Singh expanded the frontiers of his inherited domain approximately six-fold as he conquered many neighbouring territories, and the remainder of the eighteenth century remained a period of unparalleled economic and political vitality for Kota that, paradoxically, continued even after it became a tribute-paying client of the Maratha Empire in 1738.

A second reason for starting my analysis in the early eighteenth century is that it also coincides with the bringing of the Vallabha statue of Shri Brijnathji to Kota and the dedication of the kingdom to this tutelary deity, a manifestation of Krishna. The devotional (*bhakti*) sect of the Vallabha Sampraday had been growing in popularity in the urban centres of western India since the second half of the seventeenth century. In 1719, Maharao Bhim Singh purportedly took initiation into the sect and brought the image of Shri Brijnathji from Mathura, one of the sect's most sacred sites, and installed the god in a temple in his palace/citadel (*garh*). Bhim Singh's third son, Maharao Durjan Sal (r. 1723–56), then formalized and elaborated the worship of Shri Brijnathji and integrated the devotion to this deity into the rituals of the royal court. Furthermore, Durjan Sal also oversaw the arrival in Kota of the famous Vallabha image of Shri Mathureshji. This deity was brought to Kota from neighbouring Bundi in 1744 and installed in a temple in the main bazaar near the Patan Pol gate. The image of Shri Mathureshji ranked second only to Nathadvara's Shri Nathji as the Vallabha Sampraday's most revered deity and his presence in Kota made the city an important centre of pilgrimage and religious activity for the sect at large.

Taking my lead from sets of native concerns and points of reference initially suggested in both the dynastic and sectarian textual traditions of the period, the first two chapters of this book will use the religious statuary of the Vallabha Sampraday as a point of entry into an exploration of the conceptual fault-lines and disjunctures along which social contestation took place in eighteenth-century Kota. As such these chapters explore the heteroglossic conditions that quickened Kota's precolonial politics rendering them more multifarious, contentious, and truly dynamic (if somewhat less systematic) than previously appreciated. Chapter 2 opens this inquiry with an analysis of a fratricidal struggle within Kota's ruling dynasty during the decade after Bhim Singh's death. Through an exploration of how traditional histories of Kota recounted the events preceding this bloody struggle, especially with respect to the appearance, disappearance and reappearance of the kingdom's tutelary deity, this chapter shows how the system of genealogical descent that underlay royal legitimacy could be creatively repositioned in order to remoralize the murder of the heir-apparent to the throne by his younger brother. Chapter 3 then takes a relatively wide perspective and explores how this competitive politics within royal circles was also informed by the distinctive aspirations and agenda of non-royal groups in Kota, especially sectarian organizations and merchant communities. Again taking the possession and circulation of important religious statuary associated with the devotional sect of the Vallabha Sampraday as a starting point, this chapter examines the doctrinal beliefs behind attributions of their mystical powers as well as the political and economic forces through which these powers were indirectly maintained, augmented, or diminished. By unravelling several interrelated, but non-congruent, social dynamics through which doctrinal, political and economic factors could be combined, I chart how kings, sectarian hierarchs and traders were each able to define their own distinctive agendas vis-à-vis the images of the Vallabha Sampraday and how they attempted to realize those aspirations within complex social fields inhabited by other social agents with rival interests.

Chapter 4 focuses on political relations among Kota's ruling warrior elite. It explores how political authority was informed by the overlapping notions of 'service' and 'conquest' but shows how these two values entailed slightly different pragmatic orientations that often generated political and military conflict. The ubiquity of this strife will lead us to re-examine the agrarian economic foundations of the royal polity and will suggest the need to reformulate the way in which we understand the articulation between economic and political power in late precolonial India.

The last two chapters of the book collectively explore how the conceptual ambiguities and tensions informing political relations in Kota (and the material conditions that maintained them) were then implicated in instances of non-recurring political innovation and transformation. Chapter 5 analyses how Kota's powerful prime minister of the later eighteenth and early nineteenth centuries, Zalim Singh Jhala, blended traditional notions of royal service and agnatic kinship with Vallabha values associated with 'maternal devotion' into a novel amalgam in order to extend and strengthen his own grasp on power in Kota. In the process of doing this, he progressively infantilized the maharao, turning him into a figurehead who was isolated from active participation in many aspects of political practice that had traditionally fallen within his sphere of competence (as well as creating new forms of political practice from which the maharao was excluded). The last chapter of the book explores how the Maharao of Kota in the early nineteenth century attempted to take advantage of the ongoing colonial penetration into western India not only to reassert his traditional position within the polity but also to establish a more robust, originary and self-constituting form of kingship that was no longer rooted in webs of local social relations.

2 The king is dead, long live the king!: Karmic kin(g)ship in Kota

In the absence of regular and legitimate historical records, … [t]he poets are the chief… historians of Western India… There is a sort of compact or understanding between the bard and the prince, a barter of 'solid pudding against empty praise', whereby the fidelity of the poetic chronicle is somewhat impaired. This sale of 'fame', as the bards term it, by the court-laureates and historiographers of Rajast'han, will continue until there shall arise in the community a class sufficiently enlightened and independent, to look for no other recompense for literary labour than public distinction. – James Tod (*Annals and Antiquities of Rajast'han*, pp. x-xi)

On the day of the full moon in the month of Jeth of the year 1777 of the Vikrama era (or 20 June, A.D. 1720), Maharao Bhim Singh of Kota was defeated and slain in the battle of Pandhar in the Mughal province of Malwa, to Kota's southeast (map 1).[1] At the time of this unfortunate battle, Bhim Singh was fighting in the service of the Mughal emperor Muhammad Shah against Malwa's mutinous governor, Qilich Khan.[2] The date and outcome of the battle of Pandhar are surprisingly vouchsafed by numerous historical sources, some Mughal, some Rajasthani, some from Kota, and some from other Rajput polities, making it one of the earliest episodes in Kota's history amply verified by diverse documentation.[3]

1 Different sources give slightly different identifications for the place of this battle. The battle is variously placed at Pandhar, at Khandwa, at Ratanpur, and at Husainpur. All these localities are close-by in the same region of Madhya Pradesh. For a fuller discussion of the exact place of the battle, see William Irvine, *Later Mughals*, ed. Jadunath Sarkar (Calcutta: M. C. Sarkar & Sons, 1922), Volume II, p. 29.

2 From his base in Hyderabad, Qilich Khan (a.k.a. Chin Qilich Khan or, in Rajasthani sources, Khalij Khan) later succeeded in establishing one of the largest and longest-lived Mughal successor states. He became better known under his other titles of Asaf Jah and Nizam-ul-Mulk.

3 For a partial recitation of this documentation, see Joachim K. Bautze, 'Victory and Death of Maharao Bhim Singh of Kota', in *South Asian Archaeology 1989. Papers from the Tenth International Conference of South Asian Archaeologists in Western Europe*, ed. Catherine Jarrige (Madison, WI: Prehistory Press, 1992), p. 313; Irvine, *Later Mughals*, Volume II, pp. 28–34; and R. S. Mathur, *Relations of Hadas with Mughal Emperors (1568–1720 A.D.)* (Delhi: Deputy Publications, 1986), pp. 202–203.

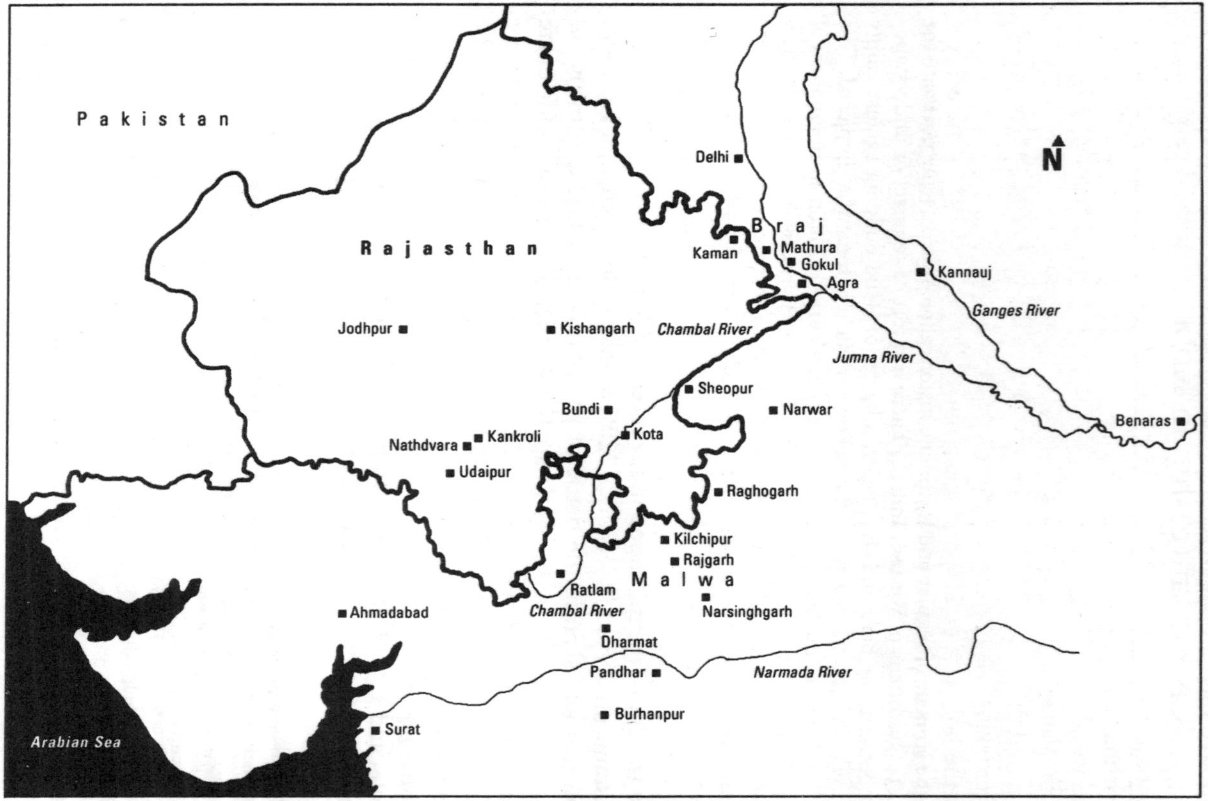

Map 1 Western India with the contemporary boundaries of Rajasthan

Unlike the Mughal sources, however, local accounts from Kota commonly endowed this date with a second loss. This tradition claims that mounted in the howdah of Bhim Singh's captured war elephant was the nine-centimetre tall, golden idol of Shri Brijnathji.[4] This manifestation of Lord Krishna was Bhim Singh's *ishtadevata* (personal, or chosen, deity) and was worshipped according to the practices of the *bhakti* (devotional) sect of the Vallabha Sampraday. According to local tradition, Bhim Singh had received this image in 1719, the year before the battle of Pandhar when, after taking leave of the Mughal emperor in Delhi, he made a pilgrimage to the holy city of Mathura where he took initiation into the sect and was given the image by one of the sect's religious leaders. Bhim Singh's devotion to Shri Brijnathji ran so deep, in fact, he dedicated his entire kingdom to the god and governed on the god's behalf as *divan*, or prime minister.[5] In a further expression of his piety to Shri Brijnathji, Bhim also changed his name to Krishnadas (slave of Krishna) and that of his capital from Kota to Nandagaon (the village of Nanda, Krishna's foster father).[6] After Bhim Singh's defeat at Pandhar, Qilich Khan is said to have taken the idol of Shri Brijnathji along with other war booty back to the Deccan where the god remained for four years before being returned to Kota in 1724.

Until this battle, Bhim Singh had been Kota's most illustrious ruler. During his thirteen-year reign (1707–20) he transformed Kota from a petty principality into one of the first important successor states that emerged during the protracted decline of the Mughal Empire. By all accounts, Bhim Singh was an exemplary Rajput. Through tireless campaigning, he not only brought under his control all of Hadauti (the traditional region of southeastern Rajasthan), but also conquered numerous cities and forts in neighbouring districts including Rajgarh, Narsinghgarh, Raghugarh, Sheopur, Umri, Bhadora, Diglodi, and Kilchipur, to name just a few. In addition, for his services to the Mughal Empire – which included the battle at which he lost his life – Bhim Singh secured great favour at the Mughal court in Delhi. In September 1713, Emperor

4 The practice of Rajput kings proceeding into battle with their tutelary deities mounted on elephant-back is most famously represented in Kavi Krishnadatta's late eighteenth-century panegyric to Sawai Maharaja Pratap Singh of Jaipur. See Krishnadatta, *Pratap prakash*, Gopalnarayan Bahura, ed. and annotated (Jaipur: Maharaja Sawai Man Singh II Museum Trust, 1983).

5 As with the ranas of Mewar who dedicated their kingdom to the deity Eklingji, the epithet 'divan' was not infrequently used by later maharaos of Kota. For a published example of this usage in connection with a portrait of Maharao Arjun Singh of Kota (r. 1720–23), see Stuart Cary Welch, ed., *Gods, Kings, and Tigers: The Art of Kotah* (Munich: Prestel-Verlag, 1997), cat. no. 22.

6 Similarly, Bhim Singh changed the name of the *qasba* and *pargana* of Mau-Maidana to Barsana, the village where Krishna's consort, Radha, lived.

Farrukhsiyar bestowed upon Bhim Singh the title of 'maharao', or 'great king', making him Kota's first ruler to enjoy the honour, and in the following years he received from the Mughal emperor other highly revered regalia, especially *naqqars* – large ceremonial kettle drums – and the *mahi-o-maratib* – the fish and dignities standard. This latter emblem was reserved for only a handful of the most eminent Mughal courtiers and, whatever its political symbolism may have been in an Islamic context, the display of the fish standard by a Rajput king also resonated with Sanskritic ideas about the king's role in maintaining social order particularly as expressed in the admonitory 'logic of the fish'.[7] Alas, after the disaster at Pandhar, Bhim Singh's heirs ruled over a much truncated dominion and it was not until fifteen years later that the polity regained its position in regional politics.

Sometime during the decade following the ill-starred battle of Pandhar, the greatest of Kota's artists, the as-yet anonymous 'Kota Master',[8] commemorated the event with a monumental (approximately 1.5 by 2.25 metres), but curious, painting on cloth that was commissioned for one of Bhim Singh's successors, either during the brief reign of Maharao Arjun Singh (r. 1720–23) or, more likely, early in the reign of Maharao Durjan Sal (r. 1723–56).[9] In this large painting (whose full view so far has eluded successful photography), the Kota Master adopted what art historians call a consecutive narrative structure in which Bhim Singh appears a total of nine times in a series of episodes that can be read, by and large, from left to right in an upside-down arc that somewhat resembles the Nike 'swoosh'™ (plate 1). The penultimate episode depicts the climactic confrontation between Bhim Singh and Qilich Khan and is remarkable insofar as the artist did not depict Qilich Khan slaying Bhim Singh, but the opposite (plate 2). Inscriptions above the two antagonists clearly indicate that Bhim Singh is decapitating his rival, who we know from numerous other historical sources actually lived for a further 28 years

[7] This symbolism of the fish ran even deeper for the dynasty Hada Chauhan Rajputs who ruled Kota insofar as they claimed descent from Vishnu and the Fish, or Matsya, was his first avatar.

[8] For more on the Kota Master and his career, see Stuart Cary Welch, 'Kotah's Lively Patrons and Artists', in *Gods, Kings, and Tigers: the Art of Kotah*, ed. S. C. Welch (Munich: Prestel-Verlag, 1997), pp. 15–38.

[9] Bautze, 'Victory and Death', p. 315. The painting has been part of the collection of the Kota royal family since its execution and thus has always enjoyed, at the very least, a royal audience. Significantly, the central scene of the painting, showing Bhim Singh's single combat with Qilich Khan, was often reproduced by the Kota atelier over the years, suggesting that there was some ongoing demand for subject if only within court circles. At least one version of this scene found its way into the Mewar royal collection indicating that it had a receptive audience in royal circles outside of Kota itself. See Joachim Bautze, 'The History of Kotah in an Art-Historical Context', in *Gods, Kings, and Tigers: The Art of Kotah*, ed. S. C. Welch (Munich: Prestel Verlag, 1997), p. 58, note 178.

Plate 1 Maharao Bhim Singh on his war elephant shoots an arrow. Detail of 'The battle of Pandhar', opaque watercolour on cloth by the 'Kota Master', c. 1725–30. Approximately 2.1 by 3.3 metres. Rao Madho Singh Trust Museum, Fort Kota. Photograph courtesy of Joachim K. Bautze.

Plate 2 Maharao Bhim Singh of Kota beheads Qilich Khan. Detail of 'The battle of Pandhar'. Photograph courtesy of Joachim K. Bautze.

after this battle![10] The rewriting of the outcome of the battle in this way is reminiscent of the *Prithviraj raso*, conventionally attributed to the poet Mahakavi Chand Bardai.[11] In this account of the last Chauhan king of Delhi, Prithviraj (ca. 1166–93) did not die at the hands of the Sultan Shahab-ud-din of Ghazni at the battle of Tarain, nor shortly thereafter in captivity at Ajmer, as is related in many other historical sources. Instead Prithviraj was captured alive, blinded, then and taken to Ghazni. Here Shahab-ud-din was persuaded, by none other than the poet Chand, to ask for a demonstration of Prithviraj's legendary archery skills which supposedly remained undiminished by his blindness. A target was erected for the purpose. But when the Sultan gave the command for Prithviraj to shoot, the blind king turned and let his arrow fly in the direction of the voice of his rival, killing him.[12]

How are we to interpret the Kota Master's (and other similar) apparently shameless misrepresentations of historical facts? Does it make a case for the accusations made by British colonial officials in the nineteenth century of India's easily excitable imagination and undisciplined historical consciousness?[13] Could it be that Bhim Singh's defeat and death were so emotionally bruising for the people of Kota that this large painting

[10] That the painting indeed represents the battle of Pandhar is confirmed by a short six line inscription at the top of the composition which gives the date (both in numbers and words) and location of the battle and the names of the two principal antagonists. The inscription also states, somewhat at odds with what is actually depicted, that everyone on *both* sides of the battle was killed (*sara uti ka va ati ka doni tarap ka sara kam aha* |). For a partial transliteration and translation of this inscription, see Bautze, 'Victory and Death,' pp. 312–313.

[11] Although some elements of this ballad may date to the thirteenth century, it is probably only in the second half of the sixteenth century that the ballad 'crystallized' in its present form in Rajasthan, where it enjoyed widespread popularity and existed in four major recensions. It is almost certain that the story would have been known in Kota at the beginning of the eighteenth century. As Mata Prasad Gupta has noted, the shortest (and earliest) of these recensions underlies the account of Prithviraj given in the tenth chapter of Chandrashekhara's *Surjana-charita*, a chronicle of Rai Surjan Singh of Bundi (r. 1554–58) that was completed during the reign of his successor, Bhoj Singh of Bundi (r. 1558–1607). The longest (and latest) of these recensions was already present in the Udaipur court by 1702. See Mata Prasad Gupta, *Raso sahitya vimarsh* (Allahabad: Sahitya Bhavan, 1962), pp. 87–108 and 141–152; Francis W. Pritchett, 'Prithviraj *Raso*: A Look at the Poem Itself', *Indian Literature* 23, 5 (1980): 56–75; Cynthia Talbot, 'The *Prithviraj Raso* in the Making of Tod's *Annals*', a paper presented at the Annual Meeting on South Asia, University of Wisconsin at Madison, 15 October 1999; and R. S. McGregor, *Hindi Literature from Its Beginnings to the Nineteenth Century* (Wiesbaden: Otto Harrassowitz, 1984), pp. 16–18.

[12] After killing Shahab-ud-din, Prithviraj then escaped to the Kuru jungle from where he ascended to the heavens.

[13] These colonial denigrations of Indian historiographical traditions bear some resemblance to earlier Islamic representations of these same traditions. Consider, for example, Alberuni's complaint of the eleventh century that 'Unfortunately the Hindus do not pay much attention to the historical order of things, they are careless in relating the chronological succession of kings, and when they are pressed for information are at

represents a psychological state of denial and total repression of historical facts that were too painful to contemplate? Or is it evidence of a peculiar Rajasthani historical sensibility – and if so, what could it possibly be? These questions will be addressed in this chapter through an examination of the specific ways in which royal legitimacy was established, substantiated, and traced in Kota through alternative modes of reckoning kinship links. In order to accomplish this goal, it will be necessary to provide some background about the actual battle of Pandhar before turning to the painting and the indigenous chronicles that informed its production and interpretation.

The Battle of Pandhar

The Battle of Pandhar was fought on 19 and 20 June 1720 near the Narmada River north of Burhanpur in the Mughal province of Malwa (present-day northern Madhya Pradesh) during the period of political uncertainty at the beginning of the reign of Muhammad Shah (r. 1719–48). At this time, Muhammad Shah was effectively the puppet of Sayyid brothers, Abdullah Khan and Husain Ali Khan, who held two of the most influential offices in the Mughal government that they used in concert to control the emperor.[14] During the previous seven years, in fact, the Sayyids had enthroned (and occasionally deposed) an alarming number of Mughal emperors. The catastrophe at Pandhar, however, was a turning point in the Sayyid brothers' political fortunes. Several other military defeats quickly followed and by year's end the two brothers had been overthrown and executed.

Unlike the Mughal emperors who claimed Central Asian descent from the great emperor Timur (Tamerlane), Abdullah Khan and Husain Ali Khan were 'indigenous' Indian converts to Islam who drew their support from the Baraha Sayyid clan from the upper Doab region between the Ganges and the Yamuna rivers. The Sayyids also carefully cultivated the support of prominent Rajput leaders, including Maharao Bhim Singh of

a loss, not knowing what to say, they invariably take to tale-telling'. The way in which European orientalist representations built upon indigenous essentialisms remains an important part of the history of orientalism that has yet to be adequately explored. See *Alberuni's India: An Account of the Religion, Philosophy, Literature, Geography, Chronology, Astronomy, Customs, Laws, and Astrology of India About A.D. 1030*, trans. Edward Sachau (London: Trübner, 1888), Volume II, pp. 10–11.

14 For fuller accounts of this period in north Indian history, see Muzaffar Alam, *The Crisis of Empire in Mughal North India: Awadh and the Punjab, 1707–48* (Delhi: Oxford University Press, 1986); Satish Chandra, *Parties and Politics at the Mughal Court (1707–1740)* (Aligarh: Aligarh Muslim University Publications, 1972); Irvine, *Later Mughals*; Mathur, *Relations of Hadas with Mughal Emperors*; and John F. Richards, *The New Cambridge History of India*, Volume I:5, *The Mughal Empire* (Cambridge: Cambridge University Press, 1993).

Kota. In return, Bhim Singh was richly rewarded with imperial honours and commands. At the time of his death, for example, he held the relatively high imperial *mansab* (rank) of 5000 *zat* and 4000 *sawar*.[15] In the face of the Sayyids' growing influence, however, elements of the older Timurid nobility mobilized to protect their privileged positions within the imperial apparatus. Qilich Khan figured prominently among this restive group. In response to Qilich Khan's opposition, the Sayyids sent an imperial army under the command of Sayyid Dilavar Ali Khan toward Qilich Khan's base of power in the Deccan in order to subdue him. This army was joined by the forces of Maharao Bhim Singh of Kota and Raja Gaj Singh of Narwar who were promised even more imperial honours and commands should they be successful against Qilich Khan. Bhim Singh, for example, was apparently assured that, in the event of victory, his mansab would be raised to 7000 zat and 7000 sawar which would have made him, after Maharaja Ajit Singh Rathor of Jodhpur, the highest ranking Rajput at the Mughal court.[16] Moreover, Bhim Singh was also given imperial help in asserting his authority over Bundi, Kota's parent state and oft-times rival from which it had split, with Mughal sanction, nearly a century earlier in 1631. The combined imperial-Kota forces captured Bundi in February 1720 on their way south towards Qilich Khan, and Bhagwan Das – Bhim Singh's foster-brother (*dhabhai*) – was put in command of Bundi which was briefly the jewel in Bhim Singh's crown. This command was short-lived as Kota was forced to relinquish control over Bundi in October 1720, some four months after the calamity at Pandhar.[17]

On learning of the approach of the army under the command of Sayyid Dilavar Ali Khan, Qilich Khan's army marched north from Burhanpur to meet the imperial forces. Hostilities commenced on the afternoon of 19 June 1720, at Pandhar near the Narmada River, and continued the following day. By the end of 20 June, the imperial army had been routed with the loss of several thousand dead while Qilich Khan's army suffered surprisingly light casualties.

[15] A mansab is a bureaucratic or military office entitling one to the revenue deriving from a specific tract of land. Under the Mughals, the mansab included a bipartite rank: a zat rank which determined the nobleman's revenue allowance, and a sawar rank, which through a series of arithmetical computations determined the number of troops to be maintained and remunerated from the proceeds of the assignment. See M. Athar Ali, *The Mughal Nobility under Aurangzeb* (Delhi: Oxford University Press, 1997 [1966]), pp. 38–59.

[16] Mathur, *Relations of Hadas with Mughal Emperors*, pp. 200–201.

[17] For a partial translation of the Mughal *parvana* authorizing Rao Raja Budh Singh of Bundi to retake possession of Bundi, see Gopal Narayan Bahura and Chandramani Singh, *Catalogue of Historical Documents in Kapad Dwara, Jaipur* (Amber-Jaipur: Jaigarh Public Charitable Trust, 1988), no. 277.

Plate 3 Raja Gaj Singh of Narwar and Ratan Singh of Ratlam advance into enemy lines. Detail of 'The battle of Pandhar'. Photograph courtesy of Joachim K. Bautze.

The visual narrative

The Kota Master's narration of the battle begins in the upper right-hand corner of the painting, where all the major commanders who fought against Qilich Khan first enter the scene mounted on war elephants. They lead a sizable force of cavalry and infantry. Bhim Singh is shown on his favourite elephant Kishan and the maharao is adorned (uniquely) by a white nimbus.[18] He is supported by several Muslim *mansabdar*s, including Sayyid Dilavar Ali Khan, and two other Rajput kings, Gaj Singh Kachhavaha of Narwar and Ratan Singh Rathor of Ratlam (plate 3). On entering the scene, they are shown as already having overrun part of Qilich Khan's encampment. As this army advances, however, they are progressively cut down by Qilich Khan's forces in various encounters including one horrific ambush by cannon fire whose depiction is a major feature in the painting. As a result of this cannon fire, one of the Sayyids' Muslim

[18] The restricted use of the nimbus, combined with the fact that the painting is currently part of the Kota royal collection, virtually assures that the painting was produced for a Kota royal patron.

Plate 4 A Muslim nawab, probably Dost Muhammad Khan, flees the ambush of Qilich Khan. Detail of 'The battle of Pandhar'. Photograph courtesy of Joachim K. Bautze.

generals, probably Dost Muhammad Khan, flees the battlefield (plate 4).[19] Nevertheless, Bhim Singh perseveres despite having to abandon his elephant and taking one arrow, rather stoically, in the middle of his forehead (plate 5). In the penultimate scene Bhim Singh is surrounded by several other kinsman and followers from Kota, including Bhai Daulat Singh Hada of Rajgarh, Raj Arjun Singh Jhala of Kunadi, Ravat Girivar Singh Hada of Ghati, and Bhat Jagjivan Gujarati. With these men Bhim Singh finally reaches Qilich Khan and they confront one another in single combat. The two warriors exchange reciprocal blows of the sword, but only Bhim's thrust finds its mark as he beheads Qilich Khan (plate 2). The final scene shows Bhim Singh, Gaj Singh, and Ratan Singh advancing further into the enemy ranks as two angels (*apsaras*?) descend from the heavens showering them with star-like blessings of, presumably, immortality.

[19] Although this personage is only identified as a '*navab mansabdar*' in the painting, several literary sources recount that Dost Muhammad Khan fled Pandhar and retreated into Malwa. See Raghubir Sinh, *Malwa in Transition, or a Century of Anarchy: The First Phase 1698–1765* (Bombay: D. B. Taraporevala, 1936), p. 140, note 2.

Plate 5 Maharao Bhim Singh dismounts his elephant. Detail of 'The battle of Pandhar'. Photograph courtesy of Stuart Cary Welch.

In each representation of the principal figures of the painting, they are identified by inscriptions in Devnagri and, in some cases, Nastaliq, and with one exception they are all known to have fought and died at the battle. The one exception is Raja Ratan Singh of Ratlam whose life and exploits are recounted in the famous late seventeenth-century *Ratan raso*.[20] Ratan Singh's presence in the painting constitutes a second major historical inaccuracy for he was long dead, having died in 1658 at the battle of Dharmat (Fatehbad) (map 1). During this battle, Ratan Singh had commanded a portion of the imperial forces of the Mughal Emperor Shah Jahan in an unsuccessful attempt to quash the rebellion of Shah Jahan's son Aurangzeb. This battle was one of the most famous events in Kota's annals for Kota's second ruler, Mukund Singh (r. 1648–58), espoused the same cause and was likewise killed along with his three

[20] Kashiram Sharma and Raghuvir Sinh eds., *Ratan raso*, Part 1, '*bhumika*' (Jodhpur: Rajasthan Prachyavidya Pratishtan, 1982), especially pp. 102–129.

brothers Mohan Singh, Kanhi Ram, and Jujhar Singh (figure 1).[21] The only brother to survive Dharmat was Bhim Singh's grandfather, Kishor Singh (r. 1684–96). Having been left for dead on the battlefield, Kishor Singh was later pulled from the carnage, nursed back to health, and eventually succeeded to the gaddi. But this was only able to happen after Kishor Singh had joined a military council that removed his nephew, Prem Singh, from the gaddi, ostensively on the grounds of incompetence. Kishor's selection as replacement rested in part on the self-sacrifice and heroism he displayed at Dharmat where so many prominent members of the ruling line had perished. By placing Ratan Singh at Pandhar, the Kota Master keyed the events at Pandhar to this other defining moment in the history of Kota's ruling line in which Bhim Singh's grandfather cheated death and kingship became vested in a junior branch of the ruling lineage through somewhat unconventional means.

In addition to these two errors of commission, this painting also evinces one conspicuous error of omission, at least from the perspective of the available local written accounts of the battle. Despite quite carefully depicting the most prized of Bhim Singh's regalia, including his nakkars and the mahi-o-maratib, the Kota Master made no direct reference to the idol of Shri Brijnathji.[22] Therefore, we must leave open the possibility that the story of Shri Brijnathji's first appearance in Kota in 1719, loss at Pandhar in 1720, and subsequent recovery in 1724 is a later accretion to the recounting of the battle. Indeed there is much contemporary documentary evidence to call into question several of the details of the story of Shri Brijnathji's appearance, loss, and recovery. We know, for example, that Kota's name was changed to Nandagaon in 1715 (not 1719) when Bhim Singh donated *qasba* Kota (i.e. his capital city) to Shri Nathji, the pre-eminent deity of the Vallabha Sampraday, whose image was situated

[21] As with the *Prithviraj raso*'s representation of the battle of Tarain and its aftermath, the *Ratan raso* also reworks historical facts concerning the battle of Dharmat, thereby compounding the apparent ahistoricism of the Kota Master's depiction of Ratan Singh at Pandhar. Though many sources indicate that Ratan Singh of Ratlam and Mukund Singh of Kota fell quickly and ineffectually in the very first assault against Aurangzeb's forces and that Shah Jahan's army then quickly fled the field of battle, the *Ratan raso* suggests that these Rajput kings survived the encounter and that Ratan Singh rallied elements of the wavering imperial forces and, along with Mukund Singh, engaged in another more sustained attack which inflicted heavy casualties against their foes before they were finally killed. See Sharma and Sinh eds., *Ratan raso*, especially pp. 102–129.

[22] Although M. L. Sharma has suggested that the idol was inside Bhim Singh's elephant howdah (and, therefore, perhaps hidden), Tod recounts that it was prominently displayed. See M. L. Sharma, *Kota rajya ka itihas* (Kota: The Kota Printing Press, 1939), p. 297 and James Tod, *Annals and Antiquities of Rajast'han or, the Central and Western Rajpoot States of India* (London, 1832), Volume II, pp. 509–510.

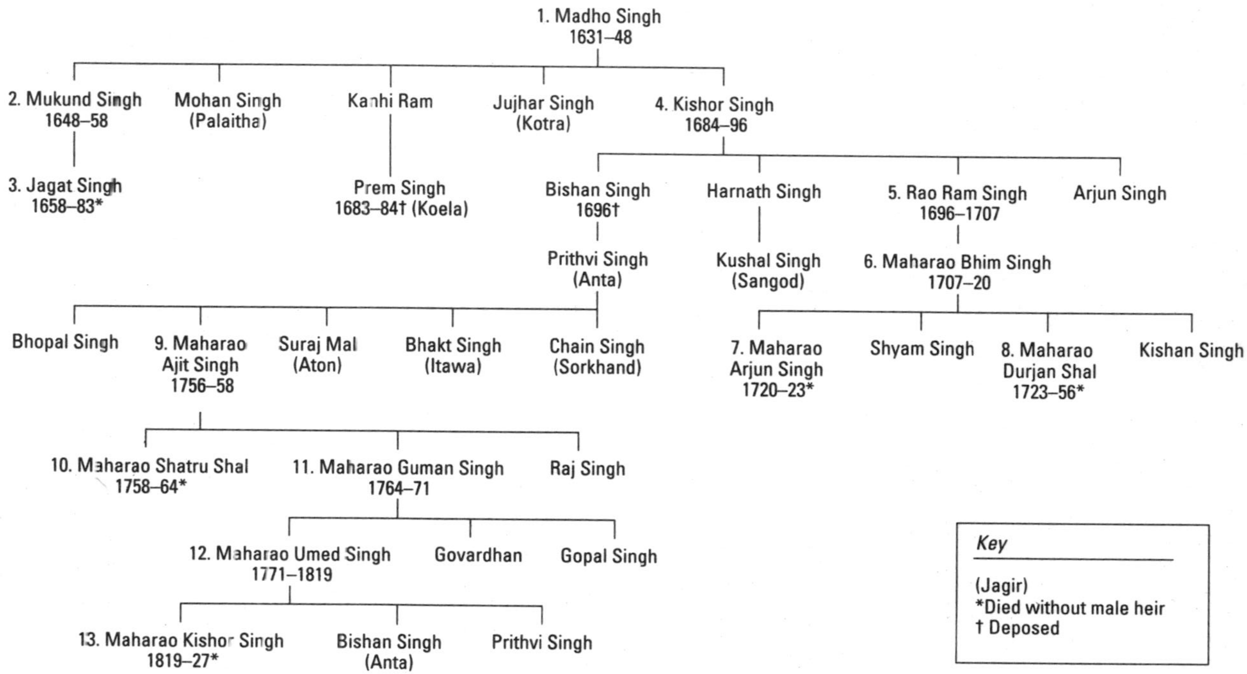

Figure 1 The ruling Hada lineage of Kota until 1827
Source: Kaviraja Lakshmandan, *'Maharao Shatru Shalji Bahadur ki vamsha prashasti'* (uncat. ms in the Thikana Kotri *daftar*, Kota)

in Nathadvara in the neighboring kingdom of Mewar.[23] Similarly, contemporary correspondence shows that Bhim Singh was using the name Krishnadas by at least 1717.[24] Thus it is quite likely that Bhim Singh took initiation into the sect somewhat earlier than generally conceded and that initially Shri Nathji was the principal object of his devotion.[25] What is clear is that the tradition of Bhim Singh bringing the idol of Shri Brijnathji to Kota from Mathura is of early eighteenth-century origin. A monumental wall painting from that period in the Chhattra Mahal in Kota's City Palace depicts Bhim Singh visiting a Mughal palace (presumably the Red Fort), then travelling to the banks of a river (presumably at Mathura) where he receives Shri Brijnathji, before finally returning with the god to Kota where, in the company of his younger son Durjan Sal, he installs the image in his palace.[26] Exactly when the tradition of the god's subsequent loss at Pandhar and recovery was accreted to the story (if it indeed is not historically accurate) remains uncertain though, for reasons discussed below, it most probably dates to early in Maharao Durjan Sal's reign.[27]

In any case, the Kota Master's use of the consecutive narrative form is highly suggestive of other sequential narrative forms (primarily oral and literary) to which this painting may have been cued. Unfortunately, at the moment no record has surfaced indicating precisely how this painting was displayed or used, but ample circumstantial evidence allows us to make an informed guess. The surface of the painting shows significant abrasions on the faces of the key antagonists that have required them to be retouched over the years.[28] Joachim Bautze has suggested that this wear

23 By the same token contemporary administrative records show that Mau was renamed Barsana in 1717. See Masanori Sato, 'The Formative Process of Towns and Market Town/Villages in South-eastern Rajasthan, 1650–1850 A. D.', in *Economy and Polity in Rajasthan: Study of Kota and Marwar, 17th through 19th Centuries*, Masanori Sato and B. L. Bhadani, pp. 57–86 (Jaipur: Publication Scheme, 1997).

24 V. S. Bhatnagar, *Life and Times of Sawai Jai Singh, 1688–1743* (Delhi: Impex India, 1974), p. 152, footnote 44.

25 Devotion to these two deities is not exclusionary, especially given that they are both manifestations of Krishna. However, considering the centrality that Shri Brijnathji was to later attain within the court of Kota, it is nonetheless significant that the earliest references in Kota are to Shri Nathji.

26 I am grateful to Woodman Taylor for pointing out the significance of this wall painting to me.

27 Among the evidence suggesting that the story of Shri Brijnathji's loss at Pandhar and subsequent recovery in 1724 was accreted to the idol's (hi)story at some later date are several contemporary paintings of Maharao Arjun Singh of Kota (r. 1720–23) worshipping Shri Brijnathji. For one such often reproduced painting, see Welch, *Gods, Kings, and Tigers*, cat. no. 19. Arjun Singh's reign, of course, coincides with the period when the idol was supposed to be absent from Kota.

28 There is no indication, however, that the identities of the antagonists have been changed in this retouching. For example, there is at least one preparatory sketch for the large composition which has not been repainted and which also depicts Bhim Singh decapitating Qilich Khan. See Bautze, 'Victory and Death', figure 37.1.

may have been the result of storytellers and/or spectators repeatedly touching the painting while pointing at it,[29] and in many parts of Rajasthan today there still is a popular bardic tradition of storytellers narrating epics, such as the epic Pabuji (concerning a Rajput Prince from Marwar), in front of large paintings on cloth (known as *pars*) depicting episodes from the narrative.[30] Given this wear it is reasonable to assume that the painting was the focus of attention, if only within courtly circles, that may have involved some sort of oral narrative and commentary about it, though we do not know precisely what this might have been. However, we do know that the events concerning the battle were recorded in several well-known and popular histories that were widely disseminated in court circles across north India and these histories would have been known to the courtiers who viewed the painting even if they themselves were not recounted in direct connection with the painting. Let us now turn to some of these literary narratives concerning the battle in order to see what light they may shed on the painting.

Literary narratives

The decade after the battle of Pandhar witnessed no fewer than three major Persian-language histories of the Mughal Empire in which the battle was described in some detail. If these literary sources concur on only one fact, it is that Bhim Singh did not kill Qilich Khan at Pandhar. Indeed a wealth of corroborating evidence establishes beyond doubt that Qilich Khan, who later became the first Nizam of Hyderabad, lived well after the battle and that Bhim Singh did not. The most detailed of these contemporary histories was Khafi Khan's *Muntakhab al-lubab* that was compiled about 1730.[31] This history confirms that both Bhim Singh and Gaj Singh commanded large armies under the overall authority of Dilavar Ali Khan and that they all fought bravely. This heroism was contrasted with the flight of Dost Mohammad Khan from the field of battle. Khafi Khan's history, however, does not mention that Qilich Khan's stunning victory was achieved, at least in part, through the deceit of an ambush. But this omission should not be too surprising given that Qilich Khan had been Kafi Khan's sometimes patron.

29 Bautze, 'Victory and Death', p. 313.

30 For more on the Rajasthani bardic tradition associated with Pabuji and pars, see John D. Smith, *The Epic of Pabuji: a Study, Transcription and Translation* (Cambridge: Cambridge University Press, 1991).

31 Khafi Khan, *Muntakhab al-lubab* (Calcutta, 1874 [ca. 1730]), Volume II, pp. 874–881. For a translation into Hindi of much of Khafi Khan's description of the battle of Pandhar, see Shyamaldas, *Virvinod*, Volume 2 (Delhi: Motilal Banarasidas, 1986 [1886]), pp. 1414–1416.

The two other accounts – Shiv Das Lakhnawi's *Shahnama munawwar kalam* and Muhammad Qasim Lahawri's *Ibratnama* – do highlight the ambush. Shiv Das's history was composed for a Mughal courtier in Delhi during Muhammad Shah's fourth regnal year (1723/24) or just a few years after the actual battle in 1720. With the exception of Bhim Singh's final triumph over Qilich Khan, Shiv Das's account otherwise confirms many aspects of the Kota Master's representation of the event. The account mentions several of the painting's inscribed personages as well as the horrific ambush by cannon fire which laid to waste much of the army that was marching against Qilich Khan. Shiv Das also mentions that Bhim Singh and Sayyid Dilavar Ali Khan bravely pushed on despite the flight and heavy loss of life of many of their compatriots before being killed themselves.[32]

Muhammad Qasim's *Ibratnama*, which was written at about the same time as Shiv Das's *Shahnama*, adds some interesting detail concerning the ambush which has important bearing upon the Kota Master's representation of Bhim Singh's triumph.[33] According to Qasim's account, the forces of Dilavar Ali Khan, Bhim Singh, and Gaj Singh were lured into the ambush by a clever deception. Qasim suggests that Qilich Khan sent out several impostors resembling himself in beard, age, and dress. They were mounted on elephant back and placed at various intervals leading to the mouth of the ravine near the Narmada River where the artillery was concealed. Dilavar Ali Khan and the others advanced towards their supposed adversary who then retreated towards the ravine. Eager to slay the man they believed to be their rival, Dilavar Ali Khan, Bhim Singh and Gaj Singh pursued steadily, disposing on their way several of the ersatz Qilich Khans until they were at last irrevocably drawn into the ambuscade. In light of this description, it is likely that the Kota Master's composition was a biting allusion by the vanquished to the victor's deception. Bhim Singh may indeed have smote down someone he *thought* to be Qilich Khan and by monumentalizing the trickery involved, the Kota Master may have aimed to demolish Qilich Khan's reputation for all of posterity.

Unfortunately, at the moment we do not have any contemporary, early eighteenth-century literary accounts from Kota describing Qilich Khan's actions at the battle of Pandhar that might confirm this interpretation. What we do know, however, is that by 1737 (and possibly earlier) Qilich Khan and Maharao Durjan Sal of Kota (r. 1723–56), son of Bhim Singh,

[32] Shiv Das Lakhnawi, *Shahnama Munawwar Kalam*, trans. Syed Hasan Askari (Patna: Janaki Prakashan, 1980), pp. 63–65.

[33] This *Ibratnama* was written in 1722/23. I am grateful to Jeevan Singh Deol for reading for me the Persian original of this hard to find text and discussing with me how the battle was narrated in it. For an English-language gloss of this text's description of Pandhar, see Irvine, *Later Mughals*, pp. 31–32.

had formed an alliance, and Durjan Sal sent an army back towards the Deccan to support his father's killer against their mutual enemy, the Marathas. Moreover, accounts from Kota dating from the beginning of the colonial era are curiously equivocal in their judgment on Qilich Khan's character. While portrayed as deceitful and dangerous in some, in others he is depicted as noble and honourable. This ambiguity is surprising given that the generally accepted effect of colonial discursive formations was to polarize Hindu and Muslim identities rather than to palliate them. The first account from Kota of which I am aware was recorded by James Tod in 1820. His source was apparently Gomund Ram's eighteenth-century *Book of Kings* which has unfortunately since disappeared.[34] Tod's gloss of Gomund Ram nevertheless is largely corroborated by other nineteenth-century Rajasthani accounts of the battle, such as in Suryamalla Mishran's *Vamshabhaskar* which was originally completed in 1841 and Kaviraja Lakshmandan's unpublished manuscript, '*Maharao Shastru Shalji Bahadur ki vamsha prashasti*', composed about 1870.[35] In his gloss of Gomund Ram, Tod followed the Persian sources in mentioning the participation of Sayyid Dilavar Ali Khan, Maharao Bhim Singh, Raja Gaj Singh of Narwar, the ambush of Qilich Khan and the valiant death of Kota's ruler. In addition, however, several other interesting details are mentioned. The first is that, prior to the battle, Bhim Singh and Qilich

[34] Most of Tod's collection of manuscripts were given to the Royal Asiatic Society in London. Gomund Ram's text is not among them, however. Tod repeatedly acknowledged Gomund Ram, or 'the Hara chronicler' as he often called him, as his source for his 'Annals of Haravati (Hadauti)' in which the events concerning Shri Brijnathji's history are recorded. Although we cannot be certain at this point, Gomund Ram may have been the same Gomund Ram who was one of Durjan Sal's closest advisors, appearing in several inscribed miniature paintings with the maharao. See, for instance, figure 41 in W. G. Archer, *Indian Painting in Bundi and Kotah* (London: Her Majesty's Stationery Office, 1959). Large portions of Tod's 'Annals of Haravati' are apparently direct translations of this text and appear in Tod's text in closed quotes. These quotations break off with events around 1760 when Gomund Ram's text was presumably written (a date which would be consistent with the suggestion that he was the above-mentioned contemporary of Durjan Sal). Although we regrettably do not have access to a firmly precolonial text concerning Shri Bijnathji's early history, many episodes of this history – including Bhim Singh's visit to the Mughal Emperor at Delhi followed by his pilgrimage to Mathura from where he brought the idol back to Kota (but, not the deity's excursion to the Deccan) – are narrated in wall paintings dating to the early eighteenth century in the Chhattra Mahal of the Fort. I thus remain confident that this story dates at least to the first half of Durjan Sal's reign (1723–56) given the way the narrative structure of Shri Brijnathji's early history so closely relates to other events of the period as will be discussed below.

[35] Suryamalla Mishran, *Vamshabhaskar* (Jodhpur, 1899), pp. 3075–3079; and Kaviraja Lakshmandan, '*Maharao Shatru Shalji ki vamsha prashasti*' (original ms, Thikana Kotri *daftar*, Kota; uncatalogued typescript copy, under the title of '*Kota rajya ke hastalikhita itihas ki pratilipi*', in the Brijraj Bhawan Palace Library, Kota). The details of these accounts are also related in the standard twentieth-century history of Kota, Sharma's *Kota rajya*, pp. 295–298.

Khan had been on friendly terms. In fact, Qilich Khan and Bhim Singh were *pagri badal bhai*, or 'brothers through the exchange of turbans'.[36] The closeness of this 'fictive' kin relationship as expressed through the metonym of swapped headgear rested on Rajput beliefs identifying the head as the source of male fertility and well-being. Norman Ziegler explains that for Rajputs of the sixteenth through eighteenth centuries the head was:

> considered to be the reservoir of stored semen, the 'Lord and Master' of the body, the storage center of the nectar which dripped down the throat and was caught by the sun inside the belly at the point of the umbilicus, keeping the body warm and giving it its vital energy.[37]

In exchanging protective headgear, the two men mixed their semen through the transfer of what Marriott has called 'coded substances' and, in effect, became brothers sharing the same source of virility and state of health.[38] Owing to their brotherhood, Qilich Khan is said to have expressed concern about Bhim Singh's safety and, prior to the opening of hostilities, reportedly sent a 'friendly epistle' to Bhim Singh requesting him to desist from the battle. Bhim Singh, as we know, refused.

Another significant detail in this account is that, along with the death of Bhim Singh, Kota sustained a second loss in the battle of Pandhar. Kota's tutelary deity, the golden idol of Shri Brijnathji, who had been installed in Bhim Singh's elephant howdah, was captured by Qilich Khan and taken back to the Deccan. Although the point is not elaborated further in Tod's gloss of Gomund Ram, Lakshmandan mentions that once back in the Deccan, Qilich Khan dutifully gave the deity to a wealthy *seth* (merchant) who spent a vast fortune on its *seva* (service or worship) before returning it to Kota some four years later at the very beginning of Maharao Durjan Sal's reign (r. 1723–56).[39] Shri Brijnathji's reputed absence from Kota thus coincided almost exactly with the reign of Durjan Sal's predecessor and elder brother, Arjun Singh (r. 1720–23). Although we cannot assess the historicity of Shri Brijnathji's loss and recovery, and must leave open the possibility that these events are a later

[36] Tod, *Annals and Antiquities*, Volume II, pp. 509–510.

[37] Norman P. Ziegler, 'Action, Power and Service in Rajasthani Culture: A Social History of the Rajputs of Middle Period Rajasthan' (PhD thesis, Department of History, University of Chicago, 1973), p. 78. According to Carstair's twentieth-century Rajput informants, the reservoir of semen in the head has the ample capacity of 'twenty *tolas*', or 6.8 ounces. See G. Morris Carstairs, *The Twice Born*: *A Study of a Community of High-Caste Hindus* (Bloomington: Indiana University Press, 1961), p. 84.

[38] McKim Marriott, 'Hindu Transactions: Diversity without Dualism', in *Transactions and Meaning: Directions in the Anthropology of Exchange and Symbolic Behavior*, ed. Bruce Kapferer (Philadelphia: Institute for the Study of Human Issues, 1976), pp. 109–142.

[39] Lakshmandan, '*Vamsha prashasti*', p. 44.

Plate 6 Maharao Durjan Sal of Kota (right) presents offerings to Shri Brijnathji as Maharao Bhim Singh (left) holds a morchal over the deity. Opaque watercolour on paper by the 'Kota Master', c. 1730. The Philadelphia Museum of Art. Photograph courtesy of Stuart Cary Welch.

accretion to the (hi)story of the battle of Pandhar, we do know that from very early in Durjan Sal's reign the deity of Shri Brijnathji for the first time became the focus of an elaborate court cult and, from this time, it figures prominently in the corpus of miniature paintings produced in the royal atelier. Plate 6, for instance, reproduces a painting that can be dated on stylistic grounds to c. 1730 in which the youthful Durjan Sal offers a plate of sweets to an anthropomorphized Shri Brijnathji while (the late) Bhim Singh stands behind the deity waving a *morchhal* (a whisk made of peacock feathers).[40]

In neither of these details – Qilich Khan's attempt to warn Bhim Singh of his impending doom prior to the battle nor Qilich Khan's turning over the Kota deity to an individual who would ensure its proper upkeep after

40 Shri Brijnathji can be identified by his distinctive iconography. The blue skinned god sits cross-legged with both hands slightly raised. One hand, held palm up, holds a small round food-offering while the other, held palm out, is positioned to grasp a flute (which for some unknown reason is almost never depicted). This miniature is but one of a large corpus of paintings dating the Durjan Sal's reign showing Durjan Sal and Bhim Singh together worshipping Shri Brijnathji. Significantly, Arjun Singh is *never* depicted in these paintings, surely a reference to the assertion that the image was absent from Kota during the reign of Durjan Sal's eldest brother.

the battle – is Qilich Khan represented as unambiguously evil, dichotomously opposed, or wholly 'other' in relation to Bhim Singh. The degree of consonance between Bhim Singh and Qilich Khan, as illustrated in these representations, is brought out more clearly in Suṛyamalla Mishran's *Vamshabhaskar* which contains an *astapad* and *doha* (a poetical form subscribing to specific metrical canons) concerning the battle of Pandhar in which the poet describes how, in the dark turmoil of battle, the identities of hero and rival become conflated. Composing in the poetical language of Dingal, Suryamalla Mishran wrote:

> [Horsemen] gather; the two armies advance with ardour to fight.
> A cloud looms, like a flood, flashing lightning.
> Horses, glaring, charge against mighty warriors who revel in battle.
> Then swords rang, great warriors fled fearfully not caring where.
> Vultures, hawks in flocks obscured the sun's brightness in the sky;
> with the incessant pounding of hooves the earth became rutted and cracked in all directions.
> As angry steel struck, hearts suffered agonies.
> As brave men ran [forward] they revealed themselves as heroes.
> As eating the [purgative] *jamal-gota* nut racks the entrails with swift pain,
> so the irresistible armed force of Kalij stirred up the whole battle.
> Many Hyderabad warriors, in attacking, tasted the savour of eternity.
> King Bhim, the lord of Kota, did not put Shiva's [protective] garland over his head;
> [His] elephants fled causing chaos, he mounted a proud active horse in the dust [of battle].[41]
> When it was wounded, he fought on foot, mighty and wreaking carnage.
> Lances are broken by swords, swords are broken and shortened,
> then shortened again into daggers, and fierce warrior enemies are cut down.
> Kalij saw his precious life confronted by (lit. mixed with) Bhim, as the rain cloud [of the month] of Bhadon,
> while Shiva beat his ash-smeared brow [in grief].
>
> On the full moon day of the month of Jeth in [V.S.] 1777
> Dilavar Khan fell in battle, and Gaj Singh along with Bhim.
> The lord [Gaj Singh] of Narwar, who had fled from the battle of Jajav [in A.D. 1707],[42] was now killed here [at Pandhar in A.D. 1720].
> Bhim Chauhan fell, having slain thousands [of his enemies] in the same manner as Bhim [the *Mahabharata* hero].[43]

[41] Although the Kota Master did not depict Bhim Singh mounting a horse, this detail is related in Khafi Khan, *Muntakhab al-lubab* (Calcutta, 1874), Volume II, pp. 876–881. For a translation into Hindi of the relevant passages, see Shyamaldas, *Virvinod*, Volume 2, pp. 1414–1416.

[42] This is a somewhat ungenerous reference to the fact that Gaj Singh of Narwar survived the battle of Jajav in 1707, while his close ally Rao Ram Singh of Kota laid down his life.

[43] Mishran, *Vamshabhaskar*, pp. 3079–3081. I am extremely grateful to R. S. McGregor for helping me translate this poem. Responsibility for the translation's final form, however, rests entirely with me.

Because the Dingal poetical tradition greatly prized highly convoluted syntactical forms, aptly known as the 'serpentine stanza', in which even short passages are open to multiple readings, several aspects of this poem deserve further comment. First, the eleventh line of the poem, which reads in the original '*haidarabad bhat bahul hani chir acchari ras rakkhyo* || ', is capable of varying interpretations. This line has been rendered, in the first instance, as 'Many Hyderabad warriors, in attacking [foes], tasted the savour of eternity [that is, death].' However, the line may also be read 'The Hyderabad warrior [that is, Qilich Khan himself], in attacking many, tasted the savour of eternity.' The number of the 'Hyderabad warrior(s)' could be either singular or plural, depending upon whether the qualifier 'many' (*bahul*) applies to *haiderbad bhat* or the implied foes. If it is singular, this then is a reference to Qilich Khan tasting 'the savour of eternity'. Although the first interpretation (that is, 'many Hyderabad warriors…') seems the stronger, given the powerful alliteration that groups the first three words of the line, the second interpretation remains nonetheless latent. This alternative reading may be an allusion to the numerous paintings that depict Bhim Singh killing Qilich Khan.

Second, the seventeenth line, reading '*dekhyo kalij jivan dulabh milat bhim bhaddhva mudir* || ', adopts a powerful hydraulic metaphor of gathering clouds to describe the confrontation between Bhim Singh and Qilich Khan in which their combat is represented in terms of their joining or mixing (*milat*). The comparison of battle with the gathering storm clouds of the month of Bhadon (a common metaphor within the bardic literature of Rajasthan) is significant because the monsoon rains traditionally had the effect of breaking down natural, social, and political distinctions as the world dissolved into unordered, segmentary parts in the quagmire of rain, mud, and swollen rivers. Within this protean firmament the rival warriors become characterized by their consubstantiality rather than by their discrete and privative essences.[44]

Finally, in the last line of the poem, reading '*mari hajaran bhim jim, paryo bhim chahuvan* || ', Bhim Singh is likened to his enemies through their shared fate of death in battle. The inference from this statement is that the slain Bhim Singh may also be likened to his slayer, Qilich Khan. Thus although Bhim Singh and Qilich Khan oppose each other in horrendous battle, that very event ties them together in a common destiny in which the identities of victor and vanquished are powerfully merged.

The blurring of selfhood among rivals as expressed in these texts also appears as a central feature in much earlier texts from elsewhere in Rajasthan. Take, for example, the mid fifteenth-century chronicle,

[44] Because of the difficulty of travel during the monsoon months, warriors traditionally stayed home during the rains to be with their wives and families. Thus the rain clouds of Bhadon were also associated with marital domesticity and the episodic reunion of husbands and wives, a point that will become significant below.

Kanhadade prabandha, composed by Kavi Padmanabha for Akhairaja, scion of another Chauhan Rajput dynasty that ruled over the western Rajasthani kingdom of Jalor.[45] This text concerns the exploits of Raval Kanhadade, ancestor of Akhairaja, who gained everlasting renown for bravely confronting the Turkish Sultan of Delhi, Alavadin, in the early fourteenth century. After a bloody seven-year siege of Jalor, Alavadin finally captured the city and killed both Raval Kanhadade and his son and heir, Viramde. In Padmanabha's text, hero and villain are joined in a most startling way. Before the final siege of Jalor, Alavadin's daughter, Khoja Ladan, reveals to her father that during her six previous lives she had been a Rajput queen married to Viramde's previous incarnations (*avatars*). After enumerating the first four of these marital unions, Khoja Ladan explains:

> The fifth time, Viramde became the avatar (*lidhau avatar*) Devraj in the house of Prithvirai,
> And I became the avatar (*avatari*) named Kumari Sahiju in the house of Jaitala.
>
> The sixth time, Viramde became the avatar Prithviraj in the house of Someshwar,
> And I became the avatar named Kumari Padmavati in the house of Palhan.
>
> In that manifestation, I sinned (*pap adariun*); I performed black magic (*kaman kariun*) and killed a cow (*gai vinasi*),[46]
> Then I recited a magical spell (*mantra*) on its womb (or foetus) that rendered the king mentally unstable.
>
> I brought the king under my control and degraded his honour; I killed the ministers and seized the kingdom.
> I later learned that Sultan Shahab-ud-din killed the king on the banks of the Ghaghar River.
>
> So I honoured the king by performing sati; I mounted his funeral pyre at Ayodhya,
> And earning merit (*punya*), I became an avatar in a great lineage (*quli*).[47]
>
> Alas, dear father, on account of committing those two sins, I became an avatar in the lineage of a Turk (*turak*).
> The seventh time, Viramde became an avatar in the house of Kanhadade,
> And I, dear father, became your daughter, the avatar Khoja Ladan.[48]

45 This text was widely copied in north India during the next 300 years.

46 *Kaman kariun*, of course, may also be read as 'an echo phrase' reinforcing the murderous action done against the cow (*gai vinasi*).

47 Here Kanhadade's use of the term *quli*, which can also mean Muslim, is a calque on the following line where it is revealed that Khoja Ladan is reborn in the house of a Turk.

48 Padmanabha, *Kanhadade prabandha*, Kantilal Baldevram Vyas, ed. (Jaipur: Rajasthan Puratattva Mandir, 1953), pp. 145–147. Hariray employed a similar mechanism in his

Two important points emerge from this passage. First, the relationship established between rivals in battle is linked with that created through marriage. Armed conflict in this context is thus understood in terms very different to those informing contemporary western moralities concerning warfare, which typically is represented as a clash of good and evil essences in which the aim of battle is to completely extinguish that which is considered evil. This passage reveals that superficially opposed enemies can be united by profound, if somewhat unanticipated, conjunctions in which the marriage-like ties that existed between rivals meant that heroes explicitly perceived their rivals as constituting an essential part of their identity in the same way that in-marrying women were necessary for the reproduction of their own lineage. In other words, the state of war in mediæval Rajasthan was not moralized as an aberrant breakdown of sociality but rather was normalized as providing the given preconditions on which any sociality was established and maintained. For this reason, enemies tended to be incorporated and subordinated, but not obliterated. Linked to this observation, we also notice in this passage an alternative mechanism through which 'genealogical' descent was traced. Padmanabha's repetition of the *avatar/avatari* form makes it abundantly clear that successive generations of hero and heroine are not united by their shared bloodlines – in each generation they are, in fact, reborn in different (and often obscure and anachronistic) households – but rather descent was traced through the residual effects of their actions, or karma, through metempsychosis, or the transmigration of souls, among unrelated persons. In the following section, I turn to Indian theories regarding fate, or karma, and how individual action is implicated in these beliefs in order to gain a greater understanding of why partisan Rajasthani sources did not demonize their enemies more fully.

Discourses on kin(g)ship in Rajasthan

Hindu scriptural sources appear to rigidly restrict sovereignty to one group only – *kshatriyas* – the 'hereditary' caste of warriors and rulers. Rajputs claimed kshatriya descent and the term 'Rajput' itself is often said to derive from the Sanskrit '*rajaputra*', meaning 'son of a king', reflecting the belief that all Rajputs have royal ancestry even if they are not kings themselves. The bardic literature concerning kingly rule in

late seventeenth-century commentary on the varta of Surdas in which he asserted that the Mughal Emperor Akbar had been in a previous birth a young Hindu man in the stage of *brahmacharya*, named Balamukunda. Unfortunately, for the sin of inadvertently drinking milk containing the hair of a cow, Balamukunda was reborn in a later life as the *mleccha* Akbar. See Hariray, *Chaurasi vaishnavan ki varta*, varta 81 (Indore: Vaishnav Mitr Mandal, 1992), p. 447.

Rajasthan made extensive use of the language of kinship, particularly patrilineal descent, in order to regulate inclusion into, and establish rank within, this aristocratic category. This practice, however, did not always enjoy universal and incontrovertible acceptance. As Dirk Kolff has argued, it was privileged, if not initially inspired, only in the sixteenth and seventeenth centuries by Mughal perceptions of Rajputs which, in a pre-form of orientalism, took patrilineal descent as the basis for Rajput social organization and consequently as the basis for their political inclusion into the empire. Prior to the Mughals, the term 'Rajput' was equally an open-ended, generic name applied to any '"horse soldier", "trooper", or "headman of a village"' regardless of parentage, who *achieved* his status through his personal ability to establish a wide network of supporters through his *bhaibandh* (lit. 'tie or bond of brothers'; that is, close collateral relations by male blood) or by means of *naukari* (military service to a more powerful overlord) and *sagai* (alliance through marriage). Thus the language of kinship remained nonetheless strong in this alternative construction of Rajput identity but collateral and affinal bonds were stressed rather than those of descent. During the sixteenth and seventeenth centuries, however,

> the top layer of Rajputs, encouraged by the openings presented by the Mughal state and helped by the expertise of their bards, tended to close ranks and to articulate new norms of Rajput behavior. Bards had always encouraged their Rajput employers to assume aristocratic self-images closely linked to myths of origin that established their status as *ksatriyas* and traced their genealogies to, for instance, the great dynasties of ancient Indian history. But now the political power and social status of the more successful lineages tended to be legitimised exclusively in the language of descent and kinship. This idiom, of course, was deeply rooted in the traditions of Indian royalty, but from the sixteenth century onwards, the political opportunities of the Mughal court and the emphasis the Mughals themselves placed on genealogy gave it a new vigour and largely pushed into the background the more ancient character of Rajputs as an open-ended status group. The tendency to interpret Rajput history in genealogical terms was later inherited by Tod and other British Indian administrators.[49]

Kota also bears witness to this tendency toward the patrilineal norms of the new 'Rajput Great Tradition'.[50] A mid-eighteenth-century king list

[49] Dirk Kolff, *Naukar, Rajput and Sepoy: the Ethnohistory of the Military Labour Market in Hindustan, 1450–1850* (Cambridge: Cambridge University Press, 1990), p. 72. For an important precursor to this argument, see two essays by Norman Ziegler: 'The Seventeenth-Century Chronicles of Marvar: a Study of the Evolution and Use of Oral Tradition in Western India', *History in Africa: a Journal of Method* 3 (1976): 127–153, and 'Marvari Historical Chronicles: Sources for the Social and Cultural History of Rajasthan,' *Indian Economic and Social History Review* 13 (1976): 219–250.

[50] The term was coined by Kolff, *Naukar, Rajput and Sepoy*, p. 74.

prepared for Maharao Guman Singh of Kota is remarkable in that only Guman Singh's direct lineal ancestors are included within the formal enumeration of the royal lineage.[51] As Acharya Parameshvar Solanki noted, several of Kota's most famous kings who were from collateral branches of the family, including Maharao Bhim Singh, are not mentioned at all.[52] However, it is worth adding that this patrilineal enumeration was only placed after a long preamble that described the wondrous beauty of various pavilions in Kota's palace whose construction and ornamentation are commonly associated with the patronage of previous rulers, including those absent from the king list. By introducing his list in this way, Krishnadatta may have been implying that the palace's present tenant also basked in the reflected glories of these previous rulers whether they were direct ancestors or not. This interpretation is strengthened by the fact that the only thing mentioned about the last member of the ruling line, the infant Maharajkumar Umed Singh, was that he was a devotee (*bhakta*) of Shri Brijnathji, the deity reputably first brought to Kota by Maharao Bhim Singh.[53]

Thus despite the apparent shift among Rajputs toward *ascribed* status reckoned through patrilineal lines, the older version of *achieved* status through the performance of archetypal exemplary actions, such as the worship of Shri Brijnathji, never entirely lost its social currency and continued to suggest alternative 'genealogies' connecting disparate individuals. This fact even holds true in Rajasthan, the region of India that Kolff suggests most thoroughly imbued the new definition of rajputhood. In fact, during the eighteenth century, with the collapse of the Mughal regime, we witness a concerted revival of these older ideals. The movement from achieved to ascribed was not unidirectional nor was it ever total. The older achieved foundation of Rajput status continued to inform

51 The king list is Kavi Krishnadatta's '*Prasad panch vimshti*' which was composed during the reign of Guman Singh just after the birth of his son, Umed Singh, in 1759. Acharya Parameshvar Solanki has published an annotated version of this as '*Kavivar Krishnadatta virchit "prasad panch vimshti",*' *Shodh Patrika* 12, 2 (December 1960): 53–63.

52 Solanki, '*Kavivar Krishnadatta virchit "prasad panch vimshti*"', p. 53. This king list thus provides an interesting variant of the type of royal genealogies studied by David P. Henige in *The Chronology of Oral Tradition: Quest for a Chimera* (Oxford: Clarendon Press, 1974), pp. 78–84. In these genealogies anybody who ever ruled was incorporated into the lineage and represented as succeeding according to the norms of father-to-son succession even though many of these rulers were actually brothers, cousins, or 'distant relations'.

53 One witnesses a similar phenomenon in the mid-eighteenth-century '*Vamsha kallola sara samuchchaya*' (Tod ms. no. 80, RAS) that was commissioned by Rao Raja Umed Singh of Bundi (r. 1739–1771). The text principally concerns with the events in Bundi during the eighteenth century during the reigns of Umed Singh and his father Rao Raja Budh Singh (r. 1695–1739). Although the first quarter of this text is devoted to establishing their genealogical pedigree, it opens with a brief panegyric to Umed Singh in which he is first and foremost praised for being a great 'avatar'.

and supplement notions of inheritance through blood such that those claiming specific Rajput identities regularly slid back and forth between different idioms of rajputhood as they exploited each in turn for their strategic potentialities in specific contexts.

Scope for the strategic negotiation of the terms constituting Rajput identity was enabled, in part, because genealogical connections based on blood did not establish uncontested hierarchies of rank among potential heirs to political office such as kingship. This was particularly true among the prodigiously polygamous Rajputs.[54] In these large families with many wives, the *patrani*, that is the wife who enjoyed senior rank within the harem, a rank itself typically dependent upon the socio-political status of her natal family, did not necessarily produce the first-born male heir. Such circumstances often pitted claims to succession based on primogeniture against claims based on the relative socio-political statuses of the claimants' mothers' natal families.[55]

Moreover, the ease with which biological genealogies can be fabricated is well known to all. Although we have no firm evidence to prove that the type of continuous royal succession from father to son (or sometimes cousin) as reconstructed in Kota's various histories rests to some extent on concocted pedigrees, there is plenty of circumstantial evidence to indicate that this practice was not unknown elsewhere in Rajasthan, if not in Kota. Any reader of the royal family histories collected by James Tod in his *Annals and Antiquities* will be familiar with the extraordinary legends of posthumous birth in exile of male heirs to apparently extinguished royal lineages, and tales of Rajput kings who were left for dead on the battlefield only to be dragged to some forest or mountain retreat from whence their heirs later reconquered their (alleged) patrimonies. These are just two common Rajasthani narratives through which warriors of obscure origin have established their legitimacy in patrilineal terms, often in the face of the stiff opposition from other warriors with stronger genealogical claims. Under such circumstance, when contested claims to genealogical status came into conflict, older notions of achieved status continued to play a vital role establishing legitimacy.

A major factor making it relatively easy to slide between the ascribed and the achieved idioms of rajputhood was that both idioms exploited the same language of kinship for, in India, genealogical connections were reckoned not only through shared blood but also through shared karma. The theory of karma posits that every action has an inevitable fruit or

[54] Madho Singh, Kota's first ruler, for example, had ten official wives in addition to his numerous concubines, and Mukund Singh, Kota's second ruler, had eleven wives.

[55] Varsha Joshi, *Polygamy and Purdah: Women and Society among Rajputs* (Jaipur: Rawat Publications, 1995), pp. 62–84.

consequence, so that an individual's identity and social station is determined by good or bad deeds in this and previous lives.[56] The most famous consequence of this belief occurs when conjoined with the belief in reincarnation through metempsychosis. Because the Hindu soul (*jiva*) is considered to be undying, when the mortal body expires the soul is reborn in another being, who need not be kin or even human, and the quality of the rebirth is determined by the excellence of the individual's past karma. Thus 'karmalogical' lineages of avatars and incarnations displayed their common pedigree through the *performance* of similar exemplary and virtuous deeds (*punya*s) in what Jayasinhji Jhala has called *karma kshetra*, 'the field of action and achievement'.[57]

What is less well appreciated, and this will become important in the concluding portion of this chapter, is that although karmalogical connections could be established between different individuals through a belief in the reincarnation of the soul, within cycles of life, death, and rebirth, similar connections also could be forged through, what O'Flaherty has called, 'the transfer of karma' among more or less contemporary individuals for whom there can be no question of sharing the same reborn soul. Furthermore, because it is karma that defines and differentiates one soul from another, transfers of karma between contemporary individuals have the effect of causing different souls to be qualified similarly, thus becoming more alike. In large measure because of the distinctiveness of the belief in reincarnation, it has become commonplace to think that the moment of reckoning, at which karmic reward and retribution are decided occurs at the time of death/rebirth: that is, a particular soul is reborn with an innate karmic imprint based on actions in previous lives. This belief is indeed closely held by most Hindus. However, it has been argued that the transfer of sin and merit associated with karma also occurs while individuals are alive. Sheryl Daniel details ethnographic examples of how karma is reckoned to be transferred between living individuals through various media, such as blood, cooked food, and co-residence or physical proximity. And intriguingly for our present purposes, Alf Hiltebeitel has pointed out similar textual examples from classical sources in which a victorious king incorporates the qualities and virtues of his vanquished

56 It has been pointed out many times that the Hindi verb *karna* (to do, to act, to perform) shares the same Sanskrit root as 'karma', reflecting the active or agentive dimension of this latter term.

57 Jayasinhji Jhala, 'Marriage, Hierarchy, and Identity in Ideology and Practice: an Anthropological Study of Jhala Rajput Society in Western India against a Historical Background (A.D. 1090–1990)' (PhD Thesis, Department of Anthropology, Harvard University, 1991), Chapter 2, Part 2, p. 41. For similar attitudes as expressed in the contemporary ethnographic record of Nepal, see Richard Burghart, 'Hierarchical Models of the Hindu Social System,' *Man* (N.S.) 13 (1978): 528–529.

rival in the course of battle through the medium of sacrifice.[58] It is perhaps for this reason that right through the eighteenth century we see north Indian warriors adopting the titles and displaying the regalia of their vanquished rivals.[59]

The most famous application of these beliefs regarding karma and metempsychosis to succession to high office (though perhaps in a more non-violent mode) occurred in the lamaist polities of Tibet, where there was ideally no blood connection between successive Dalai, Panchen, or Karmapa Lamas but, rather, soulful continuity was revealed through the common appearance of agreed-upon signs among unrelated personages. Similarly, in India those claiming to be righteous kings (*dharmarajas*) did so, in part, on the basis of their personal achievements in culturally specific arenas. For Rajputs the paradigmatic punya was the conquest of new territory with the aim of (re)establishing dharmic rule and proper social order, most typically indexed by the construction of great public works (particularly palaces, cities, tanks, and irrigation projects) and the offering of protection and patronage to Brahmans and religious institutions. Through the performance of such archetypal actions, living kings claimed to be incarnations or avatars of famous historical warrior heroes. In Rajasthan, one of the most frequently invoked champions has been Prithviraj Chauhan of the *Raso* fame. Just as Prithviraj was frequently portrayed as an incarnation of the god-king Ram,[60] so later Rajasthani kings were represented as manifestations of Prithviraj. We have already seen how, in Padmanabha's *Kanhadade prabandha*, Viramde was depicted

58 This belief also surely informs the statement made by the Maharao Kishor Singh of Kota in a letter to James Tod, dated 24 September 1821, shortly before they met in battle at Mangrol (an event that will be examined in greater detail in chapter 6). Rejecting Tod's plea to peacefully accept the conditions of a treaty alliance with the British that would have rendered Kishor Singh a 'puppet' of his prime minister, Kishor Singh wrote 'I am now forty [years old] and may live five or ten years more, but will not pass them in confinements so send your emissary and slay me. By this, my life will be rendered bright and *you will obtain credit*!' (emphasis added). Kishor Singh to James Tod, OIOC, BPC, 24/31 October 1821.

59 Wendy Doniger O'Flaherty, 'Karma and Rebirth in the Vedas and Puranas', in *Karma and Rebirth in Classical Indian Traditions*, ed. Wendy Doniger O'Flaherty (Berkeley: University of California Press, 1980), pp. 27–37; Sheryl B. Daniel, 'The Tool Box Approach of the Tamil to the Issues of Moral Responsibility and Human Destiny', in *Karma: an Anthropological Inquiry*, eds Charles F. Keyes and E. Valentine Daniel (Berkeley: University of California Press, 1983), pp. 27–62; and Alf Hiltebeitel, *The Ritual of Battle: Krishna in the* Mahabharata. (Ithaca: Cornell University Press, 1976), pp. 153, 323, and 352. See also E. Valentine Daniel, *Fluid Signs: Being a Person the Tamil Way* (Berkeley: University of California Press, 1984); and McKim Marriott, 'Hindu Transactions', pp. 109–142.

60 Sheldon Pollock, 'Ramayana and the Political Imagination in India', *Journal of Asian Studies* 52 (1993): 274–276.

as an avatar of the last great Chauhan king of Delhi. In a similar manner, Bhim Singh became this type of archetypal hero in Kota.[61]

Although biological notions of descent perhaps have come to dominate popular conceptions of kinship in modern India, one still today witnesses in Kota vestiges of this alternative way of reckoning descent. Take, for example, Kota's Dasahra festival, an annual rite whose performance celebrates the (re)establishment of the socio-political order, especially through the worship of the instruments of war. Traditionally, Dasahra marked the start of the season for warfare, coming as it does at the end of the monsoon when society quite literally had become unordered.[62] An important focal point of the contemporary manifestation of these celebrations occurs when the present maharao, Brijraj Singh, worships an early eighteenth-century portrait of Bhim Singh in a shrine located in the palace armoury (plate 7). Through this reverential act, the maharao aims to establish his axial position with regard to the rebirth of the polity. What is telling with respect to our discussion of karmalogical descent is that embodiment of this foundational past for Brijraj Singh is not the founder of the kingdom, Madho Singh, from whom the present maharao is a direct genealogical descendant, but rather a later successor from a collateral branch of the family (figure 1). That the image of Bhim Singh is also worshipped by the present maharao on his own birthday indicates the extent to which he links his biological birth with karmic descent from Bhim.

The emphasis on karmic attainment in establishing the legitimacy of Kota's kings is beautifully illustrated in a series of passages from the '*Maharao Shatru Shalji Bahadur ki vamsha prashasti*', a panegyric composed during the last half of the nineteenth century by Kaviraja Lakshmandan to honour the lineage of Kota's then ruler, Shatru Shal (r. 1866–89). Although written after nearly fifty years of colonial domination,[63] this panegyric still shares several features with praise poems from the precolonial era insofar as it continues to link royal legitimacy to the exemplary *actions* of Kota's rulers and their need to perform meritorious

[61] Later Kota kings represented themselves as manifestations of Prithviraj as well. For example, in 1826 Maharao Kishor Singh (r. 1819–27) commissioned an elegant copy of the *Prithviraj raso* that was then presented to Major J. Caulfield, the Political Agent (Tod ms. no. 120, RAS). The manuscript is fronted with a superb, inscribed miniature painting depicting Prithviraj. However, the facial features of Prithviraj are surely modelled on those of Maharao Kishor Singh. The manuscript's concluding colophon mentions that the manuscript was copied by a scribe working in the Shri Brijnathji Temple. This reference was perhaps intended to remind the reader of Kishor Singh's connection to Maharao Bhim Singh in addition to Prithviraj.

[62] Ronald Inden, 'Ritual, Authority and Cyclic Time in Hindu Kingship', in *Kingship and Authority in South Asia*, ed. J. F. Richards (Madison: University of Wisconsin South Asia Publication Series, No. 3, 1978), pp. 28–73.

[63] Kota first came under colonial indirect rule in 1817 when Maharao Umed Singh signed a treaty of subsidiary alliance with the British.

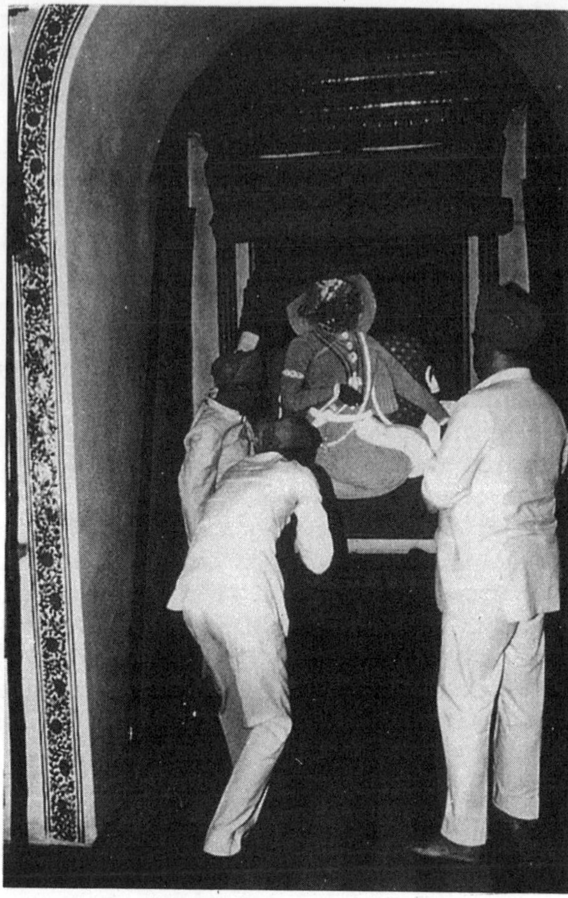

Plate 7 Maharao Brijraj Singh of Kota (right) and royal attendants worshipping a painted image of Maharao Bhim Singh on Dasahra, 1993. Photograph courtesy of Woodman Taylor.

deeds. The emphasis on the personal achievements of various monarchs in establishing their authority differs from the rather more institutionalized footings of status based on patrilineal descent or tenure of office.

This point is well illustrated in that portion of Lakshmandan's account dealing with Bhim Singh's reign, particularly with the period in 1719, the year before his death, when Bhim Singh travelled to Delhi for an audience with the recently enthroned Mughal emperor, Muhammad Shah. This audience was instigated and orchestrated by Sayyid Husain Ali Khan who was largely responsible for putting Muhammad Shah on the fabled Peacock Throne and who at that time still controlled the emperor's official actions. Of the event, Lakshmandan wrote:

> Emperor Muhammad Shah ascended the throne in the year 1775 of the Vikrama era,[64] and Vazir Sayyid Husain Ali beseeched him that 'Your Majesty should not forget that your good fortune is due to Maharao Bhim Singh'. So Muhammad Shah summoned Maharao Bhim Singh and declared, 'Ask for whatever land you want and consider it granted.' But the Maharao replied, 'I ask only that whatever land I subdue through the strength of the sword be mine.' Sayyid Husain Ali objected, 'This [request] is unacceptable and will lead to unnecessary killing.' Yet Maharao Bhim Singh insisted, 'If you are freely granting something, then do not grant that which I do not want.' So at this time Muhammad Shah gave Maharao Bhim Singh nine gold coins (*mohars*) and said, 'I grant you in perpetuity whatever land you seize by the strength of your sword and bravery.' This [proclamation] was written and taken by Maharao Bhim Singh who, having offered his respects to the emperor, departed for his capital at Kota.[65]

In this passage, we see that although the maharao accepts the Mughal emperor's prospective sanction for his rule as expressed in the imperial farman and the gold coins, he emphatically rejects the outright gift of land. Instead he insists on establishing that rule through his own personal conquest and the merit of his own deeds. The next episode recounted in the text tells of Bhim Singh's subsequent conquest of Bundi, the crowning military success of his career,[66] but not before Kota's king has stopped in the pilgrimage city of Mathura, distributed food and money to Brahmans, taken initiation into the bhakti sect of the Vallabha Sampraday, and started the worship of the Vallabha idol of Shri Brijnathji, who from that date became Bhim's ishtadevata and later the tutelary god of the entire kingdom. After recounting Bhim Singh's meritorious actions, culminating with his self-sacrifice against Qilich Khan, Lakshmandan ultimately likens Bhim Singh to 'another (or a second) Prithvi Raj Chauhan'.[67] Although the relationship between Prithvi Raj and Bhim Singh *may* have become merely metaphorical in this late nineteenth-century text, resonances of the earlier type of karmic connection remain, nevertheless, very strong.

With this understanding of the alternative ways in which kinship was reckoned in Rajasthan, let us now turn our attention to the political events in Kota during the decade after the battle of Pandhar that informed the production of the Kota Master's painting.

64 Muhammad Shah's installation took place on 14 September 1719.

65 Lakshmandan, '*Vamsha prashasti*', pp. 24–25.

66 Significantly, this account makes no mention of Mughal help in this endeavour.

67 Ibid., p. 30.

The aftermath of Pandhar

Bhim Singh was succeeded by his eldest son Arjun Singh who, in the absence of Shri Brijnathji, worshipped the image of Shri Girirajdharji (alternatively Shri Govardhandharji or Shri Giridharji). Arjun Singh ruled briefly and, by accounts, ineffectually for three years during which time Kota lost control over many of its dependencies. Arjun Singh, for example, forfeited Kota's most prized possession, Bundi, as early as November 1720. Arjun Singh then died without male heir in October 1723 and his death heralded an even bleaker period with the outbreak of civil war between his two younger brothers, Shyam Singh and Durjan Sal.[68] Shyam Singh was the elder and by rights of primogeniture had a claim to the gaddi. But he was absent from Kota when Arjun Singh died, and Durjan Sal had himself consecrated maharao on 18 November 1723. When Shyam learned of this news he gathered an army with the help of Maharaja Jai Singh of Amber (Jaipur), and marched on Kota to unseat his younger brother and, on 12 December, Durjan Sal and Shyam Singh met in battle near the village of Udaipuriya on the frontier between Kota and Bundi. Durjan Sal was victorious in the battle at which Shyam Singh apparently died. This outcome did not end the unrest, however, and for several years Kota remained agitated by millenarian movements headed by warriors claiming to be Shyam Singh.[69] As late as 1727, for example, one of these pretenders was able to put as many as 2000 troops in the field, and Durjan Sal had to request the co-operation of neighbouring rulers in order to subdue this *fitur* (rebel).[70]

In 1724, when it was clear that Shyam Singh lived on in soul if not in body, Durjan Sal *reportedly* sent an emissary to the Deccan who retrieved Bhim Singh's beloved Shri Brijnathji. We, of course, cannot be certain that the recovered idol was the same as the idol that was lost (if it was ever lost in the first place), but *in claiming* to have recovered Bhim's lost idol, Durjan Sal aimed to demonstrate that he was Bhim's worthy successor by means of their common possession of this palladium. This claim accomplished two important tasks for Durjan Sal. First, it established a direct karmic line of descent between him and Bhim Singh superseding the blood-line that privileged the position of Arjun Singh, Shyam Singh and his doubles. Thus Durjan Sal commissioned several paintings depicting himself worshipping Shri Brijnathji along with his deceased father

[68] It is tempting to speculate that these violent political ambitions were the cause of Arjun Singh's premature death.

[69] To mix metaphors, the undying Shyam Singh may be stillborn case of an immortal karmic king similar to the case of Bhim Singh.

[70] V. S. Bhatnagar, *Life and Times of Sawai Jai Singh, 1688–1743* (Delhi: Impex India, 1974), pp. 191–192.

(plate 6). Durjan Sal's brothers, unsurprisingly, do not figure in these scenes, and their conspicuous absence no doubt references that they never possessed the idol and, therefore, were not fully members of the karmalogical dynasty.

Second, by focusing public attention on Shri Brijnathji's tutelary connection to Kota, Durjan Sal privileged Bhim Singh's dedication of the kingdom to Shri Brijanthji, rather than Madho Singh's original 'founding' of the kingdom, as the exemplary constitutive act on which the polity rested. This move diffused the claims to the gaddi that were advanced by members of the more senior Hada lineages descending from Madho Singh. Thus although it may have been Bhim Singh who first brought Shri Brijnathji to Kota, it certainly was Durjan Sal who made the cult of Shri Brijnathji central to the annual cycle of court rituals. On calendrically significant days, such as the first day of the Hindu new year or Krishna's birthday, the image of the god would be taken from his temple and placed on a golden *simhasan* (lion-throne) in such prominent public locations as in the Raj Mahal (the royal audience hall) or in the Lal Chhatri above the main gates to the palace. Here Shri Brijnathji would display himself as Kota's true king and would be worshipped by the entire court and by large sections of the city.[71]

Durjan Sal's working of the (hi)story of Shri Brijnathji's loss and recovery and his elaboration of the cult of the Vallabha idol was effective in shoring up his hold on Kota's gaddi over and against his political rivals. However, this usage was not without latent consequences for kingship in Kota. As we shall see in the following chapter, Durjan Sal's move linked the stability of royal rule in Kota to other non-warrior groups, such as the sectarian hierarchy of the Vallabha Sampraday and Kota's powerful merchant community – the sect's most significant adherents – whose interests did not always harmonize with those of the maharao. Before turning to these interconnections and their repercussions, let us first return to the painting of the battle of Pandhar for one last look.

The king is dead, long live the king!

Given our understandings of how descent was reckoned in Kota, particularly as informed by local beliefs about the transfer of karma, and our knowledge of the political situation in Kota at the time when the painting was produced, we are finally in a position to better understand the curious battle scene of Maharao Bhim Singh and Qilich Khan by the

71 For a mid-eighteenth-century representation of the entire court worshipping Shri Brijnathji enthroned in the Lal Chhatri on the occasion of *janmashtimi*, Krishna's birthday, see Welch, *Gods, Kings, and Tigers*, cat. no. 30, pp. 138–139.

Kota Master. The powerful effect of this painting, apart from the sheer wizardry of the Kota Master's draftsmanship, derives from a contrapuntal polyphony in which the visual cues in the painting are self-consciously and purposefully held in opposition to other well-known textual narratives concerning the event.[72] This heteroglossic reading of the event, in which the visual anti-thesis simultaneously recalls the narrative thesis, creates what Bakhtin called 'a tension-filled interaction'[73] that, in the case at hand, serves to blur the identities of hero and rival precisely at the moment when Qilich Khan demonstrates himself to be the worthy receptacle of Bhim Singh's karma by virtue of his great military victory over the maharao. Therefore, even though the bodily Bhim Singh was defeated and killed in battle on the banks of the Narmada River in 1720, the fruit of his meritorious life, or karma, continued to be manifest in this world; and it did so in none other than the person of Qilich Khan. By virtue of his defeat of Maharao Bhim Singh, Qilich Khan *had become* Bhim Singh – and Bhim Singh, Qilich Khan. With this understanding, we are also able to appreciate why the Rajasthani sources mention that, prior to the battle of Pandhar, Qilich Khan and Bhim Singh had been *pagri badal bhai*, a kinship that caused Qilich Khan to warn Bhim Singh away from the battle. The connection established through the exchange of turbans provided an important prescience that Qilich Khan would later become a worthy and appropriate vehicle for Bhim Singh's meritorious karma. It also informs accounts of Qilich Khan's respectful stewardship of the idol of Shri Brijnathji after the battle. Finally, one should note that the Kota Master expressed something of this symmetry in his visual construction of the climactic confrontation in which Bhim Singh and Qilich Khan are shown as mirror images of one another inhabiting the same axial plane within the composition whose balance is enhanced by their parallel, reciprocal blows of the sword (plate 2).[74]

The contradictory qualities of the visual narrative of the painting were, therefore, never meant to completely obliterate or unmake the literary narrative(s) of the chronicles, and the fact that these other literary glosses

[72] For another example of heteroglossia within the multiple media of myth and ritual, see two essays by Alma Gottlieb, 'Dog: Ally or Traitor? Mythology, Cosmology and Society among the Beng of Ivory Coast', *American Ethnologist* 13 (1986): 477–488; and 'Hyenas and Heteroglossia: Myth and Ritual among the Beng of Côte d'Ivoire', *American Ethnologist* 16 (1989): 487–501.

[73] Mikhail M. Bakhtin, 'Discourse in the Novel', in *The Dialogic Imagination: Four Essays by M. M. Bakhtin*, ed. and trans. Michael Holquist (Austin: University of Texas Press, 1981 [1934–35]).

[74] It is far more common in most artistic traditions for the victor to be positioned above the vanquished. I am grateful to Lawrence Cohen (personal communication: 3 June 1997) for pointing out this facet of the painting to me.

have not been totally effaced does not indicate the failure of visual narrative to establish its authority or achieve its purpose. Rather the visual was meant to reposition, or decentre, the literary narratives by creating a multi-centred, heteroglossic domain. The multiple, contradictory readings of this larger interpretive field created dynamic tensions that produced mutable notions of self and alternative forms of historical consciousness that were not necessarily foregrounded in the texts or paintings alone. In this case at least, the intended merging of Bhim Singh's and Qilich Khan's identity was effectively created by holding two contradictory readings in view simultaneously.

3 In whose turban does the lord reside?: Kings, saints, and merchants in western India

On reaching Mathura and having bathed, Maharao Bhim Singh distributed money and food to Brahmans. While in his camp, he then changed his name to Krishnadas [servant of Krishna] and changed the names of Kota and Shergarh [Mau-Maidana] to Nandagaon and Barsana.[1] The city of Kota was dedicated to Shri Nathji and until this day the rental income from the city and the palace go to Nathadvara on a tax-free basis. Maharao Bhim Singh then worshipped Shri Brijnathji according to the practice of the Vallabha Sampraday. After which, on the pretense of being ill, he concealed himself in his tent and, proclaiming that he had died from this sickness, constructed an effigy of himself and cremated it.

This caused a great lamentation to spread throughout the land. In Bundi, Salim Singh [faujdar, or military commander, in charge of the city] heard this news and started to pillage the countryside around Kota with a formidable army... Reports of this invasion were sent to Mathura... [in response to which] Maharao Bhim Singh spread a rumour among Salim Singh's troops that his ghost would come to get them... Salim Singh became frightened... and he fled Kota... He was followed by Maharao Bhim Singh as far as Bundi... The maharao's lethal sword entered the city where his soldiers raised ladders and entered the citadel. Wherever the maharao's sword went, men fell in masses. Salim Singh fled for his life from the city. – Kaviraja Lakshmandan ('*Maharao Shatru Shalji Bahadur ki vamsha prashasti*', pp. 25–26)

When Maharao Bhim Singh of Kota purportedly took initiation into the Vallabha Sampraday at Mathura in late 1719 and received the image of Shri Brijnathji, he joined a Vaishnava sect (*sampraday*) whose most famous idol was the shiny, black stone statue of Shri Nathji residing in the busy pilgrimage town of Nathadvara in southern Rajasthan.[2] Like Shri

1 Shergarh was one of the largest fortified cities in Kota's southern *pargana* (district) of Mau-Maidana. Nandagaon was the village where Krishna's foster father, Nanda, lived, and Barsana was the village where Krishna's consort, Radha, lived.

2 For excellent analyses of Vallabha doctrine and practice, see R. K. Barz, *The Bhakti Sect of Vallabhacarya* (Faridabad, Haryana: Thomson Press, 1976); Peter Bennett, 'Temple Organization and Worship among the Pustimargiya-Vaisnavas of Ujjain' (PhD thesis,

Plate 8 Shri Nathji, worshipped by Tilkayat Dauji II, head priest of the Shri Nathji Temple. Opaque watercolour on paper, c. 1831. Approximately 25 × 20 cm. Private Collection. Photograph by Norbert Peabody.

Brijnathji and, indeed, all idols of the sect, the statue of Shri Nathji is an anthropomorphic manifestation of Krishna, the sect's paramount deity (plate 8). More than simply representing Krishna, Vallabha idols are believed to contain this deity's immanent presence and to possess (and emanate) his mystical powers. For this reason, when Vallabha idols are depicted in paintings they are often represented as fully animate subjects

School of Oriental and African Studies, University of London, 1983) and 'In Nanda Baba's House: The Devotional Experience in Pushti Marg Temples,' in *Divine Passions: The Social Construction of Emotion in India*, ed. O. M. Lynch (Berkeley: University of California Press, 1990), pp. 182–211; and Owen M. Lynch, 'Pilgrimage with Krishna, Sovereign of the Emotions', *Contributions to Indian Sociology* (N.S.) 22 (1988): 171–194.

rather than as cold stone or metal objects (see plate 6 in chapter 2).[3] As a regular feature of Vallabha practice, members of the sect worship the idols in order to partake of their special powers, and seek to make pilgrimage to important temples, such as the Shri Nathji Temple.[4] This chapter examines some of the implications of the attempts by Kota's rulers to bind these supernatural powers to the service of their rule and what consequences this had both for royal action and for the maintenance and perpetuation of the divine powers of the idols themselves.

For many years now it has been a commonplace observation in history and anthropology that the monopolistic possession of sacred objects, heirlooms, talismans, or regalia helps perpetuate political rule. Pierre Bourdieu, who has made great academic capital from the expression 'symbolic capital', has shown that the tight regulation of exchange in specially demarcated objects not only sanctions but also constitutes privilege by establishing which referential coordinates of value are natural and legitimate.[5] Igor Kopytoff has elaborated upon this insight with his discussion of how certain objects are imbued with 'cultural biographies' that singularize them, resulting in their fetishism (to expand Marx's coinage), while removing them from more promiscuous and uncontrolled spheres of exchange.[6] However, the kings in western India faced the unusual problem that the mobility of the most renowned statuary was notoriously mercurial and not subject to direct royal command. Instead it was under the management of sectarian hierarchs who, in turn, were closely linked to Rajasthan's great trading communities. The capricious mobility of idols, an essential part of their pedigree (or biography) and

[3] Following Caroline Humphrey and James Laidlaw, I use the term 'idol', despite its pejorative connotations in modern western usage, rather than the euphemistic 'image'. I do this because 'idol' best captures the assertion among followers of the Vallabha Sampraday that their gods are immanent in the statues that 'represent' them. In retaining 'idol', I think it is better to confront and reform *our* Judeo-Christian prejudices about 'idolatry' rather than submerge a central tenet of indigenous belief behind a less apt term whose principal virtue is that it is inoffensive to *us*. See Caroline Humphrey and James Laidlaw, *The Archetypal Actions of Ritual: A Theory of Ritual Illustrated by the Jain Rite of Worship* (Oxford: Clarendon Press, 1994), pp. 57–58, note 1.

[4] The Vallabha Sampraday drew its greatest support from among the three upper ('twice-born') castes, particularly among the merchant (*vaisya*) community. Other Hindus, regardless of sectarian affiliation, may (and often do) worship at Vallabha temples. In this respect Hindu sects do not display the same exclusivity as, for example, Christian sects. This tendency towards incorporation did not extend to economically and politically marginal groups (outcastes and tribals), however. These communities traditionally were denied full sectarian initiation.

[5] Pierre Bourdieu, *Outline of a Theory of Practice*, trans. R. Nice (Cambridge: Cambridge University Press, 1977).

[6] Igor Kopytoff, 'The Cultural Biography of Things: Commoditization as Process', in *The Social Life of Things*, ed. Arjun Appadurai (Cambridge: Cambridge University Press, 1986), pp. 64–91.

crucial to sustaining their powers, at the same time threatened to undermine dynastic stability and royal authority which, territorially based in Rajasthan, was not so itinerant.

One witnesses the palpable tension between the capacity of idols to legitimate kingship and the necessity for them to remain in circulation in the late seventeenth-century sectarian account of Shri Nathji's origins and migration to Nathadvara, the *Shrinathji ki prakatya varta* (or SPV), which links the presence of Shri Nathji to several Rajput kingdoms including Kota.[7] The SPV, or 'An account of the manifestation of Shri Nathji', was composed in the vernacular Brajbasha by Goswami Hariray, one of the Sampraday's most famous literary figures.[8] Contemporary popular tradition still links Hariray directly to Kota where he is said to have resided from time to time during his long life when not on one of his numerous pilgrimages.[9] According to the SPV, in 1669 the 'Patshah' (the Mughal Emperor Aurangzeb) forced Shri Nathji's priests to remove the god from his original home near Mathura (Uttar Pradesh) and seek refuge with the rajas of western India. Aurangzeb, unlike his more ecumenical great-grandfather Akbar, had recently (re)imposed discriminatory taxes on his non-Muslim subjects and had ordered the destruction of several prominent Hindu temples culminating, most famously, in the razing in 1670 of Mathura's Keshavdev Temple.[10] For two years, the temple priests kept Shri Nathji on the move one step ahead of Aurangzeb's armies. First, the image was secreted into the sometime Mughal capital of Agra, just south of Mathura, where it was worshipped clandestinely for a

[7] Hariray, *Shrinathji ki prakatya varta* (Nathadvara: Vidyavibhag Mandir Mandal, 1986). The first half of the SPV has been translated into English by Charlotte Vaudeville in 'The Govardhan Myth in Northern India', *Indo-Iranian Journal* 22 (1980): 1–45. Legends of Shri Nathji's travels also figure in royal chronicles, such as Kaviraja Shyamaldas's *Virvinod*, Volume 1 (Delhi: Motilal Banarasidas, 1986 [1886]), pp. 452–453.

[8] Hariray also substantially reworked and added commentaries to two of the sect's most important hagiographical texts: the *Chaurasi vaishnavan ki varta* (Indore: Vaishnav Mitr Mandal, 1992) (hereafter the 84V), and the *Do sau bavan vaishnavan ki varta*, 3 volumes (Indore: Vaishnav Mitr Mandal, 1992) (hereafter the 252V), whose original composition is conventionally attributed to Goswami Gokulnath.

[9] Hariray lived the proverbial 125 years from 1590–1715. His birth date, obviously, must be treated with some circumspection.

[10] Despite his reputation for ultra-orthodoxy (which has become exaggerated with time), Aurangzeb's iconoclasm was much more contextually manifest. The temples he destroyed were often those that were, in some way, connected to his enemies. It thus should be noted that Aurangzeb never actually destroyed the abandoned Vallabha temples in Braj, and the Sampraday continued to exercise authority over these properties. Moreover, during the 1660s, at least, Aurangzeb intervened to mediate disputes within the sect rather than attempting to suppress the sect altogether. As this was a time of several Jat uprisings in the Braj region, it is likely that the sectarian hierarchs were fleeing the general political instability of the period (to which Aurangzeb was a party) rather than his specific policies toward them.

short while.[11] But this arrangement did not please Shri Nathji and he was taken to Rajasthan where he temporarily graced in the kingdoms of Bundi, Kota, Jodhpur, and Kishangarh before finding more or less permanent sanctuary at Nathadvara in Mewar (Udaipur) (map 1).[12] A chorus of oral traditions concerning the wanderings of lesser Vallabha deities during the unsettled late seventeenth century echoes the literary legacy of the SPV. One of these widespread oral narratives provides background for the popular rhetorical question, 'in whose turban does the lord reside?', a lament to the fugitive nature of divine grace. This tradition recounts that Vallabha deities typically eluded the imminent arrival of hostile enemies by being concealed in the turbans of temple servants (most Vallabha idols are only a few centimeters tall) and whisked away to new (but often indeterminate) locales of safe haven.[13]

Significantly, the tension between sectarian mobility and dynastic stability also informed royal chronicles from the region, albeit in muted tones. For instance, in the passage from Lakshmandan's panegyric cited at the beginning of this chapter, the initiation at Mathura of Maharao Bhim Singh precipitated rumours of the maharao's death and emboldened Salim Singh of Bundi to invade Kota.[14] Fortunately, Bhim Singh re-emerged from his confinement in the nick of time and, with Shri Brijnathji in his possession, repulsed the attack and conquered Bundi. Lakshmandan's chronicle thus portrayed Bhim Singh's initiation, at which he was endowed with the kingdom's tutelary god, as inciting the invasion and near destruction of the kingdom! In other words, there is a tacit recognition even within this royal text that sectarian support is a potentially double-edged sword.

Before exploring the factors informing this paradoxical situation and the multiple uses to which the tensions created by it could be put by different groups within (and beyond) the kingdom, it will be necessary to provide some background about the history, philosophy, and sectarian organization of Vallabha Sampraday and some greater detail about the place of idols in the sect's worship.

11 Hariray, SPV, pp. 39–42.

12 Ibid., pp. 48 ff.

13 On the tradition of concealing images (in this case a painted one) in turbans, see the varta of Raskhan, in Hariray, 252V, Volume 3, varta 245, pp. 341–347. This practice further deepens our understanding of the blurred identities of Bhim Singh and Qilich Khan as established through their status as *pagri badal bhai* and their serial possession of the Shri Brijnathji statue.

14 This episode is an obvious calque upon the famous varta of Maharaja Askaran in which the king's total absorption with Krishna prompts an invasion by a neighbouring army. Just when things appear dire for Askaran's realm, Krishna appears to the ruler in a dream and tells him that he must fulfil his royal duties. Askaran dutifully abandons his meditations, gathers his army, and defeats the invaders. See Hariray, 252V, Volume 2, varta 123, pp. 181–200.

The bhakti sect of Vallabhacharya

The devotional (*bhakti*) sect of the Vallabha Sampraday was founded by the Vaishnava saint Vallabhacharya (1479?–1531). A Telegu Brahman from south India, Vallabhacharya is now closely associated with the region of Braj in which the 'historical' Krishna is said to have lived and in which the divine idol of Shri Nathji first appeared miraculously out of the earth. Devotional sects, with their supposed emphasis on egalitarian values and emotional congregational styles of worship, are typically characterized in the academic literature as opposed in some manner to brahmanical Hinduism, which is associated with the hierarchy of caste, ritual formalism, and the belief that liberation (*moksa*) from the karmic cycle of rebirths can only be achieved exceptionally by the individual renunciation of worldly attachments.[15] Ascetic renunciation (*samnyas*) is traditionally viewed as the fourth, and final, Hindu stage of life (*asrama*): the first three being *brahmacarya*, or religious studentship, *grhasthya*, or the stage of the married householder, and *vanaprasthya*, or the stage when the householder retires to the forest for meditation in preparation for total renunciation. Although Vallabha belief discounts the importance of asceticism to achieving liberation, it nevertheless elevates the practices of the householder (*grhastha*), the second of the four asramas, to supreme soteriological importance. Among the householder's responsibilities are the duties of procreation, performing sacrifices (especially to the ancestors), and living within the community. The last obligation, paradoxically for a devotional sect, valorizes social hierarchies based upon caste divisions.[16] The centrality of the values of the householder to Vallabha belief is well illustrated by the type of devotion that devotees are encouraged to cultivate for Krishna in their quest for union with him. The favoured inner emotion for the followers of Vallabhacharya is the maternal, or familial, love (*vatsalya bhav*) that Krishna's foster mother, Yashoda, had for her divine charge when he was an infant. This belief accounts for the somewhat unusual fact that most Vallabha images represent Krishna as a child or young adolescent. Vallabhacharyans typically contrast this type of disinterested and unselfish love with the eroticism of *madhurya bhav*,

[15] For variants of this thesis, see Milton Singer, *When a Great Tradition Modernizes* (New York: Praeger, 1972); David F. Pocock, *Mind, Body and Wealth* (Oxford: Basil Blackwell, 1973), and K. Ishwaran, 'Bhakti Tradition and Modernization: The Case of Lingayatism', *Journal of Asian and African Studies* 15 (1980): 72–83. For an important critique of this thesis, see Peter van der Veer, 'Taming the Ascetic: Devotionalism in a Hindu Monastic Order', *Man* (N.S.) 22 (1987): 680–695.

[16] For more on the significance of the householder within the Vallabha Sampraday, see Barz, *Bhakti Sect*, pp. 32–33; Rajendra Jindel, *Culture of a Sacred Town* (Bombay: Popular Prakashan, 1976), pp. 180–188; and Lynch, 'Pilgrimage with Krishna', pp. 179–180. For the duties of the householder more generally throughout Hinduism, see T. N. Madan, *Non-Renunciation* (Delhi: Oxford University Press, 1987).

the illicit love between Krishna and his consort Radha, which violates domestic order.

Vallabhacharya's positive appreciation of the householder's concerns rests in large part on his philosophical acceptance of the fundamental reality of the world and his coincident rejection of the Shankaracharyan system of *mayavada*, whereby the world is regarded as illusion (*maya*).[17] Owen Lynch suggests that Vallabhacharya's doctrine resulted in the development of what he calls 'this worldly mysticism' in which the individual 'does not try to transcend the natural and the profane to reach the supernatural and sacred... [but] rather... tries to experience more correctly that the natural, the profane, and the self *are* the supernatural, the sacred, and the divine.'[18] It is precisely because of Vallabhacharya's rejection of the sacred/profane dichotomy that his philosophy became known as 'pure non-dualism' (*suddhadvaita*).

The sect's distinctive non-ascetic position (it has no ascetic subbranches unlike, for example, the Chaitanya sect of Krishna devotees) is reaffirmed forcefully in the passage from Lakshmandan's text concerning Bhim Singh's initiation where his cremation (along with the worship of Shri Brijnathji and the changing of names) signifies his conversion and rebirth into the Vallabha Sampraday. However, such a dramatic form of conversion is not usual within the sect – receiving a sacred mantra from a religious preceptor usually suffices. Significantly, among most Hindus, ritual cremation customarily accompanies the act of renunciation. If one interprets Bhim Singh's cremation as an attempt to renounce, it is then important that Bhim Singh abandoned this intention and resumed the duties of kingship.[19]

17 These philosophical concerns were not merely the esoteric ruminations of a politically marginal priesthood. That such tenets were of vital royal consequence is attested by the considerable number of devotional tracts on Vallabha themes written by members of Kota's ruling dynasty and housed (formerly) in the Saraswati Bhandar Royal Library (now divided between the Government Museum, Kota and the Rajasthan Prachyavidhya Pratishthan, Kota). Maharao Arjun Singh of Kota (r. 1720–23), for example, composed a praise poem/song (*kirtan*) in which he expressed his understanding of the difference between Shankaracharya's '*mayavad*' and Vallabhacharya's '*brahmavad*' philosophies (ms. no. 3455, RPPK). Maharao Kishor Singh of Kota (r. 1819–27) demonstrated an even more sophisticated familiarity with the most important Vallabha treatises such as Vallabhacharya's *Subhodini*, a commentary on the tenth chapter of the *Bhagavatapurana*, the sect's most important text (ms. no. 7071/3, RPPK). More generally, the Saraswati Bandhar formerly contained a large number of religious texts of doctrinal significance to the Vallabha Sampraday. Of the large number of *Bhagavatapuranas*, several were lavishly illustrated (e.g. acc. no. 1950.1138, GMK which dates to 1759). For much more on this matter, see Woodman Taylor, 'Picture Practice: Painting Programs, Manuscript Production, and Liturgical Performances at the Kotah Royal Palace', in *Gods, Kings, and Tigers: The Art of Kotah*, ed. Stuart Cary Welch (Munich: Prestel-Verlag, 1997), pp. 61–72.

18 Lynch, 'Pilgrimage with Krishna,' pp. 190–191.

19 The dire consequences of the king's desire to renounce, of course, is a common theme in all forms of Hinduism, but I would argue that it resonates with a special intensity for adherents of the Vallabha Sampraday. See also note 14 above.

The positive religious valuation that Vallabhacharya's followers placed on the householder's worldly concerns has several outcomes, which are mentioned here only briefly. In the ritual domain, the worship of a Vallabha idol in its *haveli* (temple, literally villa) is designed to ensure the utmost physical comfort of the deity as if he or she were a sentient being. Thus the idol's raiment and decoration, musical entertainments, offerings of food, and daily activities (sleeping, bathing, playing, and so forth) are all mindfully adjusted to be appropriate to both the time of day and the seasonal cycles of weather and festivals. Similarly, the hagiography of Vallabhacharya places great emphasis on his marriage and domestic life. By comparison, the vestigial month-long period of asceticism that he underwent just before his death receives scant concern and is not at all central to his salvation quest.[20] A notable consequence of this concern with Vallabhacharya's family life has been that his progeny continue to monopolize religious authority within the sect. Members of the Sampraday believe that Vallabhacharya and his agnatic descendants are avatars of Krishna himself who intervene in this degenerate black age (*kali yuga*) in order to help devotees overcome 'their wrong perception and wrong attitude toward the world'[21] and develop the proper vision and experience of it.[22] Through this freely bestowed intercession devotees receive the gift of grace (*pusti*) that allows them to achieve salvation. For this reason, members of the Vallabha Sampraday are commonly called *Pustimargi*s (followers of the path of grace).

Initially, the supernatural power to intercede on behalf of individuals rested solely with Vallabhacharya, and sectarian authority thus remained undivided. But as 'the celestial tree of the Vallabha family' flourished, the divine legacy of Vallabhacharya devolved to all his agnatic offspring, known as *gosvami*s (goswamis) or *gosaim*s (gosains), and authority within the sect became dispersed albeit within the confines of the family. Each of these goswamis (ad)ministered to his own followers, and their prerogatives included the authority to initiate members into the Sampraday (with the *brahmasambandh mantra* that had been revealed to Vallabhacharya at Gokul in Braj) and to distribute idols for worship by lay devotees. Despite the diffusion of authority, the Sampraday is notable, however, in that spirituality has been confined to Vallabhacharya's agnatic descendants. There is no tradition or formal mechanism for electing or designating gurus from the wider lay community.

20 As David Pocock notes, some Vallabhacharyans deny that Vallabhacharya even made this small concession to renunciation. See David Pocock, *Mind, Body, Wealth: A Study of Belief and Practice in an Indian Village* (Oxford: Basil Blackwell, 1973), p. 112.

21 Lynch, 'Pilgrimage with Krishna', p. 178.

22 As agents of divine intercession, the descendants of Vallabhacharya are much like Buddhist *bodhisattva*s except that these descendants do not seek to liberate the individual from worldly attachments as a *bodhisattva* does.

Although all patrilineal descendants share in Vallabhacharya's divinity, eight members of the sectarian hierarchy claim (and generally enjoy) special status within the sect. They claim to be the senior ranking male members of eight patrilineages descending from the seven sons of Vallabhacharya's second son, Vittalnath Gosain (see figure 2). This exalted status is indexed by their possession of certain idols of divine origin known as the nine treasures (*navnidhi*) that once belonged to Vallabhacharya and that are deeply venerated within (and beyond) the sect. According to tradition, Vallabhacharya had collected these idols during his lifetime and passed them to Vitthalnath Gosain, who then dispersed them among his seven sons. These images have then been passed through the male line according to the norms of primogeniture, with the exception of the seniormost lineage which has undergone one further segmentation.[23] These eight major stem lineages, known as *gaddi*s or *pitha*s (seats) (or *ghar*s, houses), are commonly ranked according to their seniority of descent from Vallabhacharya. The gaddis are thus numbered one through seven with the seniormost gaddi remaining unenumerated in this scheme. For this reason Pushtimargis often call their most sacred deities the *satsvarup* (the seven svarups) instead of the navnidhi (the nine treasures). According to this classification, each of the seven *enumerated* svarups is associated with one of the seven *enumerated* gaddis. The supreme image of Shri Nathji and the image of his constant companion Shri Navanitpriyaji that are associated with the seniormost *unenumerated* gaddi are not explicitly listed in this classification for they are believed to contain the sum-total qualities and attributes of the other seven.

The powers attributed to Hindu images are legion, and Vallabha statues are, in this regard, no exception. Pushtimargis regularly affirm the ability of their deities to fulfill their heartfelt desires (*manorath*). The SPV itself recounts how the statue of Shri Nathji satisfied numerous entreaties of devotees such as curing infertility, finding brides for sons, returning lost cattle, and restoring good health. Some idols enjoy particular renown for their ability to grant the requests of devotees, and pilgrims from all over India travel to let their wishes be known directly to these deities and, of course, to give offerings. As a result several Vallabha temples have become extremely wealthy, and today the Shri Nathji Temple in Nathadvara is reported to be one of the richest in all of India.[24] Accounts of early European travellers to Nathadvara indicate that this wealth is not a recent

[23] However, as with the case of Bhim Singh, Durjan Sal, and the Shri Brijnathji statue discussed in the previous chapter, it is more than likely that the possession of these statues conferred kinship links among their possessors as often as it resulted from them.

[24] Jindel, *Culture of a Sacred Town*, p. 142.

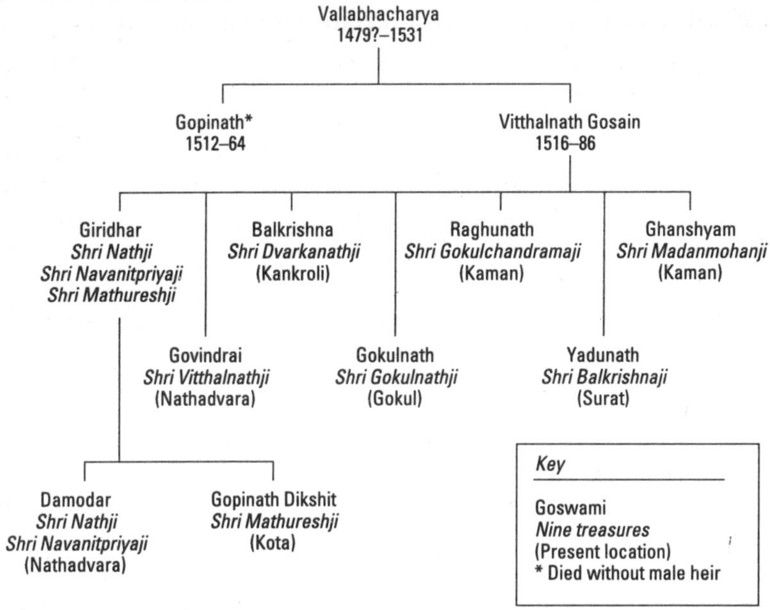

Figure 2 The 'celestial tree' of Vallabhacharya showing the distribution of the Sampraday's 'nine treasures'
Source: Amit Ambalal, *Krishna as Shrinathji* (Ahmedabad: Mapin, 1987)

phenomenon.[25] Due to this veneration, these images have become the objects of property disputes (which now involve the modern state) and famous historical instances of theft. In addition, the powers associated with these statues have made them important actors in the political struggles of western India.

The sacralization of idols

One curious anomaly in Kota is that although Shri Brijnathji is the kingdom's tutelary deity, he is far from the kingdom's most revered deity. In fact, although Shri Brijnathji figures prominently in royal chronicles, he does not even register in the sectarian varta literature. Kota's most popular deity is the Vallabha idol of Shri Mathureshji,[26] whose temple is in the heart of Kota's main bazaar about 400 metres from the maharao's

[25] Lt Col. James Tod, *Annals and Antiquities of Rajast'han or, the Central and Western Rajpoot States of India* (London, 1829), Volume I, pp. 527–531.

[26] Alternatively, Shri Mathuradhisji or Shri Mathuranathji.

palace – a peculiar location, given the normal propensity of kings to buttress their position with the strongest divine sanctions available. In order to understand why Shri Brijnathji, and not Shri Mathureshji, should be the tutelary deity of Kota, we must first appreciate the manner in which Vallabha idols are empowered through ritual and otherwise. Through this analysis I hope to establish one of the most important ways in which royal and sectarian authority were linked in Kota.

Pushtimargis oppose the terms *svarup* and *murti* to differentiate their religious statues from those of other Hindu groups. Murti is used somewhat pejoratively within the sect to mark non-Vallabha statues that pass through a consecration rite such as the life-breath ceremony (*pran-pratistha*) before being suitable for worship. During such ceremonies the immanent presence of the deity is activated in the statue by Brahman priests who transfer their vital energies to it through the recitation of Sanskrit mantras.[27] After performance of the life-breath ceremony, however, the deity may not choose to reside permanently in the statue. The deity is free to come and go as she or he pleases, and should the statue ever be damaged accidentally, it would no longer be suitable for worship. By contrast, the immanent presence of Lord Krishna eternally inheres in the material substance of a Vallabha svarup, meaning essential (*sva*) form (*rup*), which always remains divine. Hence there are no rites in which the deity is inveighed to retake residence in the idol, and the svarup must be worshipped continuously lest the deity suffer any deprivation.

The distinction between murti and svarup is informed by a similar discrimination between *puja* (the act of worship performed in ordinary Hindu temples) and *seva* (the act of worship performed in Vallabha temples). According to Richard Barz, for Pushtimargis:

> the act of *puja* is a selfish action, it is a giving of an offering to the divine in expectation of receiving a reward from the divine. In doing *puja* one does not think of the comfort of the divinity except in that the giving of something beneficial to the divinity will bring the divinity's aid to the giver. *Seva*, on the other hand, is service (*seva*), disinterested service to the divine simply because it is the duty and the delight of man to serve the divine and not because of desire for some benefit from the divine. *Seva*, in short, is unselfish love for and service of the divine being, while *puja* is worship done for the doer's benefit. There are some physical differences between organized *puja* and organized *seva* – for

[27] For fuller descriptions and discussions of the *pran-pratistha*, see Diana L. Eck, *Darsan: Seeing the Divine Image in India* (Chambersberg, PA: Anima Books, 1985 [1981]), pp. 52–55; P. V. Kane, *History of Dharmasastra* (Poona: Bhandarkar Oriental Research Institute, 1974), Volume 2, Part 2, pp. 896–903; and G. C. Tripathi, '*Navakalevara*: The Unique Ceremony of the "Birth" and "Death" of the "Lord of the World"', in *The Cult of Jagannath and the Regional Tradition of Orissa*, eds A. Eschmann, H. Kulke, and G. C. Tripathi (Delhi: Manohar, 1978), pp. 254–261.

example, worshippers doing *puja* usually offer their offering and perform their worship as isolated individuals while, on the other hand, *sevakas* perform *seva* as a group, as a *satsang*, and do not offer their gifts directly before the divine *svarupa* – but the real difference is in the attitude within the heart of the worshipper.[28]

Thus for Pushtimargis the difference between murti and svarup not only encompasses a difference in the physical properties of the images but also entails different emotional states and patterns of behaviour for devotees as well.

Among their own statuary, Pushtimargis further distinguish between the divinely created navnidhi (the nine treasures) and a theoretically limitless group of man-made images known as *pusti-svarups*.[29] Despite their anthropomorphic form, the navnidhi are considered to be *svyambhu*, meaning 'self-manifest', and numerous popular texts recount their supernatural origins. According to these traditions, Vallabhacharya and his first disciples discovered them, after they had miraculously appeared from the earth in full iconic form unblemished by the imperfections of human creation. The SPV, for example, narrates how the outstretched hand and arm of Shri Nathji emerged partially from the earth on Mt Govardhan near Mathura before the birth of Vallabhacharya but had been misidentified as a snake-god (*nag*) and improperly worshipped by the local inhabitants of the land. Later when Vallabhacharya was a young man, Shri Nathji summoned him to Mt. Govardhan, where the guru revealed the true identity of the deity and instructed people on the idol's proper worship.

The status of the nine treasures is linked to another factor, in addition to their sublime genesis, that not only validated but also sustained their potency. This is that Vallabhacharya and Vitthalnath Gosain, the sect's two greatest preceptors, both had personally performed the seva of these idols. Moreover, since the dispersal of these idols among Vitthalnath's sons, their seva has been performed continuously by patrilineal descendants of the sect's founding masters.[30] For this reason the navnidhi are often called *sevya-svarup* reflecting the fact that their status and well-being are linked to the seva performed by the family of Vallabhacharya.

The central feature of this seva has been the seven or eight daily offerings of food (*bhog*) to the idols who feed on it through their gaze. Devotees consider this offering of food to be essential to maintaining the physical

28 Barz, *Bhakti Sect*, p. 51 (diacriticals omitted).

29 Typically, there are said to be 36, 84, 252, or some other auspicious number. The lack of definitiveness on this matter will become important later in my analysis.

30 Because this task is so time consuming, the descendants of Vallabhacharya often have teams of specialist Brahman priests perform this seva on their behalf. These Brahmans traditionally have belonged to the *Audich*, *Sanchora*, or *Girinara* subcastes.

well-being of the idols (who, after all, are just children). That they understand the act of feeding to be more than a symbolic act of supplication is attested by several assertions and practices. First, like other Hindus, Pushtimargis say that through the act of worship bhog is transformed into *prasad*, a eucharistic leaving. However, Pushtimargis also routinely pledge that this prasad has a sweeter taste (*ras*) than the original bhog as a result of coming in physical contact with Krishna's saliva. Moreover, because the idol really does consume the food the sect has developed a culinary tradition which, although sophisticated and complex in many ways, always remained well suited to the delicate palate of a child. Use of salt and strong spices, such as chilies, for example, has been kept to a minimum and offerings of milk, cakes, and sweets have been favoured.[31]

The daily offering of food was elaborated and enlarged at monthly or yearly festivals (*utsavs*). At the annual Annakut Festival, for instance, food (*annakut*) consisting of a huge pile of rice surrounded by various sweets and cakes was mounded up before the deity for his nourishment and delectation. But surely the most spectacular of these feasts was the *mahotsav* (great festival) that was first performed by Vitthalnath Gosain in 1588 at Govardhan in Braj. On this occasion all of the *navnidhi* were assembled for a joint feast of 56 choice delicacies (*chhapan bhog*). This tradition has been observed by Vitthalnath Gosain's descendants on several occasions since, although it has proven impossible to reassemble all nine of the treasures at the same time ever again. Two of these latter mahotsavs are especially important in the collective memory of the Sampraday for they saw eight of the nine nidhis congregate at the Shri Nathji Temple in Nathadvara.[32] In a case of collective 'nervous eating' on a colossal scale, both of these occasions coincided with periods of deep political crisis in north India. The first of these two mahotsavs was initiated in late 1739 and continued for much of the next year during the political free-for-all caused by the near total disintegration of the Mughal Empire and the unchecked, but incomplete, rise of the Maratha *svarajya*.[33] The second mahotsav took place in 1822 when the kingdoms of western India were first entering into subsidiary alliances with the British (1817–23). These congregations were, doubtless, instrumental in reasserting *sectarian* solidarity and, with regard to the 1739–40 mahotsav, whose costs were substantially funded by Maharao Durjan Sal of Kota, it is likely that

31 Paul M. Toomey, 'Krishna's Consuming Passions: Food as Metaphor and Metonym for Emotion at Mount Govardhan', in *Divine Passions: The Social Construction of Emotion in India*, ed. O. M. Lynch (Berkeley: University of California Press, 1990), pp. 157–181; Peter J. Bennett, 'In Nanda Baba's House: The Devotional Experience in Pushti Marg Temples', in ibid., pp. 182–211.

32 On several other occasions, lesser numbers of the navnidhi have been brought together.

33 Nadir Shah of Persia sacked Delhi in 1739. A year earlier, Kota had begun paying the Marathas an annual tribute.

Kota's ruler hoped to use this *communitas* to galvanize *political* solidarity in opposition to the Marathas.[34]

The second class of Vallabha statues, those of admitted human manufacture, are sacralized by virtue of their passage through the hands, at one time or another, of a patrilineal descendant of Vallabhacharya who blesses them by bathing them in *pancamrt* (the five nectars of curds, milk, ghee, honey, and sugar) and feeding them prasad from a previously established svarup. Because the descendant of Vallabhacharya is instrumental in bestowing the 'nourishing grace' (*pushti*) of Krishna on these images, they are known as *pushti-svarups*. Although these statues are svarups, their human fabrication relegates them to a lesser order than the navnidhi.[35] Moreover, unlike the navnidhi, the man-made statues eventually may be distributed to lay devotees who perform their seva. The Shri Brijnathji idol purportedly given to Maharao Bhim Singh of Kota in Mathura falls into this category.

Although the number of the navnidhi is by definition fixed at nine, in practice a larger number of images enjoy the attribution of divine genesis without generally being accepted as one of the nine treasures. These images are often called *nidhi-svarup* reflecting their hybrid status between navnidhi and pushti-svarup. Peter Bennett has noted that:

> the prestige of many images is often enhanced in the estimation of worshippers if their biographies reveal that they were at some time in the past worshipped by the great preceptors or their eminent disciples, or if they appeared in miraculous circumstances, or if they are subsidiary manifestations of the original nine.[36]

Attempts to enhance the status of Shri Brijnathji clearly have been made in Kota. This has been accomplished principally by linking the idol more closely to the devotion of important descendants of Vallabhacharya. Thus the goswami in charge of the Shri Mathureshji Temple was often requested to perform the seva of Shri Brijnathji, especially on important festival days, such as Krishna's birth anniversary; and occasionally the head priest (known as the 'Tilkayat') of the Shri Nathji Temple in Nathadvara was even enticed to Kota to perform this task (plate 9). Woodman Taylor, moreover, has detected similar evidence of the royal desire to collapse the distinction between nidhi-svarup and pushti-svarup in the central decorative program of the Shri Brijnathji Temple in Kota. He observed that:

[34] Kanthamani Shastri, *Kankroli ka itihas* (Kankroli: Shrividya-Vibhag, 1939), pt. vi, p. 166.

[35] On the hierarchy of svarups, see Bennett, 'In Nanda Baba's House', pp. 200–204; and Lynch, 'Pilgrimage with Krishna', p. 190.

[36] Bennett, 'In Nanda Baba's House', p. 202.

above the lion-throne (upon which Shri Brijnathji is often displayed) within the inner sanctum, a painting mounted behind glass shows Maharaos Bhim Singh and Durjan Sal both worshipping Shri Nathji. The painting visually supplies the ontological equivalence of Shri Brijnathji with Sri Nathji, while also including the political rhetoric of the Kotah maharaos' long patronage and participation in Vallabha Sampraday practices.[37]

This desire to establish an ontological equivalence between Shri Brijnathji and the navnidhi is also beautifully revealed in the '*Shri Brajnathasya svarup bhavana*' of Maharao Kishor Singh (r. 1819–27).[38] This devotional poem, which was composed sometime between 1804 and 1819 when Kishor was still crown prince, equates different facets of the iconography and seva of Shri Brijnathji to each of the navnidhi and, thus, implies that Shri Brijnathji was not only equal to them individually but is also equal to them as a collectivity much in the same way that Shri Nathji is seen as equal to the sum total of the other navnidhi. However, the simple fact of having to assert this ontological equivalence belies the existence of the sectarian distinction between the two classes of idols and reveals the importance of the deities controlled by the sectarian hierarchy in setting the coordinates of sacred value.

From this taxonomy of statues one thus sees that the brahmanic line of Vallabhacharya linked both categories of Vallabha idols (divine and man-made) in a duplex circuit of consecration. As descendants of the sect's founder, the goswamis maintained the potency of the limited group of nidhi-svarups through the performance of refortification rites (just as their possession of the divine svarups validated their status as descendants of Vallabhacharya). In turn, these descendants connected the potency of the nidhi-svarups with the unbounded group of pushti-svarups. To put it simply, from a sectarian perspective, the mystical powers of a pushti-svarup, like Shri Brijnathji, derived, in large measure, from the powers of a nidhi-svarup ultimately controlled and maintained by a descendant of Vallabhacharya.[39] Unsurprisingly, sectarian chronicles typically highlighted the goswamis' privileged position in articulating

37 Taylor, 'Picture Practice', pp. 66–67.

38 Ms. no. 7071/3, Rajasthan Prachyavidhya Pratishthan, Kota (formerly the Saraswati Bhandar Royal Library). I am grateful to Woodman Taylor for first bringing this poem to my attention and supplying me with a photocopy of it.

39 Because the gift to animate statues that came with descent from Vallabhacharya was a rare and valuable source of authority, the preceptor's recognized descendants attempted to regulate tightly claims to such ancestry in order to prevent non-kin from assuming the saintly mantle. This concern accounts for the proliferation of official genealogies about the Vallabha lineage and the practice in Vallabha temples of displaying large cloth hangings with cameo portraits of the approved descendants. A number of these temple hangings are reproduced by Robert Skelton in *Rajasthani Temple Hangings of the Krishna Cult* (New York: American Federation of the Arts, 1973).

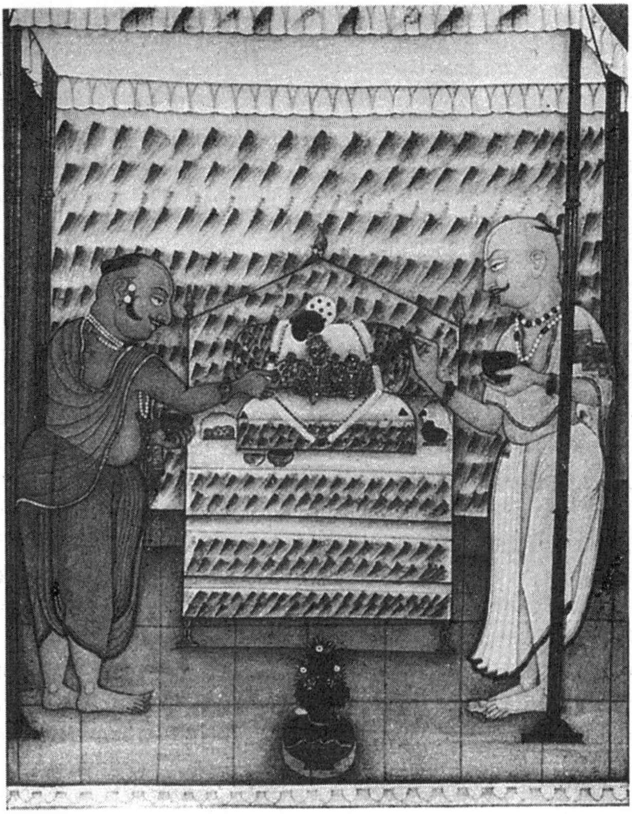

Plate 9 Shri Brijnathji, worshipped by Tilkayat Dauji II and Maharao Kishor Singh of Kota. Opaque watercolour and gold on paper, c. 1831. Approximately 25 × 20 cm. Rao Madho Singh Trust Museum, Fort Kota. Photograph by Norbert Peabody.

relations with the divine. In the SPV, for example, Vallabhacharya's descendants are represented as being most directly responsible for safeguarding the well-being of Shri Nathji by constantly performing its seva and keeping the image on the move during times of distress. Although kings from various dynasties played a role in providing temporary safe havens, they tended to come and go with great rapidity as the statue moved from place to place. The lives of the sectarian hierarchs, on the other hand, provided the narrative continuity to the story through their constant contact with and care for the statue.

Travels of the nine treasures and the legitimation of kingship in Kota

At the beginning of this chapter we encountered a paradox in Lakshmandan's account of Bhim Singh's initiation into the Vallabha Sampraday. Although Bhim Singh's initiation endowed him with the tutelary idol of Shri Brijnathji, his ritual death also directly precipitated Bundi's attack against and near ruination of Kota. In other words, although the image of Shri Brijnathji proved an effective guardian of the kingdom, it nevertheless spawned precisely the 'forces of darkness' that threatened its destruction in the first place. Presently, I shall explore this literary paradox more deeply by considering the ways in which the predicament recounted by Lakshmandan was also manifest in that sectarian activities had the dual capacity to buttress as well as undermine dynastic stability. But rather than looking to the travels of Shri Brijnathji in this regard, I shall turn to the travels of the sect's most esteemed religious statuary, the navnidhi. In focusing on these idols and how their travels became entwined with dynastic politics, I shall argue that the 'ritual' powers of the goswamis also had 'real' economic and political concomitants for the kingdoms of western India.

From the late seventeenth century the Sampraday's navnidhi were the Argonauts of western India. The course of Shri Nathji's voyages, as detailed in the SPV, presaged the travels of other important Vallabha statues. Like the image of Shri Nathji, the other navnidhi remained peaceably in Braj until the decade 1660–70 when they all dispersed during the upheavals in the region at this time.[40] Shri Nathji reached his ultimate destination of Nathadvara within a couple of years of leaving Braj.[41] Many of the other idols, on the other hand, remained on the go for several decades, and trails of abandoned temples and memorial shrines (*charan chaukis*) across western Uttar Pradesh, Rajasthan, Gujarat, and Malwa confirm the historicity of these movements.[42] By the early eighteenth century, however, all the navnidhi became relatively settled

[40] The one exception to this general pattern was the idol of Shri Vitthalnathji that moved from Braj to Kota in Rajasthan in about 1580. A little over eighty years later it moved to the village of Khimnor in Mewar.

[41] Two years, four lunar months, and seven days according to Hariray. For the precise dates, see his SPV, p. 48.

[42] For further details on the travels of Shri Dvarkanathji and Shri Balkrishnaji, see Brajbhushan, *Shri Dvarkadhis ki prakatya varta* (Kankroli: Vidya Vibhag, 1956) and Kanthamani Shastri, *Kankroli ka itihas*, pt. iv, pp. 132–144. For Shri Vitthalnathji see Jindel, *Sacred Town*, p. 26. For other deities, see Prabhudayal Mital, *Braj ke dharam-sampradayom ka itihas* (Delhi: National Publishing House, 1968), pp. 281–302 and 525–528; A. W. Entwistle, *Braj: Centre of Krishna Pilgrimage* (Groningen: E. Forsten, 1987), pp. 183–187; and Amit Ambalal, *Krishna as Shrinathji* (Ahmedabad: Mapin, 1987), pp. 54–59.

again, having found the steady patronage and protection of the most powerful Rajput kings of Rajasthan. Four of the navnidhis (Shri Nathji, Shri Navanitpriyaji, Shri Vittalnathji, and Shri Dvarkanathji) found refuge in the Maharana of Mewar's domain. Three navnidhis (Shri Gokulnathji, Shri Gokulchandrama[ni]ji, and Shri Madanmohanji) settled in Jaipur. One (Shri Mathureshji) was in Bundi and the last (Shri Balkrishna) was in Surat.[43] Although these images remained relatively rooted over the course of the next century, some of them did move on occasion, sometimes between kingdoms, sometimes within them.

During the century prior to colonial rule, Kota was implicated in two of these peregrinations. The first occurred in 1744 during the reign of Maharao Durjan Sal, after the conclusion of the mahotsav of 1739–40, when Goswami Gopinath of the Sampraday's first gaddi moved the idol of Shri Mathureshji from Bundi to a haveli in the Kota bazaar.[44] This haveli had been donated to Shri Mathureshji by Rai Dvarkadas, one of Durjan Sal's ministers, and the idol has remained in these comfortable lodgings ever since (one recent excursion aside).[45] Some sources also credit Rai Dvarkadas with giving the deity a land endowment (worth 12,000 rupees a year) as well as a daily donation of 12 rupees.[46] Shri Vitthalnathji, the idol associated with the Sampraday's second gaddi, was brought to Kota from Nathadvara during the reign of Maharao Umed Singh in 1802.[47] However, despite being installed in a palatial haveli not far from the bazaar, he remained in Kota for just under two decades. Shri Vitthalnathji returned to Nathadvara in 1821 for the mahotsav and has not been back to Kota since.[48]

Through the courses of their travels Vallabha goswamis considerably enhanced (or undermined) the political standing of the rulers into (or out of) whose territories they moved their images. This was effected in two

[43] Unlike the other *navnidhi*, this last deity did not find sanctuary in a Rajput kingdom, but in an important Mughal port city. The reason for this 'anomaly' will become apparent in the concluding section of this chapter.

[44] Both Lakshmandan ('*Vamsha prashasti*', p. 45) and Mital (*Braj ke dharam-sampradayom*, pp. 301–302) state the move took place in 1738. Sharma (*Kota rajya*, p. 410), on the other hand, records the date as 1744. The later date may reflect the idol's actual move to Kota while the earlier date may reflect the first substantial landgrant in Kota (worth 12,000 rupees annually) to the idol. Landgrants to Vallabha deities were often made in anticipation of attracting well-known images.

[45] The recent peregrination took place in 1952 when the image was taken to Jatipur in Braj before returning to Kota in 1975.

[46] Lakshmandan, '*Vamsha prashasti*', p. 45. Other sources, however, credit the land donation to Maharao Durjan Sal. See, for instance, Sharma, *Kota rajya*, p. 410 and Mital, *Braj ke dharam-sampradayom*, p. 302.

[47] This follows Shri Vitthalnathji's earlier residence in Kota from ca. 1581 to 1662. See note 40 above.

[48] Despite this god's long absence from Kota his vacant haveli in the bazaar remains readied, even today, for his hoped-for return.

interrelated ways. First, when a priest brought his idol into a new realm he (re)united the living, local king with past exemplary kings through their common worship of and devotion to the same image, thus allowing the present raja to claim that he was an incarnation of these past champions. At the same time, the goswami linked the powers of their nidhi svarup more closely with the tutelary deities of local royal dynasties thereby helping to boost the status of these idols of less august stature.

Although the divine statues remained in the physical possession of the goswamis, there were nevertheless important connections between the itineraries of Vallabha images and royal patronage. The sectarian hierarchy relied on patronage from many sources in order to maintain themselves, and kings were prominent benefactors. Indeed, the giving of land and money to Brahmans and temples was one of the most important shastric duties of the Hindu king (*rajadharma*), which additionally increased his personal merit (*punya*). To ensure that these endowments were eternal, many records of landgrants to religious organizations were permanently etched on copper plates that often included curses on future kings who might be tempted to renege on the gift.

However, the capacity of kings to give to temples was itself a function of political stability and military success and, clearly, political weakness lessened such patronage. Sectarian hierarchs therefore often searched for new benefactors and took their images on the road to do so, as in the case of Goswami Gopinath's removal of Shri Mathureshji from Bundi to Kota in 1744. During much of the early part of the eighteenth century Bundi's political situation had been precarious as both Kota and Kota's powerful northern rival, Jaipur (Amber), sought to control it.[49] Recall Maharao Bhim Singh of Kota had sacked Bundi in 1720 (and previously in 1714), plundering the treasury, dismantling large portions of the palace to be reconstructed at Kota, confiscating all cattle in the city, and even seizing common cooking pots. Rao Raja Budh Singh of Bundi (whose brother-in-law was Maharaja Sawai Jai Singh of Amber) was forced into exile and Bhim Singh's foster-brother was given command of the city. Soon after the catastrophe at Pandhar in 1720, Maharao Arjun Singh (r. 1720–23) lost control over Bundi and it fell under Amber's sphere of influence when Jai Singh returned his brother-in-law, Budh Singh, to Bundi's throne.[50] Jai Singh's support, however, did not secure lasting peace in Bundi. By 1728, Jai Singh and Budh Singh had a falling out over whether

[49] My principal sources in this paragraph are the late eighteenth-century manuscript entitled *Vamsha kallol sara samuchay* (Tod ms. no. 80, RAS); Suryamalla Mishran, *Vamshabhaskar* (Jodhpur: n.p., 1899), pp. 3096–3130; Sharma, *Kota rajya*, pp. 259–262, 289–290; and V. S. Bhatnagar, *Life and Times of Sawai Jai Singh 1688–1743* (Delhi: Impex India, 1974), pp. 213–222.

[50] Earlier, Budh Singh had been ousted from the gaddi by Bhim Singh.

Budh Singh's eight-year-old son by Jai Singh's sister would be recognized as heir. In order to subvert this plan, Budh Singh impugned the faithfulness of his Jaipuri wife and denounced the son as a bastard. Fearing that his nephew's reputation was beyond rehabilitation, Jai Singh had the boy put to death and, shortly thereafter, he deposed Budh Singh who escaped once again into exile. Jai Singh then enthroned Dalel Singh, a collateral relation of Budh Singh, who was duly married to Jai Singh's daughter. Dalel Singh, recognizing Jai Singh's strength, quickly signed a treaty naming this wife as his patrani and assured the succession to her first-born son in preference to his older sons by other wives. By this time Maharao Durjan Sal of Kota (r. 1723–56) was supporting Budh Singh who was continuing to press his claim to the throne from exile in Kota and in Mewar. Budh Singh never realized this ambition, dying in exile in 1739, but his eldest son Umed Singh did regain the throne in 1748. During the mahotsav of 1739–40, Goswami Gopinath had been a first-hand witness of Maharao Durjan Sal of Kota's lavish patronage and, by removing Shri Mathureshji from Bundi and its troubles in 1744, he no doubt hoped that Kota would provide better sources of unstinting benefactions.

A similar combination of factors was at work in 1802 when Shri Vitthalnathji came to Kota from Nathadvara in neighbouring Mewar (Udaipur). This move occurred when the power of Maharana Bhim Singh of Mewar (r. 1778–1828) had been severely compromised by the Marathas who fomented a general insurrection among the maharana's clients. In the same vein, Shri Vitthalnathji's return to Nathadvara in 1822 took place shortly after Kota's political stability deteriorated with the outbreak of open hostilities between Maharao Kishor Singh of Kota and his prime minister, Rajrana Zalim Singh.[51] Although Kishor Singh expressed his firm expectation (and desire) that the deity return to Kota at the conclusion of the mahotsav, the presiding goswami did not fulfill his wish.[52] Instead the goswami chose to keep the deity in Mewar which recently had returned to political stability with the aid of British military support that, although directed more specifically at reducing the influence of the Marathas (the East India Company's principal rival in central and western India at the time), benefited the maharana (at least in the short run). This evidence indicates that although kings did not directly control the most revered statuary of the Vallabha Sampraday, the course of their travels was susceptible to royal influence through patronage. In this sense, one can say that the travels of the statues followed the trail of

[51] The details of this conflict will be discussed in greater detail in chapter 6.

[52] Maharao Kishor Singh to Rajrana Zalim Singh, Extract from Ben. Secret Cons., 7 December 1822, OIOC, BC 1102/29697.

political success, and through the courses of these travels one is able to trace the rise and fall of political fortunes in Rajasthan during the late seventeenth and eighteenth centuries. At the same time, a history of such movements to new centres of power and patronage also confirmed and intensified the sanctioning effects associated with the statues themselves as they were popularly credited with conferring such boons in the first place.

However, if we look more closely at the new destinations to which goswamis took their idols, we see that these priests were not without significant agency in these travels as well. Take, for example, the decision of Goswami Gopinath to remove Shri Mathureshji from Bundi to Kota. This case is significant because Gopinath did not take his image to Amber, which at that moment surely had the upper hand over Kota in the contest over Bundi. Moreover, although Jai Singh of Amber is known to have maintained a particular devotion to the non-Vallabha deity Govinddevji, he also lavishly patronized the Vallabha Sampraday. As a result, earlier during his reign (1700–43) no less than three of the Vallabha Sampraday's navnidhi (Shri Gokulnathji, Shri Gokulchandramaji, and Shri Madanmohanji) had settled in and around Jai Singh's capital.[53] Yet, in 1802 when Shri Vitthalnathji fled to Kota from Mewar, which had been beset by the Marathas, this idol did not proceed to one of the emerging Maratha centres of rule as one might expect. Thus the political victor did not necessarily enjoy the spiritual spoils, and the link between travels, patronage, and political attainment did not form a closed loop. Rather there were significant conjunctures at which the sectarian hierarchy made important decisions in selecting the destinations for their idols (choosing from among several royal suitors who promised the appropriate benefactions) and, in this sense, deciding who would enjoy their propitious influences.

In the next section of this chapter I shall suggest how this agency was conjoined with the interests of merchants, sometimes in conjunction with kings and sometimes in opposition to them. But let me first mention one feature of temple land tenure that underwrote the goswamis' autonomy and mobility. Each of the nine treasures had landholdings, from which they derived rental income, that were widely dispersed across many rival kingdoms. For instance, aside from its landholdings in Mewar, the Shri

[53] Monika Horstmann has noted that certain representations of Jai Singh in Krisnabhatta Kalanidhi's near-contemporary *Ishvaravilasamahakavya* suggest his adherence to the 'pure non-dualism' of Vallabhacharya. See Monika Horstmann, 'Govinddevji of Vrindaban and Jaipur and its Kachvaha Patrons from the Mid-Seventeenth to the Mid-Eighteenth Century', in *Studies in South Asian Devotional Literature*, eds Alan W. Entwistle and Francoise Mallison, (New Delhi: Manohar, 1994), pp. 82–93, p. 93, note 14.

Nathji Temple had large estates in Jodhpur, Jaipur, Partabgarh, Kota, Karauli, Bharatpur, as well as in the Maratha dominions.[54] Kota's Shri Mathureshji Temple simultaneously held land in several other kingdoms in southern Rajasthan and Malwa, while other svarups located in foreign kingdoms had estates in Kota.[55] Perhaps of even greater importance than these land endowments, however, were the regular donations in cash and matériel sent to these temples by rulers from across north India. Many rulers even maintained a special *dak* (postal service) expressly for this purpose. Thus Thomas Broughton reported that the Maharaja of Jodhpur sent daily offerings of fresh flowers from his capital to Nathadvara (some 320 km) and that they arrived in time for the first darshan of the day at sunrise![56] Published records from the Shri Dvarkadhisji Temple in Kankroli show that it was receiving regular cash payments (*bhent*) from nearly every major ruler in Rajasthan at the end of the eighteenth century.[57] The cumulative effect of these endowments and daily donations was that no king fully controlled the purse-strings of these temples and through them the distribution of sacred allocations. Although Hindu rulers could hope to influence the movement of statues and secure their beneficial presence through patronage, this expenditure did not necessarily translate into a guarantee of control over images because the goswamis drew income from several independent and often competing sources. To rework Marx's famous insight, although Hindu kings may have been a dominant class *in sich*, they did not constitute a dominant class *für sich*. The sectarian hierarchy thereby exploited rivalries between kings in order to exert leverage against the individual rajas with whom it dealt. Thus Edwin Richardson has detailed how, during the period of decline of Mewar's power towards the end of the eighteenth century, the Shri Nathji Temple at Nathadvara was able to increase its power over all aspects of the villages under its control including not only rents and trade (transit duties, fees from public markets, duties on precious metals, gate fees, and so forth) but also the judiciary such that by the end of the century it had become a kingdom within a kingdom complete with military levies, some of which were supplied by other Rajput kings.[58] Kota's contingent at

54 Edwin A. Richardson, 'Mughal and Rajput Patronage of the Bhakti Sect of the Maharajas, the Vallabha Sampradaya, 1640–1760 A.D.' (Ph.D. thesis, Department of Oriental Studies, University of Arizona, 1979), p. 76.

55 Chaube Raghunath Das, *Report on the Administration of the Kotah State for the Year 1894–95 (Sambat 1951)* (Ajmer: Rajputana Mission Press, 1896), pp. 7–8.

56 Thomas Duer Broughton, *Letters Written in a Mahratta Camp during the Year 1809 Descriptive of the Character, Manners, Domestic Habits, and Religious Ceremonies of the Mahrattas* (London: Archibald Constable and Company, 1817 [1813]), p. 156.

57 Kanthamani Shastri, *Kankroli ka itihas*, pt. 6, pp. 219–221.

58 Richardson, 'Mughal and Rajput Patronage', passim.

Nathadvara, known as the *seva ki sena* (or 'army of service'), numbered over 250 troops while Jodhpur provided similar forces of up to 500 men.[59]

With this understanding of the dialectic between the sect's dependence on patronage from royal sources and the sect's ability to play one source off against another, the logic behind the installation of Shri Brijnathji, instead of Shri Mathureshji, as the focus of Kota's royal cult should now be clear. The maharaos of Kota directly controlled the Shri Brijnathji svarup (subject to their ability to hang onto the god in battle) whereas their authority over the Shri Mathureshji svarup was mediated by the priestly descendants of Vallabhacharya. This difference is spatially manifest in the placement of their temples in Kota – one in the maharao's palace and the other in the bazaar – and is reflected in the fact that whereas Maharao Bhim Singh is credited with first bringing Shri Brijnathji to Kota, no such royal claims were advanced regarding Shri Mathureshji, whose appearance in Kota is attributed to the devotion and generosity of Rai Dvarkadas, Maharao Durjan Sal's minister.[60]

In the following section, we turn to an examination of how pilgrimage affected the economy of the bazaar and how this implicated the business community in the dual potentialities (supportive and divisive) defining the relationship between sectarian hierarchy and king.

The pilgrimage economy and the potency of statues

So far in this chapter, we examined the importance of royal patronage (and its limits) for attracting the famous nidhi-svarups (particularly the navnidhi). We saw that an enduring source of income for Vallabha temples derived from the kingly tax-free gifts of agricultural estates and urban rental properties. However, patronage also came in the form of consumable wealth (cash and jewellery) from pilgrims and local merchants. In fact, for reasons that will become clearer in the following two chapters, this form of fungible donation came to be especially prized within the Sampraday. Although kings used land endowments to entice the Vallabha

[59] It is not known from what year Kota's seva ki sena was posted at Nathadvara; the Jodhpur force was first sent there in 1772. K. S. Gupta, *Mewar and the Maratha Relations (1735–1818 A.D.)* (S. Chand and Co., 1971), pp. 106–107; R. P. Shastri, *Jhala Zalim Singh* (Jaipur: Raj Printing Works, 1971), p. 294; and Broughton, *Letters Written in a Mahratta Camp*, p. 156.

[60] Similarly, in Mewar Shri Nathji remained at Nathadvara, 40 km from the capital, Udaipur. Mewar also remained formally dedicated to the deity Eklingji long after Shri Nathji's arrival within the kingdom's territory and despite the immense popularity of Shri Nathji dwarfing that of Eklingji. In order to profit from Shri Nathji's presence, the rulers of Mewar became *personal* devotees of Shri Nathji and altered the worship of Shaivite Eklingji to conform to the distinctive forms of Vallabha worship, such as having fixed timings for darshans when the deity may be viewed, adjusting the worship of the idol to reflect seasonal cycles of weather and holidays, and so on.

goswamis and their divine statues into their kingdoms, these divine statues often were installed in the bazaar once they arrived. Cities fortunate enough to be the home of famous Vallabha deities became, and still are, important centres of pilgrimage. The pilgrimage economy involved the temple in two interrelated ways. First, pilgrims came to the temple to offer their money to the god and thus injected capital directly into the temple. Second, pilgrims also spent money in the bazaar on other goods and services offered by merchants. Jindel has amply documented the importance of pilgrim traffic to the economy at Nathadvara,[61] a sentiment echoed, in the contemporary context, for the Shri Mathureshji Temple and Kota's bazaar.[62] Thus it is not surprising that the business communities in western Uttar Pradesh, Rajasthan, Gujarat, and Malwa (the region where Vallabha images have historically resided and circulated) have been the most enthusiastic and devoted followers of the Sampraday. This important mercantile support is reflected in the sectarian literature.[63] Significantly, it also informs the literature produced for royal patrons. Thus we noted in Lakshmandan's text that during Shri Brijnathji's four-year exile in the Deccan, the well-being of Kota's tutelary deity was preserved by a merchant (*seth*) through his sponsorship of the deity's costly seva.[64]

Booming business in the bazaar, in turn, allowed merchants to donate greater sums to temple coffers. These gifts added to the renown of the deity, for it allowed temple priests to perform ever more elaborate and costly rituals that indexed the deity's increasing status and power.[65] This lavish magnificence of worship in Vallabha temples has been one of the Sampraday's distinguishing features.[66] Recall, according to Vallabha belief, the svarup is considered a sentient being who takes delight in the seva performed for him. At the same time, increased commercial traffic in the bazaar also benefited the king, for customs duties and transit dues (*zakat*) on goods were a major source of royal revenue, along with agricultural taxes. In sum, the dynamics of a healthy pilgrimage economy bound the mutual interests of king, sectarian hierarchy, and merchants.

61 Jindel, *Culture of a Sacred Town*.

62 Judge U. C. Mehta, *State of Rajasthan* v. *Goswami Ranchodlalji Maharaj Sri* (Unpublished judgment, Kota District Sessions Court, 1972; also available at the Shri Bade Mathureshji Temple, Patan Pol, Kota).

63 Of the 252 early disciples of Vitthalnath Gosain who are extolled in Hariray's 252V, a disproportionate number are merchants.

64 As we shall see in the following section of the chapter when discussing the history of the idol of Shri Dvarkanathji, this notion of merchants providing safe haven to deities in times of distress has much older roots within the sectarian tradition.

65 The scale and splendor of certain Vallabha rites entailed a financial outlay that barred poorer temples (with presumably less potent images) from performing them.

66 Bennett, 'In Nanda Baba's House', pp. 182–183.

This dynamic helps explain why Maharao Durjan Sal of Kota so forcefully identified the kingdom with the Vallabha Sampraday in the mid-eighteenth century through his elaboration of the cycle of court rituals in which public worship of Shri Brijnathji was a central focus and activity. As the Mughal Empire declined, service to the emperor in Delhi lost importance in sustaining the authority of local kings, particularly in relation to their military clients. But by closely identifying polity with sect, Durjan Sal brought greater alignment between his own interests and those of Kota's wealthy business community, forging a king–merchant alliance in which income from pilgrimage-driven trade sustained and strengthened royal power. As C. A. Bayly has argued (in a somewhat different context and as the result of a somewhat different economic dynamic), access to greater amounts of merchant capital enabled eighteenth-century rajas to shift the basis of military organization away from prebendal levies, whose loyalties were always fickle, towards standing, professional armies that were more firmly in their employ provided the pay was forthcoming.[67]

However, there is also a down side to the dynamic uniting king, temple, and merchant. When economic conditions in the bazaar were weak, as a result of a disruption in pilgrimage due to political instability, for example, then donations to the temple decreased which was immediately reflected in the abridgment or elimination of costly rituals performed for the deity. This, in turn, adversely affected the reputation of the deity, leading to a further reduction of pilgrimage. A significant drop-off in pilgrimage then undermined the bazaar economy so that temple donations from the local business community also declined and so on. When downward economic spirals became prolonged, economic pressures mounted on the presiding goswami to remove his statue to another kingdom as in the cases of Shri Mathureshji's and Shri Vitthalnathji's travels to Kota in 1744 and 1802 respectively. The threat of removal then drove a wedge between the interests of the palace, on the one hand, and those of the bazaar, on the other. This fissure had two distinct manifestations. In the first, merchants bankrolled rival claimants to the throne who they felt would establish a more conducive pilgrimage economy, thereby permitting the image to remain sedentary. Alternatively, because the interests of merchant family corporations typically spanned several kingdoms and the tools of their trade (capital, credit and accounting expertise) were eminently portable, merchants could also encourage the

[67] C. A. Bayly, *Rulers, Townsmen, and Bazaars: North Indian Society in the Age of British Expansion, 1770–1870* (Cambridge: Cambridge University Press, 1983), pp. 14–15. This connection will be explored in greater detail in the following chapter.

goswami to move the image to the domain of a rival king in which business investments were already in place.[68]

Thus the dynamic of the pilgrimage economy when combined with the potential mobility of Vallabha idols *usually* ensured that these images remained at the centre of thriving economies and associated with exemplary kings, thus validating and intensifying their own special powers to bestow grace (pushti). In the remaining section of this chapter, however, I shall focus on one way in which contingent historical events could leave a negative imprint on the reputations of important Vallabha statuary, thereby threatening their standing within the sect and calling into question the extent of their miraculous grace-granting powers.

The schismatic sixth gaddi

Although it was most common for histories of political and religious attainment to be accumulated in important Vallabha statuary such that they became veritable repositories of power and legitimacy, untoward historical events also on occasion left a negative imprint on these images. Such lamentable events depleted these repositories, and the powers of revered images were lost or diminished, resulting in a crisis of confidence in their celestial biographies. This series of events has in fact befallen Shri Balkrishnaji, the treasure that Vitthalnath Gosain originally gave to his sixth son, Yadunath.

Although Shri Balkrishnaji was regarded as one of the original nine treasures, his status in the sect has fallen into dis(re)pute. Coincidental with Balkrishnaji's fall from grace has been the rise of Shri Kalyanrayji and, more recently, Shri Mukandrayji, and today, many Pustimargis name one of these later two deities as one of the nine treasures in preference to Balkrishnaji. According to sectarian tradition,[69] Shri Balkrishnaji's troubles date back to when Vitthalnath Gosain distributed the navnidhi among his sons. Yadunath, the sixth son, was given Shri Balkrishnaji. However, as this deity was extremely small Yadunath was not entirely happy with it. Vitthalnath Gosain's third son, whose name was confusingly Balkrishna, told his younger brother that they could share their two deities and worship them jointly (see figure 2). This arrangement continued happily enough during their lifetimes. Such co-operation,

68 For the political implications of 'transnational' business interests in Gujarat at the turn of the nineteenth century, see Howard Spodek, 'Rulers, Merchants and Other Groups in the City-States of Saurashtra, India, around 1800', *Comparative Studies in Society and History* 16 (1974): 448–470.

69 My principal sources here are Brajbhushan, *Shri Dvarkadhis ki prakatya varta* (Kankroli: Vidya Vibhag, 1956); Kanthamani Shastri, *Kankroli ka itihas*, pt. iv, pp. 119–125; and A. W. Entwistle, *Braj: Centre of Krishna Pilgrimage*, pp. 183–184.

however, proved beyond their sons. Balkrishna's son, Dvarkeshvar, refused to let his cousin, Madhusudun, worship the deities as per the prior agreement. A dispute ensued, and Goswami Gokulnath, who was in charge of the Sampraday's fourth gaddi, intervened. Madhusudun was given the deity Shri Kalyanrayji who, in addition to being larger than Shri Balkrishnaji, enjoyed the reputation in some quarters of having been a sevya-svarup of Vallabhacharya. Although this deity was not one of the original navnidhis, devotees of this god quickly came to consider it one of the group. Dvarkeshvar retained the spurned Shri Balkrishnaji along with Shri Dvarkanathji.

Shortly thereafter in 1662, Shri Balkrishnaji suffered the further indignity of being seized in a dispute between Dvarkeshvar's successor Brajbhushan and Brajbhushan's cousin Brajray (see figure 3). Although Dvarkeshvar had a son, he was disinherited (for reasons that are not entirely clear) and quickly dropped out of the story. Instead Dvarkeshvar appointed Brajbhushan, the grandson of his younger brother, also Brajbhushan, as his heir. Brajray was the grandson of Pitambar, another of Dvarkeshvar's younger brothers, and the friction between Brajray and Brajbhushan (the younger) apparently stemmed from disagreement over the birth order of their grandfathers. Brajray considered himself to be senior to his cousin in line of succession and, therefore, entitled to the deities. Fearful of his cousin's intentions, Brajbhushan took the two deities away from Braj to 'Rajnagar' (the name for Ahmadabad within the sectarian tradition), where he was offered patronage and protection by a community of seth devotees, one of whom gave his home to the deity. Brajray lobbied the Mughal court for possession of the deities and he obtained an order from Aurangzeb that granted him Shri Balkrishnaji.[70] With the help of Mughal troops Brajray seized this deity from Brajbhushan and forcibly removed it to Surat in 1670 where he established his own gaddi which is reckoned by his followers to be the Sampraday's 'sixth gaddi' in preference to the gaddi held by Yadunath's descendants who have Shri Kalyanrayji.[71] Thus, as Kanthamani Shastri has noted, the competing claims to the 'sixth gaddi' rested on stressing different bases for determining such status.[72] The descendants of Brajbhushan staked their claim to their possession of Shri Balkrishnaji, one of the original navnidhis. The custodians of Shri Kalyanrayji, on the other hand, staked

[70] In this case the Sampraday looked to the Mughal emperor in order to intercede in a sectarian dispute. There are equally cases where kings approached sectarian leaders to mediate their disputes. One of the best-known cases occurred in 1772 when the Maharana of Mewar and the Maharaja of Jodhpur approached the Tilkayat of the Nathadvara Temple to decide the fate of the disputed pargana of Godwar. See K. S. Gupta, *Mewar and the Maratha Relations (1735–1818 A.D.)*, p. 107.

[71] Kanthamani Shastri, *Kankroli ka itihas*, pt. iv, pp. 133–144.

[72] Ibid., pt. iv, p. 144.

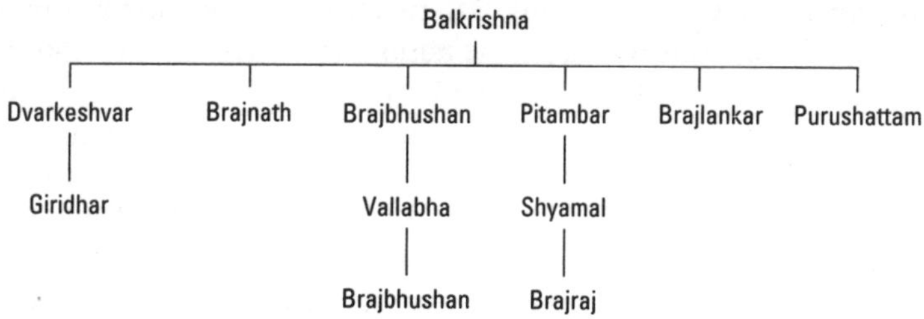

Figure 3 The quarrelsome descendants of Balkrishna
Source: Kanthamani Shastri, *Kankroli ka itihas* (Kankroli: Shrividya-Vibhag, 1939)

their claim to the 'sixth gaddi' on kinship principals. They traced direct descent from Yadunath, Vitthalnath Gosian's sixth son and progenitor of one of the sect's original stem lineages.[73]

Shri Balkrishnaji's contested status within the sect was amplified when he was the only original navnidhi not to attend the mahotsavs of 1739–40 and 1822.[74] Although the precise cause(s) of these absences is unclear, there may have been lingering fears by Brajray's descendants that Brajbhushan's descendants might use these occasions to reclaim the disputed idol. Shri Balkrishnaji's detractors, however, have used his absences from these communal festivities to call into question his status as one of the navnidhi and his absence from the 1822 mahotsav opened the door for yet another schism within the sixth gaddi. This split occurred when Goswami Girdhar, a descendant of Yadunath from a relatively junior lineage, ingratiated himself with Tilkayat Dauji (Damodar II) at Nathadvara at about the time of the mahotsav. Although the principal hagiographical account of Girdhar, the *Shri Mukundrayji ki prakatya varta*, suggests that his success rested on his extensive knowledge of the Vallabha seva, which was so thorough he was even able to instruct the Tilkayat (!), his attainment also surely also rested, in part, on the fact that his wife and Dauji's wife were sisters.[75] During the mahotsav of 1822, the

[73] An alternative sectarian tradition, favoured among devotees of Shri Kalyanraiji, claims that the idol was given to Yadunath much earlier by Vitthalnath Gosain himself, not by Goswami Gokulnath. This telling strengthens their contention that Shri Kalyanraiji was one of the original navnidhi as it was Vitthalnath Gosain's distribution of images among his sons that established this enumerative scheme in the first place. For this alternative history, see Mital, *Braj ke dharam-sampradayom*, pp. 294 and 528.

[74] Kanthamani Shastri, *Kankroli ka itihas*, pt. vi, pp. 165–166 and pt. vii, pp. 282–283.

[75] Vasudha Dalmia, 'The Establishment of the Sixth *Gaddi* of the Vallabha Sampraday: Narrative Structure and the Use of Authority in a *Varta* of the Nineteenth Century', in *Studies in South Asian Devotional Literature*, eds Alan W. Entwistle and Françoise Mallison (New Delhi: Manohar, 1994), pp. 94–117.

image of Shri Mukundrayji, belonging to Dauji and housed in the Shri Nathji Temple, was substituted for the absent Shri Balkrishnaji in some of the sevas in order to bring the number of deities up to the requisite nine. Although Shri Mukundrayji enjoyed the reputation of having been a sevya-svarup of Vallabhacharya, it was not one of the originally enumerated navnidhi. Sometime after the mahotsav of 1822, Girdhar apparently secured a promise from Tilkayat Dauji that the image of Shri Mukundrayji would be given to him. This, however, did not happen until 1827, shortly after the death of Dauji, when the late Tilkayat's widow (Girdhar's sister-in-law) gave Girdhar the idol, which he took off to Banaras where it was duly installed in a temple with the claim that it was the headquarters of the sect's sixth gaddi.[76]

By the mid-nineteenth century the reputation of Shri Balkrishnaji was trapped in a downward spiral that additionally involved the colonial state. In 1862 the goswami of the Shri Balkrishnaji Temple became embroiled with one of his devotees in a notorious libel suit that resulted in the goswami's appearance in British courts in Bombay.[77] The goswami's subjugation to the colonial legal system's imperatives further undermined his authority and provided yet another signal of the decreasing potency of Shri Balkrishnaji's idol to members of the sect. The declining status of Shri Balkrishnaji was most recently confirmed during a mahotsav held in Nathadvara in 1966, at which many of the navnidhi attended. On this occasion Shri Mukandrayji participated as one of the navnidhi and Shri Balkrishnaji remained absent.[78] From this brief history of the schismatic sixth gaddi, we thus see that the powers attributed to Vallabha images were variable over time as popular perceptions of their rank rose or fell within the hierarchy of progressively more exclusive categories of non-sectarian murti, sectarian svarup, man-made pushti-svarup, self-manifest sevya-svarup and, finally, navnidhi.

Conclusion

In this chapter we have seen how society in Kota was shot through with several competing principles of organization, each of which was loosely articulated by a different social order or group. Although these various principles inflected one another in important ways, they also mapped social spaces, agenda, and orientations that did not fully overlap and, therefore, were not fully reducible one to another. This finding thus

[76] Tilkayat Dauji II died in 1826 at a young age and without heir. For several years while it was being decided who would succeed him, the widow of the late goswami assumed a powerful role in the Sampraday's affairs. See Ambalal, *Krishna as Shrinathji*, p. 59.

[77] [Mulji], *History of the Sect of Maharajas*.

[78] Jindel, *Sacred Town*, pp. 73–74.

broadly reinforces the conclusions first drawn by Richard Burghart many years ago in his much-neglected analysis of three rival 'codes of hierarchy' as advanced by kings, Brahmans, and ascetics in eighteenth- and early nineteenth-century Nepal. Burghart showed that although these three codes overlapped to a significant extent, such that 'the Brahman, ascetic, and the king each absorbed elements of the other two codes into his own code',[79] they did not form a closed, cybernetically integrated system. Instead, the three codes were articulated according to three different principles (Burghart characterized these in terms of an organism, a continuum, and a pyramid), each of which defined overlapping and interpenetrating, but not entirely coterminous, semantic fields.[80] In this chapter we have extended these general observations by showing how the fissures and discontinuities between these multiple orders of reality established fertile spaces in which competitive local politics were waged and where rival agenda could be advanced, defended, mediated, and transformed. One important outcome of this methodological move has been the ability to recoup a culturally informed sensibility towards non-recurring historical change insofar as it has alerted us to the centrality of the travels of wandering idols and their rising and falling statuses for charting and interpreting the expansion and demise of local kingdoms. In doing so we have begun to define a culturally specific historical sensibility that remains alive to the social and political transformations as experienced by the peoples who made and lived this history.

[79] Burghart, 'Hierarchical Models', p. 533.
[80] Ibid., p. 523.

4 Military fiscalism and the cultural economy of devotion in eighteenth-century Rajasthan

During his year-long residence in 1809 with Daulat Rao Shinde's camp, which was passing slowly through Rajasthan from Agra to Ajmer via the northern part of Kota, Thomas Broughton was struck by the constant and growing demands for pay by the soldiers in Shinde's army. This clamour for money culminated just before Dasahra, in October of 1809. In a letter to his brother, Broughton wrote:

> The disturbances among all descriptions of the troops have since my last letter, been greater than ever. The Silahdars to a man have refused to stand muster, upon the terms which the Muha Raj [that is, Shinde] proposes; he has, however, been tampering with some of those who have most influence in the army, and will probably induce them, by bribes, finally to acquiesce in his plans. The regulars of Baptiste's battalions have been more violent than any others; they have thrown all their officers, together with the *Mootusudees*, into confinement, and sent a message to Seendhiya... that if the money did not come very soon, they should be under the necessity of presenting themselves at the *Deooree* [Shinde's personal tents], to make known their grievances to the Muha Raj himself. The leaders of the different detachments in *Mewar* have written word that they are unable to pursue any operations, in consequence of the troops having refused to march until they were paid.[1]

This vignette of Shinde's 'cash flow' problems at the turn of the nineteenth century alerts us to the vital role that money and, more generally, revenue played in sustaining warrior rule in the late precolonial polity. Yet during the last decade or so most ethnohistorical accounts of precolonial state formation have shied away from assessing the fiscality of the royal polity.[2] Indeed some have even suggested positively that the state was

[1] Thomas Duer Broughton, *Letters Written in a Mahratta Camp during the Year 1809 Descriptive of the Character, Manners, Domestic Habits, and Religious Ceremonies of the Mahrattas* (London: Archibald Constable and Company, 1817 [1813]), p. 209.

[2] Although highly commendable in other respects, this want can be found, for instance, in Pamela G. Price, *Kingship and Political Practice in Colonial India* (Cambridge: Cambridge University Press, 1996).

largely unconcerned with revenue. Perhaps the strongest statement in this regard has come from Dirks who was struck by the *apparently* large percentage of the territory in Pudukkottai that was given away by the raja in tax-free *inams* (estates) to his clients.[3] By the late nineteenth century over two-thirds of Pudukkottai's territory had been alienated from direct royal control.[4] From the perspective of a revenue-centred polity this would appear to be sheer folly as Eric Stokes lamented, echoing so many British colonial officials.[5] But from an indigenous perspective, Dirks argued, such a redistribution was a fundamental part of the royal exercise of gifting that defined and established the king's sovereignty in the first place.

The fact that landgrants did not inflect the maximizing aims of economic rationality and therefore should not be taken as political weakness (that is, an inability to maintain control over valuable material resources) was further inscribed in the counter-intuitive spatial pattern underlying the distribution of estates in Pudukkottai. According to Dirks:

> If inams represented royal weakness, we would expect that inams would be 'given' in the border areas where the king would have had less control over the countryside and its inhabitants. In Pudukkottai, this expected pattern is reversed. Only the Cervaikarars [affinal relations of the raja who generally commanded large contingents of troops] were uniformly situated near the borders of the state, though this was for obvious strategic reasons. If we take them all together, inams were more heavily concentrated in the central portions of the state than at the periphery.
>
> From the perspective of Stokes's argument, it would seem natural that the strength of the state would fall off increasingly towards the peripheries. It would also seem natural that, given collections in kind, the king should hold on to rights to the royal share near the centre of the state and give away lands at the periphery, minimizing, all other things being equal, substantial transportation costs. But we

[3] Nicholas Dirks, *The Hollow Crown: Ethnohistory of a South Indian Kingdom* (Cambridge: Cambridge University Press, 1987), especially pp. 111–138.

[4] Dirks's problematic use of data deriving from the height of the colonial era for reconstructing characteristics of the precolonial period has been noted by many. One such difficulty arises from his use of the category 'inam'. Although this term is Persian in origin, its meaning was considerably reshaped in south India by British usage during the colonial period. Perhaps most significantly, colonial use of the category 'inam' lumped together many different types of alienated lands that in Tamil were distinguished by such terms as *maniyam*, *umpalam*, *jivitam*, and *lavanam*. If one adopts the Tamil categories as the relevant units of analysis, one finds that in Pudukkottai the king held roughly 33 percent of the land, collateral branches of the ruling lineage held 23 percent, military retainers held 11 percent, village servants and officials held 11 percent, and religious endowments a further 20 percent. Thus the king was by far the single largest landowner in the state, and, as we shall see below, probably commanded the largest market-share of the vital trade in grain. Any assessment from a neoclassical perspective of whether the size of the royal domain was large or small must be made against some estimate of the size of the potential market in grain. Dirks fails to do this.

[5] Eric Stokes, *The Peasant and the Raj: Studies in Agrarian Society and Peasant Rebellion in Colonial India* (Cambridge: Cambridge University Press, 1978), pp. 60–61.

see here conclusively that more units of inams were given away in the centre than in the periphery. Clearly the simple economic rationality proclaimed by neo-classical economics must yield to other explanations.[6]

In decoding a cultural logic guiding the redistribution of land, honours, and service tenures in Pudukkottai, Dirks has done valuable work in unlocking a set of meanings informing political relations in the precolonial Indian polity. I shall argue, however, that he overshot the mark in characterizing the extent to which these political relations did not influence fiscal considerations. Although transactions involving land in late precolonial India do not reveal the consistent operations of a maximizing mentality in every respect (then again, in what society does it?),[7] I shall suggest several ways that the constitution of warrior rule through the management of land had vital economic concomitants involving distinct strategies of maximization that Dirks has ignored at his peril.

Part of the reason why Dirks succeeded with his legerdemain of banishing the operations of political economy from his consideration of the precolonial polity is that he presented a highly idealized, top-down view of the traditional state that is largely oblivious to dispersive tendencies that simultaneously threatened to displace royal power onto other centres. Rather than presenting Pudukkottai within a field of overlapping polities, paramount powers, and political dependencies, Dirks treated the kingdom in isolation, one of whose principal effects was to endow the king with a 'monopoly over public goods in his kingdom' whose redistribution underpinned an enduring 'spirit of unity and centricity'.[8] As a result of his monocentric view of the precolonial polity, Dirks failed to see how rival centres advanced competing claims to kingship, sovereignty

[6] Dirks, *Hollow Crown*, pp. 136–137.

[7] Two interrelated ways in which India did not develop a maximizing logic regarding land, particularly agricultural land, were in the absence of the concept of private property in land and the absence of the abstract concept of rent. With regard to the first want, rights to the produce of the land were always shared between landlords, any intermediaries, and the cultivating peasants. This meant that risks regarding the success harvest, in theory, were shared between cultivators and landed elites (though as we shall see below there were nonetheless important ways in which landlords could attempt to shift, at least, some risks to peasant cultivators). One important manifestation of this arrangement is that the landlord, subject to the abstract forces of supply and demand, did not set the revenue rates in land. Instead revenue rates were tied to the crop that a peasant chose to bring under cultivation. That is, if a peasant brought the land under poppy cultivation he paid one revenue rate; if he brought it under barley, he paid another. Whether the cultivator brought the land under poppy or barley was determined by prices in the market and not by the demands of the landlord. Thus 'rent' (to the extent it existed) was not determined by the demand for land but, rather, by the demand for the produce of the land. This system may have developed in part because land in itself was relatively abundant in many parts of India until the nineteenth century.

[8] Dirks, *Hollow Crown*, p. 135.

and divinity based on alternative symbolic constructs, how the distribution of power was then constantly renegotiated among these centres, and the ways in which such negotiations were linked to and informed by fiscal concerns.[9] Put yet another way, in a Hindu universe populated by the proverbial '330 million gods' (*tentis karor devata*), how truly extraordinary was the godliness claimed by one 'little king'?

That the king's monopoly over culturally valued allocations was not complete is tellingly manifest in the perennial rebellions, cutthroat politics, and shifting political alliances – André Wink's *fitna* (drawing away of allegiance; sedition) – that quickened most precolonial Indian polities in the eighteenth century.[10] During the hundred years prior to the establishment of British indirect rule in Kota in 1817, the kingdom was periodically disrupted with mutiny, internecine conflict, and changing loyalties. In chapter 2 we encountered Maharao Durjan Sal's civil war with Shyam Singh and his doubles involving strategic interventions from Maharaja Sawai Jai Singh of Amber (Jaipur). These hostilities occasioned several other rebellions in Kota at roughly the same time when we find important members of Kota's nobility – such as Rawat Chitar Singh Hada of Ghati and Rao Balbadhra Singh Hada of Guger – switching their allegiances back and forth between Durjan Sal of Kota and Rao Sangram Singh Chandrawat of Rampura.[11]

Insurrection was such a prominent feature of the polity because kings did not enjoy authority over discretely bounded territories administered by 'rational-bureaucratic' chains of command. Rather kings were implicated in multiple hierarchies of authority that intersected not only with the hierarchies of sectarian organizations, as discussed in the previous chapter, but also with the hierarchies of rival kings. The overlapping, layered, and non-exclusive sovereignties that were defined by these cross-cutting hierarchies meant that a king rarely enjoyed 'a monopoly over public goods in his kingdom'. Cross-cutting links often were created when individuals established relationships with different (sometimes rival) overlords. The best example of this was the eight Kotriat Thikanas along Kota's northern frontier with Jaipur and Bundi. At the end of the eighteenth century, the holders of these estates sent tribute to the Maharaja of Jaipur (as well as to the Marathas), provided military levies to the Maharao of Kota (as well as to the Marathas), and performed acts

9 Ibid., p. 133. In Kota the multiply-constituted and multi-centred character of kingship even permeates the first royal title enjoyed by the ruling dynasty: *maharajadhiraj*, or 'supreme king of great kings'.

10 André Wink, *Land and Sovereignty in India: Agrarian Society and Politics under the Eighteenth-Century Maratha Svarajya* (Cambridge: Cambridge University Press, 1986).

11 V. S. Bhatnagar, *Life and Times of Sawai Jai Singh, 1688–1743* (Delhi: Impex India, 1974).

of personal service to the Rao Raja of Bundi (as well as to the Marathas).[12] Claims to kingship were always contested and its terms negotiated among kings, clients, allies, and rivals.

The anxiety of precolonial kings concerning the polity's active dispersive tendencies underlay many well-known political practices designed to prevent local clients from developing alternative bases of power. These included: 1) the splitting of estates of individual clients, where possible, among far-flung portions of the kingdom; 2) adopting forms of 'administrative involution' whereby the duties of local officials were made to overlap in order to establish a system of checks and balances upon their actions; 3) dividing military and revenue assignments so that clients did not hold both forms of authority over the same territory; 4) employing extensive networks of royal spies and newsrunners throughout the kingdom in order to report on local officials and military clients; and 5) maintaining salaried, standing armies which were paid directly from the royal treasury alongside the prebendal levies that were provided by estate-holders. These 'royal' (*raj*) or 'personal' (*khas*) troops, whose loyalties were tied directly to the king and were not mediated through clients, have been neglected too often in recent ethnohistorical studies of the precolonial Indian polity, but they were a crucial dimension of its military constitution. They were already an important feature of the Vijayanagar Empire in south India by the sixteenth century and, although surely an exceptional case, by the early nineteenth century the standing army in Kota accounted for perhaps as much as two-thirds of the men under arms.[13] In order to maintain this indispensable arm of the polity, the king

[12] Similarly, in the mid-seventeenth century, each of Mukund Singh's younger brothers held imperial Mughal mansabs, some with attendant jagir assignments, from the Mughal Emperor Shah Jahan in addition to the patrimonial rights that they held in Kota by virtue of their descent from Madho Singh. As a result, ambiguous lines of hierarchical authority existed among the brothers. One witnesses this ambiguity at the Battle of Dharmat at which these Hada brothers fought in support of the Mughal Prince Dara-Shikoh against his brother Aurangzeb. The Hadas were unified in their support of Dara-Shikoh, but contemporary records show that while two brothers fought under the immediate command of the eldest brother (Mukund Singh), two other brothers (Mohan Singh and Kishor Singh) fought separately under their own banners. See Satish Chandra, Raghubir Sinh, and G. D. Sharma, eds, *Jodhpur hukumat ri bahi*: *Marwar under Jaswant Singh, 1658–1678* (Meerut: Meenakshi Prakashan, 1976), pp. 8, 13–14. Furthermore, G. D. Sharma reports, with reference to Jaipur, attempts by subordinate Rajput nobles to establish mansabdari relationships directly with the Mughal emperor were viewed as acts of defiance by Rajput rulers. See G. D. Sharma, *Vakil Reports Maharajgan (1693–1712 A.D.)* (Delhi: Radha Krishna, 1987), pp. 27–28, 51–53.

[13] For the role of the standing army in the Vijayanagar Empire, see Burton Stein, 'The Segmentary State: Interim Reflections' *Purusartha* 13 (1991): 217–288. For figures regarding the composition of Kota's military in 1802 and 1817 respectively, see R. P. Shastri, *Jhala Zalim Singh* (Jaipur: Raj Printing Works, 1971), pp. 350–351, and Sir John Malcolm, *A Memoir of Central India Including Malwa, and Adjoining Provinces, with the History, and Copious Illustrations, of the Past and Present Condition of that Country* (London: Parbury, Allen, and Co., 1832 [1824]), Volume II, p. 230.

perforce needed revenue. Significantly, the troopers who were employed in this army and received a salary continued to participate in the other forms of gift-giving that were associated with the royal gift of land. That is, they continued to desire, demand, and receive robes of honour (*siropavs*), titles (*khitabs* or *padvis*), turban bands and turban ornaments, pashmina shawls, pedigree horses, jewelled weaponry, palanquins, ceremonial umbrellas (*chatras*) and other 'necessary things' (*lavazma*; that is, 'regalia'). It thus appears that the symbolic constellation surrounding salary was not fundamentally opposed to that surrounding the gift of land. Notions of 'service' could just as easily be articulated through a cash wage as through a prebendal estate. Yet salaries had radically different pragmatic implications for state formation in the royal polity.

This chapter, then, will suggest that Dirks is far too unnuanced in the way he banished concerns about tax collections and revenue enhancement from his deliberations on precolonial state-formation. In doing so, he recapitulated, without formally admitting as such, the grossly simplistic formalist v. substantivist dichotomy that sidetracked the development of economic anthropology during much of the 1960s and 1970s.[14] Although Dirks was correct to highlight the important symbolic meanings attached to the redistribution of land, this does not necessarily mean that kings were unconcerned with the fiscal implications of these gifts. Royal anxiety over revenue arose precisely because revenue was not simply 'revenue' but was also laden with important symbolic meanings that had profound implications for how royal authority was conceived and articulated. These cultural meanings associated with the circulation of more fungible forms of wealth were being informed by new orientations towards the world deriving from bhakti devotionalism, particularly that brand associated with the Vallabha Sampraday that was becoming increasingly influential in Rajasthan during the late seventeenth and eighteenth centuries.

Before addressing this important matter, however, it will first be necessary in the next section to examine several textual representations concerning kingship and sovereignty in order to reveal how the dissonant politics of 'sedition' described above did not emerge from some extra-symbolic domain of naked ambition or realpolitik but, rather, grew out of tensions, incongruities, and disjunctures within the cultural coordinates of kingship and sovereignty themselves. Here I shall show that political clients often discounted, denied, or hedged the positive cultural valuation of the royal gift in favour of other cultural coordinates associated with conquest and bio-moral affinity with the soil. The following

[14] In this regard Dirks would have done better to draw on the Marshall Sahlins of *Culture and Practical Reason* (Chicago: University of Chicago Press, 1976) rather than the Marshall Sahlins of *Stone Age Economics* (New York: Aldine de Gruyter, 1972).

three sections then turn from the cultural representations of kingship to actual social institutions associated with agrarian revenue assessment, the grain market, and forms of land tenure through which income was raised in order to support and maintain, among other things, the standing army. Finally, the last section of this chapter will show how the state's fiscality and the military institutions built on it were informed by religious attitudes concerning 'liquidity' as expounded in bhakti doctrine.

An excursus on the rhetorics of service and conquest in Rajasthan

In chapter 2, during our examination of Lakshmandan's account of the audience of Maharao Bhim Singh of Kota with the Mughal Emperor in Delhi in 1719, we witnessed a palpable tension between the Kota ruler's acceptance of an imperial farman and gold coins, on the one hand, and his rejection of the emperor's outright gift of land, on the other. By insisting on conquering land himself 'through the strength of [his] own sword', Bhim Singh indicated that land that was given to him in the context of service was not as desirable as land that was conquered. Sovereignty had to be established from the ground-up as well as from the top-down and these two processes often gave rise to divergent pragmatic possibilities.

That these two bases of sovereignty were not always fully assimilatable and at times could be uncoupled is brought out even more starkly by Munhata Nainsi, the famous seventeenth-century chronicler of Rajasthan from Jodhpur (Marwar), in his *Bundiri dhaniyanri khyat* where he gave several conflicting accounts (*vat*s) that he heard concerning how Rao Deva Hada first conquered Bundi and established his seat of rule there in 1341.[15] It was from this base at Bundi that, a generation later, the Hadas conquered Kota. At stake in these stories, the first two of which shall concern us here, was Bundi's relationship to Mewar, which from time to time had claimed sovereignty over Bundi. From the relatively disengaged perspective of Jodhpur, Nainsi was able to recount the conflicting versions without feeling compelled to adjudicate their veracity or synthesize their differences, and for this reason he reveals, in close and stark juxtaposition, the heteroglossic dimensions of Bundi's founding that are often more muted in a single text.

All the stories agree that prior to Rao Deva's gaining sovereignty over Bundi, it was controlled by Minas, who seemed to have had a certain weakness for strong drink. At the time, Deva was ruling at Bainsrod,

[15] This date is much disputed. More out of convenience than conviction, I follow R. S. Mathur, *Relations of Hadas with Mughal Emperors (1568–1720 A.D.)* (Delhi: Deputy Publications, 1986), pp. 5–9.

which is some 60 kilometres due south of Bundi. Beyond these few details, the stories disagree on important matters, giving each tale very different implications regarding the basis of Deva's sovereignty over Bundi. The second story recounted by Nainsi establishes Deva's sovereignty within cultural coordinates of service and gift-giving that are consonant with those revealed by Dirks:

> Deva Hada, son of Banga, was flat broke when he came to Bundi from Bainsrod with a group of followers (*vasis*). Previously, Deva had married off his daughter to Rana Arsi, son of Lakhamsi, who brought a large army with his wedding entourage. After the wedding, Rana Arsi asked Deva how things were going, and Deva told him that times were tough. So the Rana said, 'Why do you stay here? Come join me.' Deva replied, 'Let's talk in private; I have a request to make of you.' When they were alone, the Rana asked Deva what he wanted, and Deva said, 'Nearby at Bundi there is some excellent land under the authority of the Minas who are hopeless drunkards. With backing from the Rana's army, I'll defeat the Minas, seize the land, and then serve the Rana (*Divanri chakri karun*).' So the Rana gave Deva as many men from his camp as Deva needed. Deva took command of the army, marched to Bundi, and attacked the Minas at night. He blockaded the city gates and, in the ensuing battle, all the Minas were killed or fled. In this way Deva established his command (*ann*) over the city.
>
> Having defeated the Minas, Deva then came to pay his respects to the Rana. The Rana was very pleased with Deva and asked him if there was any other work that still needed doing. Deva said, 'Thanks to the Rana's muscle everything is fine. Yet I could use the help of 500 of your horsemen for another four months.' Before returning to Chitor, the Rana gave Deva the horsemen. With the help of these troops Deva defeated the landlords (*bhomiyas*) in the countryside around Bundi and those who had remained on the land, fled. Deva then assembled his *bhaibandh*, and installed his followers throughout the countryside. After his men and animals were settled, the land became bountiful. Deva then dismissed the Rana's army but, thereafter, he served Mewar (*Mewari chakri karan lago*) by attending the Rana at Dasahra with a large number of troops.[16]

This account thus domesticates Deva's conquest of Bundi within his (sub)servience to Mewar. Not only does Deva, who was impoverished at Bainsrod, require the help of Rana Arsi's army in order to seize his future capital, but this assistance has been offered by the Rana during the course of his marriage to Deva's daughter. In north India where hypergamy was greatly idealized (if not always realized), this marriage instantiated Deva's subordination to the Rana, which was reconfirmed annually thereafter through his service (*chakri*) to the Rana at the Mewar Dasahra which he attended with a large contingent of soldiers.

The first account related by Nainsi, however, situates Deva's conquest quite differently.

16 Munhata Nainsi, *Munhata Nainsiri khyat*, Volume 1, ed. Badriprasad Sakariya (Jodhpur: Rajasthan Pracyavidya Pratishtan, 1960), pp. 98–99.

Deva Hada, son of Banga, had gone from Bainsrod to Bundi, where Minas had been living and which was in the state of disorder (*vikhayat thako*). The Minas had asked the Brahmans who lived in Bundi to give them a daughter in marriage. The Brahmans of Bundi were indignant and rebuffed the proposal, but the Minas remained insistent. So the Brahmans requested help from Deva, their *jajman* (patron), who was living at Bainsrod. Deva said, 'Agree to give a daughter to the Minas, but after determining the appropriate time for the wedding, claim that you do not know the proper rites and that you must ask your jajmans, the Hadas who live in Bainsrod, to make the necessary arrangements.' The Minas consented to this ploy, and the Hadas made preparations for the wedding.

Due to their fondness for strong drink, the Minas walked blindly into the trap that was set for them. Before the wedding started the Hadas built a large hut and on the floor of the hut they laid explosives, which they then covered with grass fodder. The bride's people then invited the Minas to sit in the wedding hut and plied them with liquor. When the Minas finally passed out drunk, the Hadas fell upon them and set the wedding hut alight killing them in the explosion. Afterwards the Hadas attacked and seized Bundi killing the Minas there. Those who survived the attack fled, and they are now called Bundelas.[17]

In this version of the tale, Rao Deva is represented as an upholder of a differentiated social order through his prevention of an improper mixing of castes as threatened in the Mina marriage proposal to the Brahman maiden. In flattening the Mina town and killing the offending inhabitants, Deva is also depicted as an awesome destroyer of a degenerate age meting out stiff punishment to those who threaten the dharma. Finally, and most significantly, Deva is represented as a conqueror in the complete sense of someone who forces others to bend to his will while he, himself, submits to no other. This account thereby establishes Deva's authority solely in the grounds of his conquest that leads to the (re)establishment of proper social hierarchies. Crucially, this version censors any reference to Deva's service to Rana Arsi.

Nainsi, unfortunately, did not mention his sources of these stories. Circumstantial evidence from the nineteenth century, however, gives a strong indication that these two stories derived from Mewar and Bundi respectively. Surajmal Mishran's *Vamshabhaskar*, composed for the Bundi court in 1841, tells a version of the tale in which Deva's conquest was motivated by a desire to champion the cause of Bundi's Brahmans and this victory was achieved without aid from Mewar.[18] Shyamaldas's

[17] Ibid., p. 97.

[18] Suryamalla Mishran, *Vamshabhaskar* (Jodhpur: n.p., 1899), p. 1624. The *Shatrusalyacharitamahakavya,* which was composed at Bundi ca. 1635, similarly neglects any mention of Rao Deva's service to the Rana of Mewar. Although this text mentions that Deva was involved in conflict with the Minas, it claims that the Hadas had first established their capital at Bundi during the reign of Deva's great-grandfather, Chandraraja (no mention of service to the Rana here either). And even those portions of the text dealing with those Hada rulers who fought with the Mughal army use the

Virvinod, published for the Mewar court in 1886, privileges the version of the vat that highlights Rana Arsi's aid in conquering Bundi.[19] Furthermore, evidence internal to the two tales reflects these two different perspectives. Although both tales mention that Deva's ambition to conquer Bundi was motivated by states of misfortune, the misfortune is situated differently in each tale with divergent implications for understanding Deva's status. In the 'Mewar' version, the misfortune was located in Bainsrod. Deva was impoverished. In the 'Bundi' version, however, the misfortune resided in Bundi. The Minas were attempting to transgress proper marriage practices. Thus in the 'Mewar' version Deva is the *subject* of misfortune who is redeemed by Arsi. But in the 'Bundi' version he is the *destroyer* of misfortune who redeems Brahmanical honour.

That the significance of conquest was not always neatly subsumed within the cultural coordinates of service was inscribed in the fact that Rajputs maintained qualitatively different attitudes toward lands they held through conquest as opposed to lands they held in connection with service. This difference was witnessed in their much prized *vatandar* status within the Mughal Empire.[20] *Vatan*s were ancestral estates that, in theory at least, had been conquered and ruled by Rajputs prior to their incorporation into the Mughal Empire and over which they maintained special authority after their annexation. Vatans contrasted with the mansab or jagir estates, which Rajput chiefs also held along with the majority of the Mughal nobility, that were geographically dispersed among far-flung territories in the empire and periodically reassigned and in which the holder only had a revenue interest. Vatandars, on the other hand, maintained hereditary control – involving revenue, judicial, and military rights – over their specific home territories which could only be reassigned at the risk of provoking strong resistance, if not insurrection.[21]

At the height of Mughal power in the late sixteenth and seventeenth centuries, Rajput vatans tended be extremely small and they were circumscribed by territories over which they exerted little direct influence. As Mughal power waned during the eighteenth century, however, these

language of alliance rather than service in describing their conduct. See Mahakavi Viswanatha, *Shastrusalyacharitmahakavya*, ed. Bholashankar Vyas (Jodhpur: Rajasthan Prachyavidya Pratisthan, 1996).

19 Shyamaldas, *Virvinod*, Volume 2 (New Delhi: Motilal Banarasidas, 1986 [1886]), p. 107.

20 G. D. Sharma, *Vakil Reports Maharajgan*, pp. 2 and 26–29; Dilbagh Singh, *The State, Landlords and Peasants: Rajasthan in the 18th Century* (Columbia, MO: South Asia Publications, 1990), pp. 8–12.

21 The one famous exception to this general rule was during Akbar's reign when Rao Raja Surjan Singh Hada of Bundi (r. 1554–1558) exchanged his vatan in Rajasthan for a Mughal jagir including Banaras and Chunar. Surjan Singh's desire to hold Banaras and Chunar, however, did not arise from its connection to Akbar but, rather, from Banaras's religious status as one of India's great *tirtha*s. Significantly, Surjan Singh's son, Bhav Singh, reclaimed Bundi after Banaras and Chunar had been resumed.

vatans became the nuclei from which many of the Rajput successor kingdoms emerged as Rajput rulers eschewed dispersed land holdings elsewhere in the empire in favour of more concentrated holdings surrounding their vatan.[22] Thus, for example, the vatan of Maharaja Jai Singh of Amber (Jaipur) consisted only of pargana Amber at the time of his accession in 1699, but by the time of his death in 1743 he had substantial rights in well over fifteen contiguous parganas in eastern Rajasthan. Jai Singh claimed some of these new territories, such as parganas Toda and Chatsu, as part of his vatan (even if the Mughal emperor did not always concede these claims). Other neighboring parganas were held as part of his imperial jagir, and yet more were held on *ijara* (tax farming) tenure from other Mughal mansabdars.[23] In this way he developed a consolidated, if variable, authority over a sizable contiguous territory surrounding his vatan.

The special links that Rajputs forged with specific tracts of land – particularly land where they had fought – was symbolized, as Norman Ziegler has noted, by the *pinda*, 'a ball of food or clay made either from the sustenance of the land or the land itself, which [was] offered up to... ancestors, who had conquered and enjoyed mastery over the land before them'. Ziegler further recounts episodes from Marwari chronicles, such as the seventeenth-century *Aitihasik batan*, in which mortally wounded Rajputs mixed their blood with the soil where they had fallen in battle in order to form pandas, which were then offered up before death. 'Such acts', he explains, 'represented the return of strength to the land and its nourishment of the brotherhood [an internal segment of the Rajput clan], which preserved the "body" and enabled it to continue to rule.'[24] Through the trope of the blood-soaked pinda, Rajputs thus dialectically linked their strength and well-being to the fertility of specific tracts of land. Because each, in turn, was deemed to nourish and strengthen the other, Rajput mastery over the land and the fertility of the land gained through the spilling of one's own blood became powerfully conjoined in a bio-moral order. This attitude accounts for the reluctance of Rajputs to part with their ancestral lands even in exchange for equally, or more,

[22] Sometimes this grab of local territory was a matter of reasserting rights that had been enjoyed prior to the Mughals. More often than not, however, Rajputs used the discourse of vatan to legitimize the seizure of lands which had previously not come under their rule.

[23] G. D. Sharma, *Vakil Reports*, p. 28.

[24] Norman P. Ziegler, 'Some Notes on Rajput Loyalties during the Mughal Period,' in *Kingship and Authority in South Asia*, ed. J. F. Richards (Madison: University of Wisconsin South Asia Publication Series, no. 3, 1978), p. 223. For similar dialectical connections between persons and the land on which they live in contemporary south India, see also E. Valentine Daniel, *Fluid Signs: Being a Person the Tamil Way* (Berkeley: University of California Press, 1984).

valuable lands elsewhere.[25] Rajputs held that such exchanges ultimately diminished their power for it separated them from the earth to which they had become particularly well suited over time. It also informed the numerous literary representations, in texts such as the *Kanhadade prabhanda* discussed in chapter 2, of the (idealized?) mediæval Rajput practice of *jauhar* in which Rajput womenfolk, when faced with the certain conquest of their homeland, committed mass suicide by throwing themselves from the ramparts while their husbands allowed themselves to be cut down in hopeless battle rather than surrendering or retreating. In soaking the soil with their own blood they impregnated the land with their own distinctive qualities, making it (con)substantially theirs and, in effect, poisoning it for the victors.[26] This belief explains why victorious kings often resettled the lands where rivals had been killed with the relations of the vanquished, for only these people were suited to the soil and able to make it productive.[27]

Assessing agrarian land revenue in eighteenth century Rajasthan

The rhetorics of conquest and bio-moral affinity with the soil clearly animated strong, from-the-ground-up, centrifugal pressures within Rajasthani kingdoms that, at times, discounted the 'spirit of centricity'

[25] One is tempted to see in these practices and attitudes an incipient form of nationalism, as early colonial commentators such as James Tod did. Such a presumption would not be incorrect insofar as this term highlights a close attachment between a people and specific tracts of land. However, one must appreciate that the 'imagined community' that was included within this *patriæ* privileged the position of warriors – those who spilled blood and whose blood was spilled. This national sentiment thus remained limited and hierarchical and did not become the basis for a 'deep, horizontal comradeship', to borrow Anderson's turn of phrase, encompassing other communities (for better or worse). Perhaps a better point of departure for comparative purposes would lie in more pluralistic notions of patriotism (as opposed to homogenizing nationalisms) as outlined by Maurizio Viroli in his essay on patriotism and nationalism. Moreover, unlike European notions of nationalism in which it was the land that determined the character of those residing on it, in the Rajasthani conception the relationship between people and land was conceived more dialectically. See Benedict Anderson, *Imagined Communities: Reflections on the Origins and Spread of Nationalism*, 2nd edn. (London: Verso, 1991 [1983]), p. 7 and Maurizio Viroli, *For Love of Country: An Essay on Patriotism and Nationalism* (Oxford: Oxford University Press, 1995).

[26] This belief similarly underlies the seemingly defeatist Rajput tradition of glorifying battles at which ancestors lost their lives. The *Ratan raso*, for example, devotes considerably more space to recounting the gory events of the battle of Dharmat where Raja Ratan Singh of Ratlam died, rather than the numerous victories he had enjoyed earlier in his career.

[27] For example, Sanjay Subrahmanyam has noted that, in the *Karnataka rajakkal cavistara carittiram* by Senji Narayanan Pillai, the family of the Bundela Rajput Tej Singh was given revenue rights to land nearby to where he was killed by the victorious Saadatullah Khan. See Sanjay Subrahmanyam, 'Friday's Child: Or How Tej Singh Became Tecinkurajan', *Indian Economic and Social History Review* 36 (1999): 86.

established through top-down, royal gift-giving. These fissiparous tendencies are seen not only in the ubiquity of revolt against royal authority, but also in the fiscal measures kings put in place to underwrite supplementary locations of royal military power. While Dirks's description of what we might call a fiscally innocent polity ('the original affluent polity'?) may have applied to his small, remote corner of south India (and even here I have my doubts which I shall raise at the end of this chapter), it cannot be seen as a general model, in and of itself, for the larger and more complex state-formations in the eighteenth century. The body of evidence concerning the fiscal interest of the king in land, in which he often displayed considerable financial acumen, is overwhelming.

This section examines measures taken by the privileged land-holding strata of society, be it the king himself or one of his political clients, in order to enhance their revenues at the actual point of collection in the village. An abiding trend within South Asian economic anthropology during the last twenty years – a trend that often has been nested within analyses of the cultural construction of power in the precolonial Indian polity – has characterized the 'traditional' village economy, most commonly known by its north Indian manifestation the *jajmani* system, as being regulated according to the terms of a 'moral economy' of shared risks in which the hereditary rights and privileges of cultivators, village servants, and landlords were joint and complementary, rather than unitary and separable. Although the jajmani system enshrined distinct hierarchical asymmetries among the participants, thereby allowing landlords to enjoy the benefits of a considerable percentage of the agricultural product, economic relations were not informed, it has been argued, by an 'anti-social', maximizing, or market-oriented, mentality. Instead the jajmani system was more a redistributive system in which the flow of things (produce, goods, and services) was embedded in the flow of social relations, and economic transactions served to express the interdependence of different social beings rather than being a marker of possessive individualism.[28]

[28] Many anthropologists have made this 'substantivist' argument. Louis Dumont and Pauline Kolenda have offered the classic statements, but even recently Gloria Raheja has offered a variant of this position (despite her many valid criticisms of Dumont). This position has been subject to occasional criticism, most notably by C. J. Fuller. Curiously, the substantivist position continues to inform most ethnohistorical accounts of the precolonial polity, such as those offered by Dirks. See Louis Dumont, *Homo Hierarchicus*; Pauline Kolenda, 'Toward a Model of the Hindu Jajmani System', in *Tribal and Peasant Economies*, ed. G. Dalton (Garden City, NY: American Museum of Natural History, 1967); Gloria G. Raheja, 'Centrality, Mutuality, and Hierarchy: Shifting Aspects of Inter-Caste Relationships in North India', *Contributions to Indian Sociology* (N.S.) 23 (1989): 79–101; Dirks, *Hollow Crown*, especially pp. 31, 117–128, 195–198; C. J. Fuller, 'Misconceiving the Grain Heap: A Critique of the Concept of the Indian Jajmani System', in *Money and Morality of Exchange*, eds J. Parry and M. Bloch, pp. 33–63 (Cambridge: Cambridge University Press, 1989).

One of the defining features of this non-market system of economic exchange was that, apparently, it was not monetized. The values of goods and services were not established against an abstract counter of value as in market-based economies. Instead, participants in the economy were sustained and rewarded through a share system based on a fixed division of the crop, known as *batai* in north India, that took place at the time of the harvest. After the harvest had been brought in from the fields and the crop threshed, the grain heap would be divided on the threshing floor among the co-sharers according to traditional formulae. Tod witnessed one such division of the crop in Udaipur at the turn of the nineteenth century in which village servants (night watchmen, accountants, blacksmiths, potters, barbers, washermen, and so on) collectively received approximately 25 percent of the crop, the royal treasury 30 percent, and the cultivator 45.[29]

While it is clear that the complementary share system provided the ideological underpinnings for revenue extraction at the village level and, thereby, precluded certain forms of economic rationality associated with the private ownership of land, evidence of fiscal pragmatism can be witnessed in other arenas of the agrarian economy. This form of narrowly economic calculation can be seen at work in the persistent attempts (sometimes successful, sometimes not) by landlords in large sections of north India during the sixteenth through eighteenth centuries to introduce alternative systems of revenue assessment in favour of batai. Although these alternative revenue regimes continued to be *formally* rooted in the share system, they were preferred by landlords because they not only reduced administrative costs, thereby enhancing the incomes of landed elites, but they also shifted certain risks to the cultivator. Significantly, money figured conceptually in both these alternative modes of assessment, even where no coin physically changed hands and the revenue continued to be collected in kind. In other words, money was used as an abstract counter of value even when it was not involved in the economic transaction.[30]

[29] These proportions, however, varied with the season, the crop under cultivation, and the social status of the cultivator.

[30] Money enjoyed at least limited use in India from ancient times. During the seventeenth and eighteenth centuries, however, its use expanded dramatically as Europeans brought vast quantities of specie and bullion to India for the purposes of trade. Kota had three mints dating most probably to the third quarter of the eighteenth century (at Kota, Gagron, and Shahabad) and a fourth was added at the turn of the nineteenth (at Jhalrapatan). These mints produced Kota's own bimetallic currency (known as the Gumanshahi rupee) for which there were standardized exchange rates into currencies used elsewhere. Other financial instruments, such as the ubiquitous *hundi* (bill of credit), were also used, especially in contexts where specie was either too cumbersome or in short supply. For money in Kota, see B. L. Gupta, *Trade and Commerce in Rajasthan during the Eighteenth Century* (Jaipur: Jaipur Publishing House, 1987), pp. 168–174. For the use of money elsewhere in India, see also Fuller 'Misconceiving the Grain Heap', especially

For the landlord, batai had several important drawbacks. First, batai afforded cultivators plenty of opportunity for 'pilfering' insofar as they were able to make sure that considerable quantities of grain never reached the threshing floor. Two means of accomplishing this goal were commonplace: 'eating the crop green', or harvesting a portion of it before it had fully matured, in advance of the landlord's arrival in the village to collect his share; and leaving considerable quantities of produce in the fields at harvest-time for later gleaning after the landlord had left the village. Under the batai regime the landlord also was left with the costs and risks of disposing of his portion of the crop, a particular concern where the crop was of the highly perishable 'garden' variety and exceeded his immediate consumption needs. Additionally, the landlord's income was subject to fluctuations associated with the success or failure of each season's crop, itself dependent upon the vagaries of the monsoon and the periodic appearance of blights and pests (especially locusts).

The two landlord-favoured modes of revenue collection addressed several of these drawbacks. The first, known as *latai* in Kota and as *kankut* elsewhere in north India, consisted of an assessment reckoned in cash terms based on the yield of the crop estimated while it was still standing.[31] During the growing season when the crop was well up, the landlord sent agents to the fields where, together with the cultivators, they estimated the crop's yield and valued it at current market prices in the local qasba.[32] The cultivators would then be held liable for the cash equivalent of the landlord's share. In other words, the landlord's revenue was still fixed, at least initially, as a percentage of the crop, but this percentage was then converted into a monetary equivalent. Because the revenue assessment was made while the crop was still standing in the fields, the cultivator had considerably less chance to appropriate a greater share of the grain by stealth. Furthermore, this revenue regime also shifted the costs and risks of disposing of the landlord's share of the crop to the cultivator. In many cases, however, the cultivator continued to pay his land revenue in kind (for reasons which will be discussed below) when the crop was eventually brought in, but the appraisal of his in-kind payment was based on its monetary value as established in the grain market rather than on a percentage of the actual harvest. There was often a discrepancy between

pp. 43–47 and K. N. Chaudhuri, 'European Trade with India', in *The Cambridge Economic History of India*, Volume I: *c. 1200–c.1757*, eds Tapan Raychaudhuri and Irfan Habib (Cambridge: Cambridge University Press, 1982), pp. 382–407.

31 M. L. Sharma, *Kota rajya ka itihas* (Kota: The Kota Printing Press, 1939), pp. 148–149.

32 Tod reported that these conjectures were very accurate and rarely deviated from the actual harvest by more than 5 percent. See James Tod, *Annals and Antiquities of Rajast'han or the Central and Western Rajpoot States of India* (London: Smith, Elder and Co., 1832), Volume II, p. 537.

the two forms of reckoning as grain in the market was typically at its lowest price during the harvest season. Despite these advantages for landlords, latai retained one distinct disadvantage insofar as it continued to link revenue assessment to the size of the actual (or anticipated) harvest and, thereby, did nothing to smooth out the consequent fluctuations in income that occurred between years of good harvests and bad.

The second alternative mode of assessment, known as *kuntai* in Kota, was introduced to ameliorate this problem. It was similar in many ways to the Mughal system of *zabt* that was introduced by Akbar to several parts of Rajasthan in the early sixteenth century but perhaps did not achieve widespread usage in Kota until the eighteenth century.[33] Under this regime, the assessment was only tied to a division of the harvest in the most abstract of ways. That is, the amount of land revenue was determined by the *average yield* for each particular crop within a specified field over a number of preceding years. As with latai this mode of assessment was fixed in cash terms but could be paid in kind at market rates after the harvest. In comparison with latai, kuntai further reduced the landlord's administrative costs, for once the initial assessment of the average revenue rates had been established, the landlord no longer had to employ agents to go to the fields to estimate the actual crop. Moreover, this revenue regime insulated the landlord from the burden of variable crop yields, leaving the cultivator to bear the risk in its entirety.

Although variants of latai and kuntai were known across north India at least since the late sixteenth century, attempts by landlords to introduce these revenue regimes faced certain limitations. The most serious inhibitor was the flight of the peasantry. Masanori Sato has noted that during the course of the first half of the eighteenth century agricultural labour in Kota regularly fled oppressive conditions, and the government tried to prevent the flight by instituting measures of 'collective responsibility' that made entire communities of agricultural labourers responsible for the financial and labour obligations of individual members.[34] This observation supports Harbans Mukhia's more general suggestion that the north Indian peasantry was not formally tied to the land in a state of 'serfdom' but remained *relatively* 'free' in comparison to their European counterparts insofar as Indian farmers continued to control the means of production (ploughs, seeds, and so on) as well as the processes of production

[33] Irfan Habib, *The Agrarian System of Mughal India (1556–1707)* (London: Asia Publishing House, 1963), pp. 190–219; See also Stewart N. Gordon, 'The Slow Conquest: Administrative Integration of Malwa into the Maratha Empire, 1720–1760', *Modern Asian Studies* 11 (1977): 20–29.

[34] Masanori Sato, 'The Chamars of South-Eastern Rajasthan, A.D. 1650–1800', in *Caste System, Untouchability and the Depressed*, ed. H. Kotani (Delhi: Manohar, 1997), pp. 31–53.

(how they organized their labour).[35] These factors made it somewhat easier for the Indian peasantry to flee oppressive tax regimes than was the case in Europe. Not infrequently, however, conditions did prevail that restricted the ability of farmers to move and thus permitted landlords to extract revenue more aggressively. One condition that impinged heavily on peasant mobility was political disruption in neighbouring realms to where farmers could reasonable hope to move.

Agrarian revenues and the urban grain market

The possibilities for landlords to enhance their incomes from land revenues did not end, however, with the collection of their share of the harvest from the peasantry, especially when that share was realized in kind, for only a limited amount of this grain was actually consumed by the landlord. The rest was shipped off to the grain market for sale. For the largest landlords, such as the king, this meant they became deeply involved in the grain trade. In eighteenth-century Jaipur, for instance, the royal treasury derived half of all its agrarian revenue in kind.[36] As the kingdom's largest landowner, the king thus became a major supplier of grain on the wholesale markets in the larger urban centres (qasbas) as well as in the smaller market towns (*mandi*s or *ganj*s) and weekly village markets (*hat*s).

These markets were considerable in size and had a major impact on the social and military dynamic of the royal polity. Yet, when discussed in the academic literature at all, recent assessments of the economic foundations of most precolonial South Asian polities have generally underestimated their importance. As early as 1662, however, one finds Munhata Nainsi collecting census data on Marwar's major qasbas. Merchant groups figure prominently in these enumerations – they are invariably listed first attesting to the growing importance of commerce and mercantile expertise in managing capital and credit.[37] Even for the smaller towns and villages of Marwar where he did not have reliable census data (or did not think it important to collect it) he still noted wherever mahajans were settled.

Nainsi's enumerative interest in mahajans and their growing role in the constitution of the polity also find literary expression in several of the tales he related in his *khyat*. Take for example the story he collected about Chaju and Siva, two Chandravat Sisodiyas (father and son), who gained

[35] Harbans Mukhia, 'Was There Feudalism in Indian History', *Journal of Peasant Studies* 8 (1981): 273–310.

[36] Bajekal, 'The State and the Rural Grain Market', p. 445.

[37] Munhata Nainsi, *Marvar ra parganan ri vigat*, Volume 1, ed. Narayansinh Bhati (Jodhpur: Rajasthan Prachyavidya Pratishtan, 1968), pp. 391 and 497 and Volume 2 (Jodhpur: Rajasthan Prachyavidya Pratishtan, 1969), p. 83.

authority over a stretch of territory in northern Malwa during the fifteenth century. According to the tale, Chaju and Siva were *bhomiya*s (local landlords) living on their vatan (ancestral land) in the village of Pathar in pargana Antri of northern Malwa. This pargana was within the dominion of the Patshah of Mandu. Chaju and Siva lived alongside other relations (*bhaibandh bhomiya*s) who held land in the same and surrounding villages. However, Chaju and his relations were constantly wrangling over damage to the village crops caused by the uncontrolled grazing of animals. These disputes eventually came to a head and Chaju's and Siva's relations forced them to leave Pathar. The exiles then settled in the village of Milsiyakhedi situated just a few miles from the qasba town of Antri, headquarters of the pargana bearing the same name. Here they built a stronghold with a small following of 20 or 25 Rajput families. However, events in Antri brought about a change in their fortunes. Nainsi explains:

> The qasba of Antri is a big city with a large business district. But the city was infested with thieves and, in the surrounding district, the royal officials could not control the bhomiyas. This lawlessness disheartened the merchants who thought – 'These royal officers are incompetent. But the Sisodiyas, Chaju and Siva Chandravat, are noble Rajputs and powerful bhomiyas. If we give them responsibility for protecting the town, they will put matters right.' The merchants deliberated and appealed to Chaju for help and he accepted their overture. The merchants paid him one rupee a day as protection money. They also paid a tax on births and marriages. Chaju and Siva, father and son, then served (*tahal karai*) the qasba. Chaju prevented his bhaibandh bhomiyas, who were living close-by, from robbing the town. He also arrested and executed those who previously had stolen. After this there were no more robberies and the merchants of the qasba enjoyed peace of mind. As the deeds of Chaju and Siva increased, they became renowned, and a multitude of Rajput horsemen rallied round them.[38]

In this story, the qasba is represented as a crucial site where the dispossessed Chaju and Siva are able to overcome the misfortune of their exile, gain a large following of supporters, and even punish their earlier foes (their bhaibandh bhomiyas).

By the early 1700s, Kota included several important urban, commercial centres – notably qasbas Kota, Baran, Mau, and Gagron – as well as a considerable number of smaller qasbas. During the course of the eighteenth century the number of qasbas, as well as smaller mandis and ganjs, within Kota expanded rapidly, and by mid century there were well in excess of fifty towns with the designation of qasba in the kingdom.[39]

[38] Munhata Nainsi, *Munhata Nainsiri khyat*, Volume 3, ed. Badriprasad Sakariya (Jodhpur: Rajasthan Prachyavidya Pratishtan, 1964), pp. 242–243.

[39] Masanori Sato, 'The Growth of Towns (Qasbas) of South-Eastern Rajasthan under the Mughals – A Case Study of Jhalrapatan', in *Economy and Polity of Rajasthan: Study of Kota and Marwar, 17th through 19th Centuries*, Masanori Sato and B. L. Bhadani, pp. 31–56 (Jaipur: Publication Scheme, 1997).

While most of these qasbas had populations of just a few thousand people, some of them were quite large. The Comte de Modave estimated in 1776 that qasba Kota was home to 25,000 or 30,000 inhabitants.[40] Mau's population was probably at the lower end of this range and Gagron's population surely exceeded 10,000.[41] If Kota's total population in the eighteenth century was similar to its late nineteenth-century numbers, then it is quite likely that the urban- and town-based inhabitants of Kota accounted for about a fifth of the total population.[42]

These cities and towns were both centres of manufacturing as well as entrepôts of trade. The production of textiles was particularly important to this urban economy. Kota was home to several distinctive, luxury hand-looms – one of which was an airy, gauze-like weave in cotton whose production was centred in the town of Kethun, 20 kilometres southeast of qasba Kota, and which became well-known throughout India. These cities and towns engaged both in long distance trade with other metropolises across north India, the Middle East, and Southeast Asia, and in more local commerce with nearby villages, much of it being conducted through a system of rotating weekly markets. A wide range of goods were bought and sold. Textiles were naturally extremely important. Other items traded included other manufactures such as metalwork for domestic and agricultural use, cash crops such as opium, cotton, indigo and, especially, grain.

Madhavi Bajekal has documented for Jaipur, with supporting evidence from Kota, that befitting his large stake in the grain market, the king had an extensive system of inventoried storage facilities, networks for transportation and distribution, and marketing strategies that included systematic accounting procedures that monitored the daily and seasonal fluctuations of grain prices in the bazaar. The price at which the 'royal share' was sold, the quantities sold and their total value were then recorded in revenue abstracts, known as *jamabandi*s and *arhsatta*s.[43]

40 Comte de Modave (Louis Laurent de Federbe), *Voyage en Inde du Comte de Modave*, ed. J. Deloche (Paris: Ecole française d'Extrême-Orient, 1971), pp. 478–501.

41 In the late seventeenth century, Nainsi estimated that Gagron had 10,000 inhabitants and, although he did not venture a total figure for Mau, he stated that Mau had about two and a half times the number of (joint) households (*ghar*) as Gagron (2000 households in Mau as compared to 700 or 800 in Gagron). This would suggest that Mau's total population might have been as high as 25,000. See Munhata Nainsi, *Munhata Nainsiri khyat*, Volume 1, pp. 114–115.

42 Kota's total population was estimated at 433,000 in 1876. See C. U. Aitchison, *A Collection of Treaties, Engagements, and Sunnuds Relating to India and Neighboring Countries*, Volume III: *The Treaties, &c., Relating to the States in Rajpootana, Central India, and the Mediatized Chiefs in Central India and Malwa* (Calcutta: Foreign Office Press, 1876), p. 137.

43 Madhavi Bajekal, 'The State and the Rural Grain Market in Eighteenth Century Eastern Rajasthan', *Indian Economic and Social History Review* 25 (1988): 443–473, especially

Bajekal furthermore noted that the king used his political authority to intervene in the local grain markets in order to maximize his own revenues by:

> monitoring and negotiating the price and conditions for the sale of grain, coercing the merchants to purchase state grain either directly through forced sales or indirectly by restricting commercial transactions and the intra-regional movement of [non-state] grain until its stocks [of state grain] were sold'.[44]

William Hunter observed precisely this phenomenon at work in 1793 when passing through Shinde's territories around Ujjain just to the south of Kota. He noticed royal officials attempting to inflate the price of grain by creating conditions of scarcity.

> The scarcity [of grain] was artificially increased, by the rapacity of Cablee Mul, the person entrusted by Sindiah with collecting the revenues of the district. His wealth and influence enabled him to hoard up large magazines of grain, and thereby keep the price far beyond its natural standard. And when Sudasheu Naick, an eminent banker,... attempted to throw open his stores, and fell the grain to a moderate price, no means of obstruction and intimidation, that the union of artifice with power could afford, were left unemployed to make him desist from this purpose.[45]

Therefore, even though the 'routinization' of a market-orientated, maximizing mentality may have been restricted (and even here only unevenly) by cultural norms and expectations within the domain of primary production, it is clear that a 'fiscal acuity' was highly developed in other important economic spheres that were linked to agrarian production.

Thus rather than seeing a single undifferentiated logic underlying economic exchange in the precolonial polity, a picture begins to emerge of different 'spheres of exchange', to utilize Paul Bohannan's enduring insight, each of which was governed by its own morality involving its own pragmatics and possibilities for calculation.[46] Moreover, also following Bohannan, we see that these spheres often existed in a segmented relationship one to another and that profit or advantage that was gained in one sphere could be 'converted' for use in another sphere albeit then

pp. 446–448. James Tod mentions that these same practices operated in Kota in the early nineteenth century. Tod, *Annals and Antiquities*, Volume II, pp. 538–544.

44 Bajekal, 'The State and the Rural Grain Market', pp. 464–465. For a description of similar practices in Kota, see Tod, *Annals and Antiquities*, Volume II, pp. 539–545.

45 William Hunter, 'Narrative of a Journey from Agra to Oujein', *Asiatick Researches* 6 (1808): 56.

46 Paul Bohannan, 'Some Principals of Exchange and Investment among the Tiv', *American Anthropologist* 57 (1955): 60–70; and 'The Impact of Money on an African Subsistence Economy', *Journal of Economic History* 19 (1959): 491–503.

subject to different norms and evaluations.[47] This view of the late precolonial economy, then, does not chart the differences between India and the west in terms of a moral economy v. market economy polarity. We know too well that western societies cannot be seen simply as economics writ large – they also have their cultural designs. This fact becomes readily apparent when we reflect on the practice of 'revenue farming' which was widespread in India (and which will be discussed in far greater detail in the following section). The creation of 'revenue farms' is clearly an example of the precolonial state creating a marketable commodity in an area that we in the west, as yet, have refused to utilise in this way. Our abhorrence at the commodification of revenue rights rests on the way we perceive it infringing on the sovereignty of the state (especially when regarded, surely somewhat naïvely, as an embodiment of the 'public good'). But why we recoil at the commoditization of rights to revenue collection and not of rights in revenue production (through notions of private property in land and the ownership of other 'means of production') remains entirely arbitrary (that is, it is a culturally determined matter). From this example,[48] we see that both western and Indian societies incorporated both forms of exchange, but the boundaries between the spheres were defined differently as were the ways in which these spheres were ordered and linked in specific sequences to produce larger social and economic forms.[49]

[47] Of course, where one would want to modify Bohannan's model to better suit the Indian context lies in his suggestion that western expansion was responsible for the appearance of the 'market' segment of the economy in which money was the medium of exchange. While this may have been the case among the Tiv, money-based exchanges existed in India well before the arrival of the 'hat-wearing merchants' (*topiwalas*) of the East India Company.

[48] Another area where the cultural dimensions of the western 'capitalist' economy have become apparent lies in the recent controversy in the European Parliament regarding attempts by biotechnology companies to patent specific genes or gene sequences that have diagnostic use in health care. Much of this debate was shaped by the western nature/culture dichotomy that underlies the distinction between the 'discovery' of a naturally existing phenomenon (which cannot be patented) and phenomena whose existence requires human intervention, i.e. inventiveness (which are patentable). This sort of distinction would be largely incomprehensible in other cultures, yet it has had a very real impact on the way in which the bio-tech market is developing.

[49] This view also substantially revises Karl Polyani's 'ports of trade' argument that contended, where impersonal markets did exist in traditional kingdoms, they tended to be insulated from the internal or domestic workings of economic exchange and only involved 'overseas' exchange with foreign powers. In late precolonial north India, at least, markets were integral to patterns of exchange within the polity and had a significant impact in how royal power itself was built.

The distribution of revenue rights among landed elites

But surely, the strongest evidence suggesting that precolonial elites were perfectly capable of and often quite willing to view the alienation of land in terms that had significant fiscal dimensions lies in the revenue-farming practice – known, in Kota, as *muqata* or, more generally elsewhere in north India, as *ijara* – in which contracts to collect revenue for the king were put out to competitive bid. This practice appears to have been Mughal in origin. It knew limited application in north India, at least, since of the reign of Akbar, and it appears to have expanded considerably in scope at the beginning of the eighteenth century during the reign of Farukhhsiyar.[50] Many of the Mughal successor kingdoms of the eighteenth century, including Kota, 'naturalized' ijara tenures within their domains. According to this practice, at the beginning of the year (or at the beginning of a single growing season), agents would bid to pay a fixed sum to the king, half of which was tendered in advance on acceptance of the bid, in return for the right to collect the actual land revenue from a specified territory when the harvest eventually came in. The revenue agents tended to be drawn from the localities where they hoped to collect the revenue and came from a wide variety of backgrounds that included not only 'traditional' landed elites (*jagirdars* and *zamindars*), but also bankers (*sahukars*), other prominent businessmen (mahajans), and even prosperous peasants. Quite simply, the muqatadar, or ijaradar, aimed to use his knowledge of local production conditions, as well as his locally based coercive means, to collect land revenues that exceeded what had been promised to the royal treasury.

For its part, the royal treasury shifted the burden of revenue collection to the muqatadar and, more importantly, as the muqatadar paid the treasury part of his bid in advance, this system afforded the king ready cash in times when agricultural income was not normally forthcoming. That kings were conscious of the fact that this form of economic expediency sometimes entailed a loss to the royal treasury in terms of revenue skimmed off by the muqatadar is witnessed in periodic attempts by kings to resume the farmed-out territories and to take direct control over them once again. However, often the muqatadars provided real 'value-for-money' insofar as their local knowledge allowed them to collect revenues at a far higher rate, and therefore bid far higher sums, than the king could hope to collect on his own. This was particularly true in newly conquered

[50] Irfan Habib, *The Agrarian System of Mughal India (1556–1707)* (London: Asia Publishing House, 1963), pp. 277–278. It was also known to be widespread in the Nayaka kingdoms of south India by the early seventeenth century. See Velcheru Narayana Rao, David Shulman, and Sanjay Subrahmanyam, *Symbols of Substance*: *Court and State in Nayaka Period Tamilnadu* (Delhi: Oxford University Press, 1992), pp. 100–107.

lands where the king had no previous knowledge of local conditions of production. Moreover, we also know that this revenue vehicle was used by kings to provide incentives to muqatadars to invest in expensive capital inputs, such as irrigation systems, in order to bring new lands under production or to rehabilitate old lands that had been abandoned due to war or natural disaster. This involved a variation on the revenue-farming contract which was based on an escalating scale of recompense in which stepwise increases in revenue obligations were payable by the revenue farmer to the king over a fixed period, typically three to ten years. This system thus allowed the king to increase his revenue base by fostering 'agricultural development' on otherwise non-productive lands, the costs of which were borne, in the first instance, by the muqatadar.[51]

These muqata tenures in which the alienation of land involved considerable fiscal considerations and calculations by both king and muqatadar existed alongside the type of 'tax-free' tenures discussed by Dirks. In Kota, as throughout most of north India, land in which the king *formally* renounced his revenue interest to others was known as *jagir*.[52] The category of *jagir*, in turn, consisted of two main subtypes: *mafi jagir* and *chakri jagir*. The term *chakri* derives from *chakar* meaning 'servant' or 'attendant' and, unsurprisingly, this 'tax-free' tenure was granted to clients who provided service, particularly military service, to the king. In Kota the holders of these estates, or jagirdars, were quintessentially Rajputs but they also included among their numbers Gujars, Jats, Minas, Marathas, Ahirs, Bhils, and Muslims.[53] Service *ideally* preceded the granting of the jagir so that the value and size of the jagir was pegged to the number and quality of horsemen, foot soldiers, or musketeers that a jagirdar provided to the king.[54]

The term *mafi*, on the other hand, means 'forgiven' or 'excused' and indexes that the king expected no service from the holders of these 'tax-exempt' estates. Religious institutions – such as temples, feeding and rest houses for pilgrims, colleges of religious learning, and lineages of Brahmans – were the quintessential recipients of these estates, which they

[51] Stewart Gordon describes this arrangement in considerable detail with respect to Maratha revenue practices in Malwa in the mid-eighteenth century. See Stewart N. Gordon, 'The Slow Conquest: Administrative Integration of Malwa into the Maratha Empire, 1720–1760', *Modern Asian Studies* 11 (1977): 1–30. See also Habib, *Agrarian System*, pp. 234–236 and D. Singh, *State, Landlords and Peasants*, pp. 129–130.

[52] In this regard it is significant that muqata was typically classified as a subset of khalsa, or royal land where the king maintained a direct revenue interest in the land. For example, see D. Singh, *State, Landlords and Peasants*, p. 134.

[53] Sharma, *Kota rajya*, pp. 143–144.

[54] Ibid., p. 146, points out, for example, that the written *patta*s (assessments of obligation) confirming jagir assignments not only stipulated the number of horses a jagirdar was to furnish the king but also their breed.

held in perpetuity. They were thus associated with the merit (*punya*) making activities of the king whose duty (*rajadharma*) included maintaining and upholding religious institutions. The fact that mafi was distinguished from chakri suggests that the relationship between Brahmans and the king was not conceived as a service relationship but was informed by other meanings associated with their religious standing.

Despite the formal precision of the land tenure scheme of classification, in practice the distinction between muqata and jagir – especially chakri jagir – was scarcely watertight. Let us turn to evidence from neighbouring Jaipur, which has produced the most detailed data on land tenure arrangements in the late precolonial era. As Dilbagh Singh has noted, revenue farms, which in Jaipur generally went under the ijara label, varied considerably in duration and scope.[55] Minimal tax farms, known as *qarar ijara*, involved very short-term contracts varying from one season to a few years and were restricted to land revenue only. Other local taxes (on grazing, on cutting wood from forests or fodder from wastelands, on agricultural and artisanal implements such as ploughs or potters' wheels, on irrigation, on local markets, transit duties, and so on) were not included. Nor were judicial or policing rights. These remained vested with the king. Other tax farms, however, were granted for longer terms and included a greater array of levies, not merely land revenue. These were known as *ijara istamrari*. The specific terms and scope of the rights and the length of tenure were negotiated between the ruler and the agent, and the agreed upon terms were then set down in written 'contracts', or pattas. The most desirable ijara tenures, however, were the *vatan zamindari va istamrari ijara*, which included not only a hereditary right to a wide range of taxes but also military (*faujdari*) rights involving the local maintenance of law and order.

Dilbagh Singh further notes that the rights and obligations of these latter tenures did not differ considerably from those of the jagirdars who rendered service to the king. This is especially apparent if we consider that, although kings alienated their revenue rights to jagirdars, they nevertheless imposed a large number of cesses on them, many of which were loosely pegged to the estimated revenue of the jagir, thereby establishing an indirect financial interest in the alienated agricultural land. The best known of these cesses was *peshkash*, a tribute paid by the jagirdar to the king in semi-annual installments. But the king also collected *matami* (a 'condolence' fee when the jagirdar succeeded to the rights of his deceased father), *nyota* (a fee paid to defray the cost of royal marriages), and several other dues in times of military crisis. The sum

[55] D. Singh, *State, Landlords and Peasants*, pp. 129–143.

of these various levies could mount up considerably and jagirdars not infrequently found themselves in arrears.[56]

As a result of these convergences, Singh finally notes that some revenue farmers were able to transform their ijara tenures into jagirs. Such were the circumstances leading to the establishment of several new *thikanas* in Jaipur such as Barawa and Dhula. Conversely, however, he describes the existence of standardized procedures for making revenue calculations when the reverse process took place.[57] Although Singh does not give a concrete example of this event, Stewart Gordon notes the case of the Maratha dominions in Malwa on Kota's southern frontier. Here Gordon charts how various 'alienated' lands were progressively incorporated into the royal fisc as the Peshwa consolidated his control over the region. For example, during the 1740s the *zamindaris* of Bhopal, Bhilsa, Chanderi, and Kurwai were all resumed and enter in the Peshwa's documents as directly administered areas through the vehicle of ijara (muqata) tenures based on escalating scales of revenue payment.[58] The incremental, institutional arrangements bridging ijara and jagir thus apparently afforded considerable opportunity for conceptual slippage between the two, and the meanings associated with one type of land tenure could be turned to inform the other and vice versa. The effect of these competing ways of looking at alienated land can be detected in longitudinal variations in the amount of land that was transferred from royal control to jagir. Again we turn to Jaipur for the best diachronic data concerning khalsa:jagir ratios in the eighteenth century. In analyzing the copious mass of indigenously produced revenue statistics from between 1700 and 1785, Madhavi Bajekal discovered that the amount of land in jagir in Jaipur fluctuated between about 60 and 40 percent.[59] It thus appears that local kings not only gave land away to their clients but that at times they found it necessary and expedient to take it back where they could. While some of this land was quickly redistributed to new clients, this was not always the case. Often it remained in the royal domain for

[56] Ibid., pp. 151–152.

[57] Ibid., pp. 133–135.

[58] Stewart N. Gordon, 'The Slow Conquest: Administrative Integration of Malwa into the Maratha Empire, 1720–1760', *Modern Asian Studies* 11 (1977): 19.

[59] Bajekal, 'The State and the Rural Grain Market', pp. 443–473. For even more variable khalsa:jagir ratios, see Satya Prakash Gupta, 'The Jagir System during the Evolution of Jaipur State (c. 1650–1750),' *Proceedings of the Indian History Congress* 34 (1974): 171–179. There is similar, albeit more circumstantial, data with regard to Kota. Evaluating evidence from the mid-seventeenth century relating to five selected parganas, M. L. Sharma indicates that approximately two-thirds of the territory was held in jagir. Tod, however, noted that by the beginning of the nineteenth century only a relatively small proportion of the land in Kota was held in jagir. See Sharma, *Kota rajya*, p. 145 and Tod, *Annals and Antiquities*, Volume II, pp. 531–547.

considerable periods during which time the king made strategic use of the fiscal revenues deriving therefrom.

Bhakti, capital, and kingship

In their masterful study of Nayaka period Tamilnadu (sixteenth through eighteenth centuries), Velcheru Narayana Rao, David Shulmman and Sanjay Subrahmanyam have charted the interconnections that were forged among new forms of embodiment emerging from Tamil bhakti devotionalism, 'liquidity' (particularly in food and cash), and the rhetorics of kingship. They observe that the 'world-affirming' stance of Tamil bhakti, like the 'this-worldly mysticism' of Pushtimargi devotionalism discussed in the preceding chapter, heralded a shift in how the human body and its senses were perceived within the quest for transcendence. Tamil bhakti, like Pushtimargi devotionalism, positioned itself against the 'yogic' traditions which deeply distrusted the human senses as miring the soul in illusion (*maya*), and which exalted forms of asceticism that aimed to discipline or negate the senses. Within bhakti, the human body became the 'primary… instrument of transcendence', through which the devotee 'is meant to open himself, imaginatively and sensually, to the god, who is at least partly accessible to contact through the sensory modes (especially taste, smell, and touch)'.[60] Again in contradistinction to the austerities and forms of self-mortification privileged within yogic traditions, a central feature of bhakti, both in its Tamil and Pushtimargi variations, was the soteriological position given over to *bhog*, or 'enjoyment' in all its sensual immediacy, aesthetic hypertrophy, and transient exuberance.

The significance of 'enjoyment' with its emphasis on consumption, the sensual, and the here-and-now overflowed from the human body into the body politic through the newly elaborated form of gift-giving – *annadan*, or the gift of food. Although annadan has generally been conflated in the literature with other forms of gift giving, quintessentially in land, Narayana Rao et al. reveal that they contained significantly different conceptual orientations as well as different pragmatic entailments.[61] The gift of land had a more permanent existence and, therefore, established a more or less stable and ongoing relationship between donor and recipient, albeit one that offered a less immediate and less direct experiential basis for that relationship. The gift of food, on the other hand, established a

60 Velcheru Narayana Rao, David Shulmman, and Sanjay Subrahmanyam, *Symbols of Substance, Court and State in Nayaka Period Tamilnadu* (Delhi: Oxford University Press, 1992), p. 114.

61 Here Narayana Rao et al. are primarily concerned with royal gifts of land to Brahmans (*brahmadeya*). However, I would argue that their argument could be expanded to include landgrants made to military clients as well.

more directly visceral relationship between donor and recipient, albeit one that was more evanescent. The instability of this relationship required the gift's constant repetition if the relationship were to be maintained, but it was precisely this transient quality that was prized within this devotional framework.[62] Changes in the medium of the gift and the foreshortening of its temporal horizons, furthermore, required fairly complex organizational skills to sustain the polity. Political relations, previously maintained through the alienation of landed property, now depended 'on ready access by the centre to massive fluid resources'.[63] Although Narayana Rao et al.'s discussion about annadan is mostly concerned with the gifting of food, it is clear that similar attitudes and beliefs coalesced around that most fungible of all substances – money. Indeed their analyses of Nayaka-period devotional texts show how central cash became in the quest for transcendence on account of its extreme liquidity.[64]

The philosophical parallels between south Indian bhakti traditions and Pushtimargi devotionalism are profound. This should not be surprising considering that Vallabhacharya was a south Indian Brahman whose family had close connections to the Vijayanagar court where he occasionally resided and where he is said to have engaged in his greatest debates with the philosophers of the *mayavad* school of Shankaracharya.[65] The affinity between the two bhakti traditions even extends to the positive valuation accorded to the circulation of capital. It has long been recognized that Pustimargi devotionalism held a special appeal for merchant groups in north India.[66] David Pocock, for example, has noted that 'More than any other sect..., the Pushti Marga provided an arena in which wealthy merchant classes could display their wealth and earn at once distinction and merit.'[67] The popularity among this community accounts for the disproportionate number of the merchants whose life stories are recounted in Hariray's 84V and 252V.

One even witnesses the valorization of 'mercantile' forms of 'liquidity' as a basis of power in eighteenth-century representations of royalty in Kota. This was perhaps most forcefully expressed in Kota's annual

62 This evanescence of the annadan was even manifest in the material forms used to record it. There was 'a dramatic decrease in the use of stone and copper-plate for donative inscriptions; [as a result of which] the act of prestation, like its substance,... [took] on more fluid less permanent contours'. Narayana Rao et al., *Symbols of Substance*, p. 68.

63 Ibid., p. 68.

64 Ibid., pp. 117ff.

65 Richard Barz, *The Bhakti Sect of Vallabhacarya* (Faridabad: Thomson Press, 1976), pp. 43–44.

66 Max Weber, for example, noted the connection in his *The Sociology of Religion*, trans. Ephraim Fiscoff (Boston: Beacon Press, 1963), pp. 92–93.

67 Pocock, *Mind, Body, and Wealth: A Study of Belief and Practice in an Indian Village* (Oxford: Basil Blackwell, 1973), p. 117.

annakut (mountain of food) festival, which dates to Durjan Sal's reign and was modelled on the annakut festival at Nathadvara, which the maharao attended several times.[68] In Kota, this was one of several important occasions during the year when Shri Brijnathji would be brought from his temple and placed on a golden throne in the *rajmahal* (royal hall of public audience) where the maharao, courtiers, and townspeople would come to worship the deity in an appropriately royal setting. On this day, the large open-air courtyard in front of the rajmahal was covered with trays of sweets and other delicacies at the centre of which was a large mountain of rice some 2.5 metres tall which would be 'looted' at the end of the ceremonies by those assembled in a frenzy of devotional ecstasy. Increasingly during the eighteenth century, one finds reference to other occasions in which expressions of royal authority revolved around the maharao's distribution of vast quantities of food to his subjects, such as the *nagar bhojan*s associated with royal weddings when the maharao was expected to feed the entire city. Moreover, as Woodman Taylor has noted, it is for such expressions of evanescent generosity that Durjan Sal is most remembered in texts such as the *Sri-ji ke pas sato svarup padhare*, in which the maharao is explicitly praised for his unbounded expenditure (*dhanya dhanya kharchyo*) on the occasion of the mahotsav of 1739–40 at Nathadvara.[69] Durjan Sal's reputation for financial generosity extended beyond Kota and continues to be remembered in sectarian histories of the Sampraday as well.[70]

The special significance of 'liquidity' in Vallabha belief, however, did not lead to a full-blown 'rational, or bourgeois, capitalism' at least as Max Weber has imagined it. In the Pushtimargi soteriology which is built upon a 'this-worldly *mysticism*', rather than the Calvinist 'this-worldly *asceticism*', it is the consumption of liquid resources and their circulation that are stressed, not their accumulation and perspicacious reinvestment. This consumption-driven fiscalism is well illustrated in the varta of Surdas, one of the sect's great early poets, which is contained in the 84V. This varta includes a description of an encounter between the poet and a greedy merchant who had his shop at the bottom of Govardhan Hill in Braj where the temple of Shri Nathji was originally located (before its relocation to Nathadvara). Although this merchant made a fortune selling

68 Lakshmandan, 'Vamsha prashasti', p. 49.

69 Woodman Taylor, 'Visual Culture in Performative Practice: The Aesthetics, Politics and Poetics of Visuality in Liturgical Practices of the Vallabha Sampradaya Hindu Community at Kota' (PhD dissertation, Department of Art, University of Chicago, 1997), pp. 70 and 182–183. Several versions of this text still exist in the erstwhile royal library (Saraswati Bhandar) at Kota. For example, see ms. nos. 1226, 3204, and 3206, RPPK.

70 Kanthamani Shastri, *Kankroli ka itihas* (Kankroli: Shrividya-Vibhag, 1939), pt. vi, p. 166.

goods to the devotees who passed his shop on the way to and from the temple, he himself never bothered to take darshan of the deity. Moreover, he committed a great deception.

Each day before opening his shop, the merchant would ask the first Vaisnava to pass by on his way home from the *darshana* periods at Shri Nathaji to describe the dress and adornment (*shrngara*) of Shri Nathaji on that day. Then the merchant would put on the Vaisnava necklace made of *tulasi* beads, apply the Vaisnava *tilaka*, make the Vaisnava marks on his body, and open his shop. Then, he would hail each group of Vaisnavas to pass by and glorify that day's *darshana* before them... The merchant did all this as a sham; in fact he never had been to have *darshana* of Shri Nathaji. When he gave such accounts of the love of Shri Nathaji, the Vaisnavas were very pleased and considered the merchant to be a true Vaisnava. They used to buy things at his shop. In this way the Vaisnavas were deceived by the merchant's hypocrisy. The merchant made a great deal of money, but spent as little as possible.[71]

Surdas knew the merchant was committing this deception and over the course of several days tried to convince him to walk to the top of the hill to take the deity's darshan. The merchant always promised that he would attend the next day but, when the time for the darshan came, he found some excuse or another not to leave his shop. Eventually, Surdas threatened to compose verses about the merchant's perversity and sing them to the Vaishnava community thereby exposing his deception to his clientele. With this threat, the merchant hastily attended the next darshan with Surdas at which

Shri Nathaji gave that shopkeeper such a wonderful *darshana* that his heart was enraptured. When the *darshana* period was over, the merchant seized Suradasaji's feet and begged, 'Maharaja! I have spent my whole life in vain piling up wealth. Now I want to spend the money that I have hoarded on whatever you command me to buy. I want to become a Vaisnava; help me become a *sevaka* of Shri Gusainji [Vallabhacharya]... Then Shri Gusainji summoned the merchant and seated him in the presence of Shri Nathaji. He gave him the divine name and initiated him by means of the *Brahmasambandha* rite. In this manner, that merchant's thought became pure and, ever after, he attended all of the *darshana* periods. He gave many presents to Shri Gusainji for Shri Nathaji and he had clothing, jewelry, and food purchased for Shri Nathaji.[72]

Significantly, this varta thus does not disparage wealth in and of itself. Provided it is spent in the right manner in the service of Shri Nathaji, it has the capacity of generating merit. The hoarding of wealth, however, is viewed as a grievous sin.

71 Barz, trans., *Bhakti Sect*, pp. 127–128.

72 Ibid., p. 131.

Early nineteenth-century colonial officials who were dealing with Kota also commented on this ethic of consumption (even if its *raison d'être* eluded them). James Tod wrote the following about Zalim Singh Jhala, Kota's famous prime minister of the later eighteenth and early nineteenth centuries:

> The indefatigable perseverance which makes him even sacrifice decorum to increase the income of the State is only to be equaled by the magnificent liberality with which he dispenses it. In Kotah the total absence of all sorts of penury, an appearance of substance everywhere reigns and pervades throughout – from the cavalcade of the Prince to the meanest member of it – and it becomes a matter of speculation when you learn of the harmful and laborious acquirements to know by what secret the mind can be brought to oppose its very self, in dispensing it.[73]

Although strategies of gift-giving in both its substantial and its liquid forms were typically pursued in tandem as supplementary activities, occasionally they became more distinct one from the other in competitive local politics. In the following chapter we shall examine one such case that occurred in Kota during the later eighteenth and early nineteenth centuries when Zalim Singh Jhala purportedly 'usurped' all 'substantive' power in Kota and reduced two successive generations of 'legitimate' sovereigns to 'titular' figureheads. But before turning to this matter, let us return to Dirks's discussion of the distribution of inams in Pudukkottai and offer a reinterpretation of his data in light of the issues and concerns discussed in this chapter.

Epilogue: A reappraisal of Dirks's late precolonial Pudukkottai

In revealing ways in which the 'symbolic' dimensions of the royal gift encoded moral obligations binding clients to kings, Dirks has made a valuable contribution. Yet the gift of land was not devoid of vital fiscal implications for the king and the extensive alienation of land from direct royal control did index weakness in royal power, in part, because the collection and expenditure of revenue carried important symbolic meanings elaborated within bhakti soteriology. In suggesting that the royal gift of land was an *unequivocal* and *inexhaustible* source of royal legitimacy whose symbolism was unproblematically shared by all, Dirks remains tied to an older style of symbolic anthropology that views culture as internally

[73] James Tod to Charles Metcalfe, OIOC, BPC, 17/22 April 1820. Later in the same letter Tod pithily described Zalim Singh's attitude towards money as 'parsimonious in the acquirement, liberal and lavish in expenditure'.

consistent, thoroughly integrated and largely consensual. This assumption ultimately informs Dirks's monovalent, raja-centric view of the precolonial state that substantially underplays any active dispersive tendencies animated by other non-congruent, cultural meanings. Dirks's claims that the efficacy of giving land did not implicate fiscal considerations rests on the counter-intuitive distribution of inams in Pudukkottai which were more concentrated in the central portion of the kingdom and did not seem to follow the imperatives dictated by a desire to maximize revenue. Recall this latter position would anticipate that:

> the king should hold on to rights to the royal share near the center of the state and give away lands at the periphery, minimizing, all other things being equal, substantial transportation costs [of grain to royal granaries in the capital].[74]

But this apparently was not the case in Pudukkottai.

Unfortunately, Dirks's conclusions on land tenure were based on data collected in 1886, that is after nearly three-quarters of a century of colonial 'indirect rule', and one ought to be circumspect in its use for reconstructing a picture of the precolonial era. One area where the impact of colonialism was significant was precisely in the spatial distribution of alienated lands for, with colonialism, the permeable and militarily contested frontiers of 'little kingdoms' were replaced by fixed and colonially policed boundaries. Thus precolonial pressures and imperatives stemming from a highly competitive military environment and shaping the distribution of estates no longer applied when Dirks's data was collected.

However, if one looks at firmly precolonial land-tenure data, such as in Richard Saran's painstaking mapping of land holdings in Marwar based on mid-seventeenth-century documentation, one finds, as one would expect, that royal lands were concentrated near the royal capital and other important towns while alienated lands tended to be found on the fringes of the kingdom.[75] There are, naturally, some notable exceptions to this general pattern and not infrequently one does find royal lands in far-flung locations. However, these exceptions do not display any sort of anti-market mentality, just the reverse. As Madhavi Bajekal has shown for eighteenth-century Jaipur, the state in fact rarely transported its share over long distances.[76] When such long distance transport did occur, it was done in order to take advantage of sellers' markets in areas where the

[74] Dirks, *Hollow Crown*, p. 136.

[75] Richard D. Saran, 'Conquest and Colonization: Rajputs and Vasis in Middle Period Marvar' (PhD thesis, Department of History, University of Michigan, 1978), pp. 145–175.

[76] Bajekal, 'The State and the Rural Grain Market', pp. 446–450.

grain crop had failed and where the state hoped to make windfall profits. Instead the state disposed of most of its grain locally. To this end, the state's share was usually stored in royal granaries in the very villages where it was grown and where it remained until needed. A small portion of this grain was used to provision royal garrisons in nearby forts. More importantly, however, most of royal share was sold in the wholesale grain markets of the qasbas located in most districts. By keeping centres of grain production close to royal garrisons and the wholesale markets, it should be clear that, contrary to Dirks's assumption, the dispersed distribution of the royal fisc *reduced* the state's cost of transporting grain.

Finally, it is possible to reconfigure Dirks's data on the spatial distribution of inams in Pudukkottai in order to reveal a perspective from which the alienation of some estates can be linked to royal weakness. Moreover, this weakness can be shown to manifest itself precisely in terms of the king's variable control over territory, with more estates being '"given" in border areas where the king [had] less control over the countryside and its inhabitants'.[77] In order to do so, however, one must remember that not all inams were the same order and did not pose an equal political threat to the king. Land given in perpetuity to religious institutions for the purposes of earning religious merit did not represent royal weakness to the same degree as did land distributed in perpetuity to military clients. Dirks's argument against the linkage between the inams and royal weakness rests however on the even distribution pattern of *all inams* in Pudukkottai regardless of the status of the assignee.[78] But if one breaks Dirks's data down according to different types of inam a different picture emerges. For example, the *cervaikarar*s (the class of military retainers who held the largest estates) were uniformly assigned inams on the peripheries of the kingdom where one might imagine that the authority of the raja was weakest.[79] In addition, Dirks's data on inams granted to religious institutions, which shows them more heavily concentrated at the centre of the polity, provides us with the exception that proves the rule.[80] In order for these religious gifts to be meaningful and the merit they generated efficacious, these inams had to be concentrated in those areas closest to the raja where the deed of land could be properly enforced and protected and where his authority was strongest. Thus if we keep in mind where various sub-types of inam were granted relative to the centre, we see that their distribution was informed by a logic that understood alienated land in relation to royal weakness but that weakness was inflected differently by each distinct category of inam.

[77] Dirks, *Hollow Crown*, p. 136. [78] Ibid., p. 137.
[79] Ibid., p. 176. [80] Ibid., pp. 429–434.

5 From 'royal service' to 'maternal devotion' during the Jhala Regency: Local politics at the end of the old regime

The individual most closely identified with Kota during the second half of the eighteenth century and the early years of the nineteenth has been, without doubt, Rajrana Zalim Singh (b. 1739; d. 1824), the kingdom's influential prime minister (*musahib-i-ala* or *divan*) of over fifty years. A Rajput of the Jhala clan, Zalim Singh was one of a number of prime ministers who had assumed Peshwa-like powers over the administrative, judicial, and military apparatuses of several kingdoms in Rajasthan, including not only Kota but also Mewar and Jaisalmer. Maharao Umed Singh of Kota (r. 1771–1819), whose reign coincided with most of Zalim Singh's regency, appears to have been largely divorced from the affairs of state and remained secluded within his palace or removed from court altogether on endless, closely supervised, hunting expeditions to Kota's numerous forest preserves.

The maharao's seclusion from public affairs elicited European comment as early as 1776, when the Comte de Modave spent over a month in Kota. Although Modave misidentified Zalim Singh as a Brahman,[1] he nevertheless observed that the maharao:

> only very rarely appears in public, and he does not take the slightest hand in his affairs. It is a Brahman [*sic*] who takes care of sparing him any burden, and who reigns in his name. When I was in Kota, [Umed Singh] had gone to a house in the country in order to entertain himself with hunting. This house was on my route. He was still there when I passed and he had not once left it.[2]

[1] This error may reflect the erroneous assumption that all administrators in India were Brahmans (owing to their reputation for literacy). Furthermore, as Zalim Singh was away from Kota (campaigning in Mewar) when Modave visited, the Frenchman never had the opportunity to meet the rajrana and correct this false impression.

[2] Comte de Modave (Louis Laurent de Federbe), *Voyage en Inde du Comte de Modave*, ed. J. Deloch (Paris: Ecole française d'Extrême-Orient, 1971), p. 480.

To Modave, Umed Singh's seclusion was a prime manifestation of 'oriental despotism' in which his self-abandonment 'to the facile pleasures of the seraglio'[3] stemmed from his possession of unlimited and uncontested powers. But in 1793 when William Hunter passed through Kota, he turned this interpretation on its head. Hunter offered that Umed Singh was subject to an enforced confinement with his prime minister the jailor. Hunter wrote:

> The present Rajah is Ummeid Singh. His uncle, who was his immediate predecessor, was assassinated about twenty or twenty-five years before, by his Dewan Zalim Sing, a Rajpoot of the tribe Jhala. He seized, and still retains the administration, having left nothing but the name and the pomp of Rajah, to the present incumbent.[4]

Zalim Singh's power and Umed Singh's seclusion were also noted by Thomas Broughton who, while passing through the northern portion of Kota in 1809, wrote that 'the legitimate Raja of Kota is, with his family, kept in close confinement by a person named Zalim Singh, who has long usurped the entire management of public affairs; and is indeed recognized as ruler by all the states of Hindoostan'.[5] When James Tod visited Kota a decade later, he too noted Zalim Singh's control over the cosseted maharao and, like Broughton before him, he branded the rajrana a 'usurper'. Tod further suggested that Zalim Singh maintained the maharao as figurehead in order to exercise power behind the scenes away from the glare of public attention, thereby escaping public censure for his actions. Tod described the charade of kingship thus:

3 Ibid. p. 489.

4 William Hunter, 'Narrative of a Journey from Agra to Oujein', *Asiatick Researches* 6 (1801): 65. In claiming that Zalim Singh assassinated Umed Singh's uncle 'who was his immediate predecessor', Hunter has made an error that blends two different accusations of murder that long have been levelled against Zalim Singh by his detractors in Kota. Umed Singh was preceded on the gaddi by his father, Guman Singh, not an uncle (figure 1). However, Guman Singh did die of some sort of an ulcerous condition in January 1771, and it has long been claimed that Zalim Singh applied poisoned bandages to the maharao's wounds in order to, at least, hasten his death. Similar aspersions have been cast on Zalim Singh with respect to the murder, two years later, of Maharaja Swarup Singh Hada. Although Swarup Singh's actual murderer was one Dhabhai (or foster brother) Jaskaran, Zalim Singh generally stands accused of masterminding the deed. Swarup Singh was an uncle of the newly installed Umed Singh and was Kota's musahib-i-ala, a post he had held since the reign of the late maharao. Swarup Singh's demise thus cleared the way for Zalim Singh, who at the time only held the post of faujdar, to consolidate his authority over the second of Kota's two most important offices. For an early Rajasthani source repeating both these accusations, see Suryamalla Mishran, *Vamshabhaskar* (Jodhpur: n.p., 1899), pp. 3816–3818.

5 Thomas Duer Broughton, *Letters Written in a Mahratta Camp During the Year 1809 Descriptive of the Character, Manners, Domestic Habits, and Religious Ceremonies of the Mahrattas* (London: Archibald Constable and Company, 1817 [1813]), p. 28.

If an envoy came from a foreign state, he was introduced to the prince, delivered his credentials to him; and from him received a reply, but that reply was his minister's. If a foreign noble claimed protection, he received it from the prince; he was the dispenser of the favours, though he could neither change their nature or amount... The archives, the seal, and all the emblems of sovereignty, remained as in times past in the custody of the personal servants of the prince, at the castle, though none durst use them without consent of the Regent.[6]

Similarly, Tod remained incredulous at statements of loyalty by the rajrana toward the maharao. When the rajrana once told Tod that 'he would cling to his sovereign's skirts, and "chakri kar" (serve him); that he would rather retire to Nat'hdwarra than blacken his face with any treason towards his master', Tod dismissed the sentiments as an embarrassingly transparent subterfuge.[7] For Tod, these expressions of deference and loyalty toward the maharao were intended to divert attention from the new foundations of power in Kota that were articulated, in fact, by Zalim Singh and that were based, according to Tod, on a regime of extortionate taxation, the summary seizure of land, and an army of 'foreign mercenaries' that Zalim Singh had recruited in north India's vibrant, military labour market. In short, Tod transposed onto Zalim Singh the label of 'oriental despot' that Modave had earlier applied to Maharao Umed Singh.

There were groups in Kota during this era, no doubt, among whom Zalim Singh became deeply unpopular, as attested by the rumours of his murderous past recorded by Hunter. The most prominent group to resent Zalim Singh was the old, largely Hada Rajput, landed military elite whom Zalim Singh opportunistically, if not systematically, dispossessed of their estates during his regime (more on this matter below). Thus when pondering Kota's reputation for political stability and economic vitality under Zalim Singh's regency, Tod posed, and then answered, the question:

But is this propriety?... Was it to entertain twenty thousand mercenary soldiers from the sequestered fields of the illustrious Hara [Hada], the indigenous proprietor? Is this government, is it good government according to the ideas of more civilized nations, to extend taxation to the limits in order to maintain this cumbrous machinery?... But as it is, whilst the corn which waves upon the fertile surface of Kotah presents not the symbol of prosperity, neither is his well-paid and well-disciplined army a sure mean of defense; moral propriety has been violated; rights are in abeyance, and until they be restored, even the apparent consistency of the social fabric is obtained by means which endanger its security.[8]

[6] James Tod, *Annals and Antiquities of Rajast'han or, the Central and Western Rajpoot States of India*, Volume 2 (London, 1832), p. 553.

[7] Ibid., p. 566.

[8] Ibid., pp. 546–547.

Yet despite Tod's condemnations of Zalim Singh's regime, which have informed the judgments of historians of the region ever since,[9] this chapter will argue that Zalim Singh's administration enjoyed significant support from important segments of society precisely because it directly and explicitly appealed to broader cultural values and social expectations. In fact, Tod himself grudgingly noted:

> How far Zalim Singh went... to avoid public stigma to reconcile general opinion with the positive possession of power in his situation appears so incompatible that at first sight the desire may have the appearance of mere parade, but there is nothing more certain than next to the possession of this power is the wish in the application thereof to stand well in the eyes of the world.[10]

Indeed much of Zalim Singh's exercise of power was not hidden from view but was plainly visible for all to see. Not only did every European visitor to Kota comment upon it (including those who visited Kota only briefly),[11] but there is much evidence that Zalim Singh actively engaged in the highly public display of his power. Although he never attempted to separate the maharao from *his* symbols of authority, Zalim Singh did engage in many conspicuously unmistakable expressions of his own status. For instance, in the early 1770s, immediately after assuming guardianship of the young Maharao Umed Singh, Zalim Singh started construction on an opulent, 80-room palace within the very precincts of the citadel (*gadh*) in the heart of the capital city that overlooked and to some extent dominated the maharao's palace. This palace, known as the *Jhala ki haveli*, was just one of several palaces bearing his name that he constructed and/or renovated in the city and around the kingdom. Similarly, official records show that when Zalim Singh went out on tour, he was accompanied by a mounted escort of 631 men that dwarfed the 156-man cavalcade that accompanied the maharao.[12] He was also a noticeably lavish (and discerning) patron of the fine arts, especially painting.[13] And as recounted at the end of the previous chapter, Zalim Singh engaged in many highly public displays of liberal alms-giving and generosity to priests, holy men, and charitable institutions that gained him a reputation of fabulous

[9] Twentieth-century accounts of Zalim Singh that continue to reproduce Tod's attitudes include Sharma, *Kota rajya*, p. 489 ff. and R. P. Shastri, *Jhala Zalim Singh* (Jaipur: Raj Printing Works, 1971).

[10] James Tod to George Swinton, OIOC, BPC, 69/24 November 1821.

[11] In this regard, it is significant that these comments came from both French and British travellers who were unlikely to have ever read each other's accounts of Kota.

[12] Cited in Shastri, *Zalim Singh*, p. 294.

[13] Joachim K. Bautze, 'Jhala Zalim Singh of Kotah: A Great Patron of Rajput Painting', in *Festschrift Klaus Bruhn*, eds Nalini Balbir and Joachim K. Bautze (Reinbek: Inge Wezler, 1994), pp. 105–125.

wealth. These were surely not the actions of someone cynically hiding his power and influence behind the illusory façade of a puppet-king.

This chapter shall argue that Zalim Singh's explicit display of his power and the concomitant confirmation of the maharao's weakness and vulnerability were central features around which Zalim Singh constructed his authority. I shall suggest that during this era Zalim Singh decentred the traditional notion of warrior service (*chakri*), which was defined by the straightforwardly hierarchical relationship of king and client, or master and servant (*svami* and *malik*), by suffusing it with the Vallabha notion of service (*seva*), particularly as informed by the emotive state of 'maternal devotion' (*vatsalya bhav*). This definition of 'service' entailed a far more paradoxical relationship of interdependence between subordinate and superordinate beings in which Zalim Singh cultivated the role of the human foster mother, Yashoda, opposite the maharao's Krishna, Yashoda's divine foster child. According to this reformulation of 'service', the rajrana's expressions of devotion towards the maharao were not a disingenuous or cynical subterfuge that aimed to mask his exercise of power. Rather the maharao's powerlessness was explicitly *foregrounded* precisely because such vulnerability was taken both as a token of his complete trust in Zalim Singh as well as proof of Zalim Singh's 'disinterestedness' in selfish gain. Within this line of reasoning, if the rajrana's motives were not pure, he surely could have, and would have, deposed the utterly defenseless maharao. Zalim Singh's exercise of power, therefore, was not a matter to be hidden from public view but rather was to be held up to sustained public scrutiny.

But first it will be necessary to provide some background about Zalim Singh and chart his rise to power. Building upon the findings of the previous chapter, we shall see how he put the kingdom on a new military footing that was based increasingly on a waged, standing army and articulated through liquidity. In particular, we shall see how several economic and geo-political factors (some local in origin, others regional, and yet others truly global) conspired to allow this military transformation to proceed to an extent that had not been possible before.

Zalim Singh's background and early career

Zalim Singh belonged to a lineage of Jhala Rajputs that traced its early origins to the mediæval dynasty that ruled the kingdom of Halvad in Gujarat.[14] By the mid-seventeenth century, however, a series of dynastic reversals had forced his great, great-grandfather Bhav Singh and a small

[14] Unless cited otherwise, the information in this section has been culled from Shastri, *Zalim Singh*, pp. 17–36.

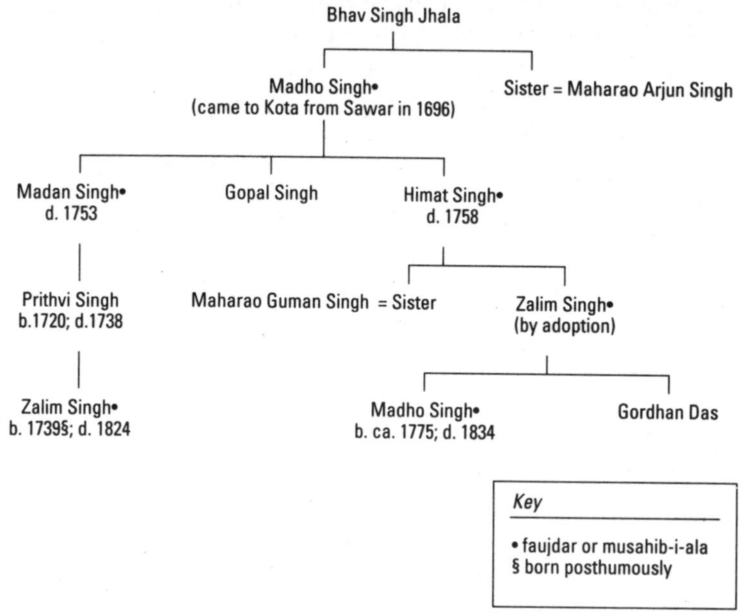

Figure 4 The lineage of Jhala Zalim Singh
Source: R. P. Shastri, *Jhala Zalim Singh* (Jaipur: Raj Printing Works, 1971)

group of followers to leave Halvad for Rajasthan where he sought military work (figure 4). Bhav Singh eventually joined the service of the Raja of Sawar who had a stronghold not far from Ajmer. Here Bhav Singh married a daughter of the raja and had a son, named Madho Singh. Despite his maternal links to Sawar, Madho Singh left the place as a young man and, with 25 mounted followers, looked for opportunity elsewhere. After briefly stopping in Bundi in 1695, Madho Singh moved on to Kota the following year. Here Madho Singh found settled employment for nearly half a century during which time he served no less than four of Kota's rulers – Rao Ram Singh (r. 1696–1707), Maharao Bhim Singh (r. 1707–20), Maharao Arjun Singh (r. 1720–23) and Maharao Durjan Sal (r. 1723–56). Madho Singh's service was appreciated and, during the reign of Bhim Singh, he was rewarded with the office of *faujdar*, or commander of the army, and was granted the prosperous jagir of Nandta. This estate, a few kilometres west of Kota, occupied a considerable portion of the only tract of land belonging to Kota that lay on the left bank of the Chambal River which, otherwise, formed the boundary between Kota and Bundi. During Bhim Singh's reign, Madho Singh also consolidated his standing in Kota by having his sister marry the maharao's eldest son, Maharajkumar (later Maharao) Arjun Singh.

After his death in 1740 Madho Singh was succeeded in the office of faujdar by two of his sons, Madan Singh and Himat Singh. Himat Singh was especially influential at court and played an important role in securing the succession of Maharao Ajit Singh to Kota's gaddi after the death of Maharao Durjan Sal (figure 1). At some point, most probably after 1753, Himat Singh adopted Zalim Singh, the fatherless grandson of his eldest brother, and on Himat Singh's death in 1758 the young Zalim Singh, in turn, became faujdar. Within a few years, he proved his military capabilities in spectacular fashion. In 1761, a large army from Jaipur invaded the northern portion of Kota and Zalim Singh led the forces that routed the invaders at the battle of Bhatwada. This was one of Kota's greatest military victories of the later eighteenth century. Zalim Singh's triumph not only safeguarded Kota's independence from Jaipur but it also allowed Kota to extend its influence over the eight northern Kotriat Thikanas, which also were claimed by Jaipur and Bundi (map 2).[15] Zalim Singh's victory also yielded rich war booty including 17 elephants, 1800 horses, 73 field cannon and the five-coloured Jaipuri ensign that, thereafter, festooned the image of the demon-king Ravan at Kota's Ramlila.[16] On the accession to the throne of Maharao Guman Singh of Kota on 28 December 1764, Zalim Singh was appointed to the post of prime minister (musahib-i-ala) giving him overall charge of the kingdom's 'civilian' administration.[17] Like Madho Singh Jhala before him, Zalim Singh immediately strengthened his position by arranging for his (adoptive) sister to marry Guman Singh. These two marriage alliances earned Zalim Singh the title of 'mamaji' (maternal uncle), which he bore in everyday usage as well as in much official correspondence.

Zalim Singh's rapidly growing influence in Kota during this period, however, seems to have sparked alarm within some quarters at court, and Bhopat Singh Bankrot, another maternal uncle (mamaji) of Guman Singh, somehow engineered a falling out between the maharao and his prime minister. Guman Singh removed Zalim Singh from office and confiscated his ancestral estates at Nandta, which he then gave to Bhopat Singh along with the office of faujdar. The office of prime minister was

[15] The eight Kotriat Thikanas were Pipalda, Gainta, Karwad, Pusod, Indragarh, Khatoli, Balwan and Antarda.

[16] Lakshmandan, '*Maharao Shatru Shalji Bahadur ki vamsha prashasti*', (Uncatalogued manuscript in the Thikana Kotri *daftar*, Kota. Uncatalogued typescript copy, under the title of '*Kota rajya ke hastalikhita itihas ki pratilipi*', in the Brijraj Bhawan Palace Library, Kota), p. 54.

[17] In all likelihood, this appointment re-conferred on Zalim Singh a post that he first had assumed late in Maharao Ajit Singh's reign.

Map 2 Kota state ca. 1820

given in due course to Maharaja Swarup Singh Hada, a cousin of the maharao (figure 5), who was also a close ally of Bhopat Singh. Working in tandem, Swarup Singh and Bhopat Singh briefly became tremendously influential in Kota's affairs. Zalim Singh, on the other hand, left Kota in disgust and sought service in the court of the Maharana of Mewar where he remained for about four years. While in the rana's service, Zalim Singh was granted a new jagir and the title of 'rajrana', which became the other principal title by which he was known throughout the rest of his life.

In 1769, Bhopat Singh, in turn, fell out of favour with the maharao on account of his inability to effectively deal with the growing incursions of the Marathas along the southern and eastern frontiers of the kingdom. Bhopat Singh was dismissed from office, and Guman Singh invited Zalim Singh back to Kota to reoccupy his former estates at Nandta and once again take up the position of faujdar.[18] The prime ministership, however, remained vested with Maharaja Swarup Singh, and Zalim Singh's recall also may have been motivated by the maharao's desire to establish a more effective counterbalance to Swarup Singh's influence.[19] This neverending reshuffling of offices and the constant balancing of opposing factions at court during this period shows Guman Singh to be a consummate player in the game of 'rule by managed dissension'. And the dying Guman Singh bequeathed this state of affairs to his 12-year-old son two years later when he named Zalim Singh guardian of Umed Singh with Swarup Singh retaining the prime ministership.

Zalim Singh's rise to power

Although Zalim Singh's predecessors had enjoyed considerable influence in Kota, the type of authority he commanded during the later nineteenth century was in many ways unprecedented. To some extent, the power of the prime minister grew in inverse proportion to that of the traditional, landed military elite. During his tenure as prime minister Zalim Singh took several opportunities to undermine the standing and privileges of the jagirdars particularly with respect to their control over their estates, the great many of which he resumed and (re)incorporated into the royal fisc (khalsa). Three moments in this campaign stand out in particular. The first occurred during the early years of Maharao Umed Singh's reign (while he was still a young teenager) when the holders of three important

[18] For Maratha intelligence on the ongoing rivalry between Bhopat Singh and Zalim Singh at this time, see G. S. Sardesai, ed., *Selections from the Peshwas' Daftar*, Volume 29; *Peshwa Madhavrao I, 1761–1772* (Bombay: Government Central Press, 1933), no. 253.

[19] Conversely, by retaining Swarup Singh in the office of prime minister, Guman Singh was clearly hoping Swarup Singh would prevent Zalim Singh from becoming too powerful.

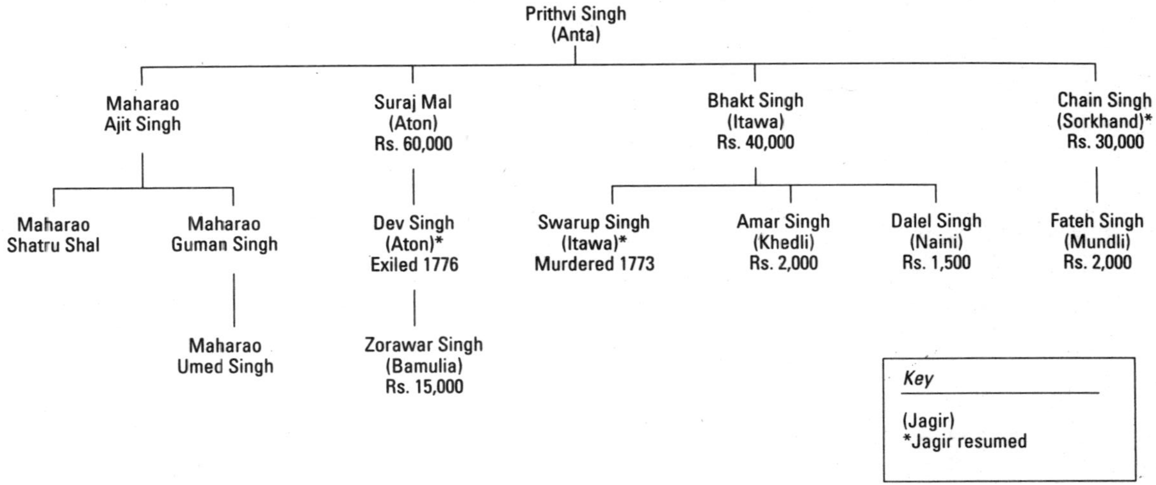

Figure 5 The Jagirdars of Aton, Itawa, and Sorkhand
Source: Kaviraja Lakshmandan, '*Maharao Shatru Shalji Bahadur ki vamsha prashasti*' (uncat. ms in the Thikana Kotri *daftar*, Kota)

estates in Kota were dispossessed of their lands. Although their heirs were eventually granted new jagirs, they were a fraction of the size of those formerly possessed. The three original estates—Aton, Itawa, and Sorkhand—were valued at 60,000, 40,000 and 30,000 rupees per annum respectively and had been granted to the younger brothers of Maharao Ajit Singh, and on the accession of the youthful Maharao Umed Singh, they were held by his cousins (figure 5). The estate of Itawa, moreover, belonged to Swarup Singh Hada who held the office of prime minister after Guman Singh's death. Two years after Umed Singh's accession, however, Swarup Singh was murdered by a rival courtier,[20] and in the ensuing power vacuum Zalim Singh assumed the prime ministership. He also reincorporated the Itawa estate into the royal khalsa. A couple of years later when it became clear that the surviving brothers of Swarup Singh would not be allowed to inherit their dead brother's lands, they joined a rebellion led by their cousin Maharaja Dev Singh Hada of Aton and their uncle Maharaja Chain Singh Hada of Sorkhand. Several other disgruntled courtiers (including the former faujdar, Bhopat Singh Bankrot) also joined the revolt, which culminated in a long, drawn-out siege at Dev Singh's principal stronghold at Aton. After holding out for several months the surviving rebels broke through the blockade and fled into exile. The estates of these exiles were reincorporated into the royal khalsa as well.

At the turn of the nineteenth century there was another failed insurrection, the so-called 'Conspiracy of Mohsian'. Taking its name from its leader, Bahadur Singh Hada of Mohsian, this *coup d'état* aimed to rid Kota of Zalim Singh by assassinating him, members of his family, and his chief supporters. But the plot was exposed before it could be carried out, and the organizers were executed or exiled and their estates resumed. Finally, a few years later attention was turned to the *biradari* (brotherhood) of the Apji of Palaitha, the seniormost ranking noble in the kingdom whose estate consisted of some 20 villages and who had one of the strongest forts in the country. The biradari included several middle-ranking jagirdars (offshoots of the Palaitha jagir) including Dabri, Nagda, Kunjer, Darva, and Rajgarh, each of which had estimated incomes of between 20,000 and 25,000 rupees per year. The biradari took refuge in the Palaitha fort, which after another siege was razed to the ground. Those rebels who survived fled into exile and once again their estates were resumed.

Several contemporary sources (as well as most later histories) have blamed Zalim Singh for masterminding the murder of Swarup Singh in order to consolidate his grip on power in Kota. This accusation may well be true; there is little doubt he benefited from the murder. Similarly, the

[20] The rival was another former musahib-i-ala named Dhabhai Jaskaran.

ensuing rebellions and attempted *coup d'états* generally have been understood as principled attempts by the nobility to dislodge the rajrana in order to restore the maharao to power. On this matter, however, the evidence is more ambiguous. For one, each of the revolts involved, at least, the counter-accusations that the rebel leaders were advancing rival claimants to the gaddi and did not accept the legitimacy of Umed Singh.[21] Thus when Comte de Modave visited Kota soon after the siege of Aton in 1776, he reported that it was Umed Singh himself who ordered the attack on his cousins in order to remove these rivals to the throne.[22] That some Rajputs saw things this way is attested by the fact that many joined Zalim Singh in prosecuting the siege. The most prominent among this group was Maharaja Nath Singh Hada of Gainta who commanded the day-to-day operations of the campaign against Aton.[23] At this long remove from the actual events, we cannot hope to establish the veracity of these accusations and counter-accusations, but what is clear is that Umed Singh never formed common cause with the rebels and, as we shall see later, he seems to have felt that his personal safety was best safeguarded by Zalim Singh, and by and large supported his actions against the jagirdars.

To some extent, the confiscation of jagirs was offset by the granting of other estates to new jagirdars. But this recycling of lands introduced subtle changes into the composition of the jagirdari class that benefited Zalim Singh. The new jagirdars were drawn principally from several new warrior groups—including Marathas, Pindaris, and Pathans—that came from outside Rajasthan and whose links of service and kinship to the ruling Hada lineage were, as yet, relatively undeveloped and often conflicted by loyalties to other regional powers. The most important of these new warrior groups were the Marathas. Although they had begun to obtain military jagirs in Kota by the mid-eighteenth century, the growth in their numbers accelerated during the early years of Zalim Singh's regency. By 1781, for instance, there were 39 Maratha sardars holding a total of 71 villages in jagir with an aggregate valued income of 128,000 rupees per annum.[24] At this point, it is unclear to what extent the influx

[21] For rumours concerning Swarup Singh's aspirations to the throne, see Sharma, *Kota rajya*, p. 472. For accusations that Bahadur Sigh of Mohsian wanted to place one of Umed Singh's younger brothers on the throne, see Tod, *Annals and Antiquities*, Volume 2, pp. 526–527.

[22] Modave, *Voyage en Inde*, pp. 489–490.

[23] Sharma, *Kota rajya*, p. 476.

[24] Ibid., p. 457. A similar picture holds true for the Pindaris who by the late eighteenth century had begun to carve out several small but powerful realms (often within the ambit of the Maratha Empire) on Kota's southern and eastern frontiers. As Pindaris began to push into Kota towards the end of the eighteenth century, Zalim Singh decided to settle some of them (after initial attempts at outright resistance proved unsuccessful) and, by 1790, 43 Pindari leaders had been granted a total of 51 villages worth nearly 64,000 rupees. See, Shastri, *Zalim Singh*, pp. 188–189.

of Maratha jagirdars was the result of a conscious policy of Zalim Singh or the result of pressure from the Maratha regimes further south to settle their military representatives in Kota in order to better safeguard their interests in the region. What is certain is that the Maratha jagirdars constituted a pool of military labour in Kota whose interests were only tenuously bound to the Hada military elite of the old regime. Despite the creation of new jagirdars, it is nevertheless clear that the number of estates that were given out during this period were dwarfed by the number of estates that were resumed.

These actions against the jagirdars were dramatic, but only ever sporadic. They did not constitute a sustained and proactive policy on the part of Zalim Singh insofar as he never attacked the jagirdars without justifiable cause, such as rebellion. Conflict with the jagirdars, therefore, was pursued in fits and starts only when opportunity permitted, and it was precisely because Zalim Singh did not target the jagirdars as a group that for many years they did not rise up in a united front against him. If Zalim Singh had a determined and consistent policy aimed to secure his position in Kota, it was rooted elsewhere in changes he instituted in the basic organization of military power. The later eighteenth century did not witness so much an attack on the jagirdars as their marginalization, with a pronounced shift away from reliance upon their irregular, seasonally mobilized levies to a new standing army that increasingly was paid wages in cash. In the previous chapter we saw that Rajasthani kings had long maintained levies of royal or personal troops whose loyalties were not mediated through military clients. But it appears that the size of these forces remained relatively small in comparison to the combined contributions of the jagirdars. Royal troops rarely amounted to more than a third of a kingdom's total forces in the mid-eighteenth century. In Kota by the turn of the nineteenth century, however, these proportions had been reversed: the standing army now totalled some 16,000 soldiers while the jagirdari levies amounted to just slightly more than 7,000.[25] Although the jagirdars remained deeply embedded in the cavalry, providing nearly half of the total force of horsemen, the royal forces controlled virtually all the newly emergent and strategically important technologies of warfare, such as the artillery.

Of course, the dramatic expansion of Kota's salaried, standing army required increased revenue. But three interrelated factors during the last half of the eighteenth century conspired to allow the rajrana to raise the 'ready money' that was necessary to pay this type of army. These were Kota's strategic alliance with the Marathas, the settlement and development of the kingdom's 'inner frontiers', and finally, after about 1790, the growth of the opium trade.

[25] Shastri, *Zalim Singh*, pp. 287 and 351.

Kota and the Marathas

Since the first appearance in the early nineteenth century of James Tod's *Annals and Antiquities of Rajast'han*, the latter half of the eighteenth century in Rajasthan has been treated as a dark age characterized by political disarray, shrinking commerce, declining agriculture, and cultural decadence. Tod himself succinctly dismissed this period as an era of 'civil strife and external spoilation',[26] and his opinions broadly fall in line with other British colonial commentaries on the condition of Indian politics, which tended to see strong governance, economic prosperity, and cultural vitality in steep decline everywhere on the subcontinent during the eighteenth century. C. A. Bayly's revisionary history of burgeoning commerce and cultural florescence in many of the sub-imperial qasba towns of the Gangetic plain during the age of British expansion provides a valuable corrective to these ideas which appeared to be informed principally by what was happening in the old imperial centres such as Delhi and Agra—or in Tod's case, his much beloved Mewar.[27] And more recently, Ronald Inden has shown how these lamentations on the Fall in India were part of a self-serving campaign that aimed to delegitimate indigenous society and politics on the eve of British mastery over India in order to justify colonial intervention.[28]

From Tod's time on, blame for the apparently chaotic situation in Rajasthan has been directed towards the intervention of 'foreigners' who were not 'native' to the region.[29] In Tod's estimation, the principal alien culprits were the Marathas, a 'warrior' (but non-Rajput) group from the Deccan who in the preceding century had expanded their empire

26 Tod, *Annals and Antiquities*, Volume 2, p. 438.

27 C. A. Bayly, *Rulers, Townsmen, and Bazaars: North Indian Society in the Age of British Expansion, 1770–1870* (Cambridge: Cambridge University Press, 1983). Bayly's thesis is not a simple assertion that everything was rosy right across north India during this period. He accepts the notion of decline (at least within specified domains of social activity) as applied to many of the Mughal centres of rule. Instead he charts how certain forms of political and economic collapse in these older centres permitted the redirection of economic and human resources to new centres of rule, sometimes reproducing dimensions of the previous system and at other times introducing subtle changes.

28 Ronald Inden, *Imagining India* (Oxford: Basil Blackwell, 1990).

29 Tod's interpretation has been uncritically accepted, by and large, by most twentieth-century historians of region. Raghubir Sinh produced the classic statement in this regard in his revealingly titled, *Malwa in Transition, or a Century of Anarchy: The First Phase 1698–1765* (Bombay: D. B. Taraporevala, 1936). But see also K. S. Gupta, *Mewar and the Maratha Relations (1735–1818 A.D.)* (New Delhi: S. Chand, 1971), Beni Gupta, *Maratha Penetration into Rajasthan through the Mukandara Pass* (New Delhi: Research Publications in the Social Sciences, 1979), Anil Chandra Banerjee, *Aspects of Rajput State and Society* (New Delhi: Rajesh Publications, 1983), and Jadunath Sarkar, *A History of Jaipur, c. 1503–1938*, ed. Raghubir Sinh (Hyderabad: Orient Longman, 1984). For the classic Hindi language statement of this position, see Gaurishankar Harichand Ojha, *Rajputane ka itihas*, Volume 1 (Ajmer: Vedik Yantralya, 1925), pp. 288–292, especially p. 291.

northward into Malwa, Rajasthan, and the interfluvial Doab between the Jamuna and Ganges Rivers. Not coincidentally, the Marathas were also the principal indigenous rivals of the British in north India during the late eighteenth and early nineteenth centuries. There were no fewer than three Anglo–Maratha wars between 1774 and 1818, and for many years after 1818 a lingering paranoia about yet another Maratha uprising, perhaps in collusion with the French or Russians, periodically unsettled British confidence in the ultimate stability of their rapidly expanding empire.[30]

Although by the latter half of the seventeenth century the military power of the Marathas in the Deccan already rested upon the integrated deployment of infantry and highly mobile artillery, it was the Maratha cavalry that caught the British imagination and defined their military power. To the British the Marathas' superb horsemanship was symptomatic of a more generally unsettled, or 'nomadic', way of life that Tod considered 'lawless' and 'predatory'. Thus it was claimed that the defining characteristic of Maratha rule was that the rights and prerogatives of the government vis-à-vis the people were in no way defined or codified. The Maratha penal regime was portrayed as irregular and arbitrary, and its revenue 'system' was nothing more than random and wanton pillage. Tod pulled no punches when he wrote that the Marathas were 'distinguished for mean parsimony, low cunning, and dastardly depredation' or when he likened them to 'vampires, who drained the very life-blood wherever the scent of spoil attracted them'.[31]

The fly in the ointment of Tod's thesis was Kota. Of all the Rajasthani kingdoms, Kota had been under the Maratha sphere of influence longest and, on paper at least, owed the Marathas massive sums in tribute and punitive fines. Kota first began paying *khandani*, what Stuart Gordon has called 'a stabilized annual tribute', to the Marathas in 1738.[32] This sum was initially fixed at just under 100,000 rupees per year and a Maratha revenue official (*kamavisdar*) was posted in Kota to collect the tribute that was paid on an installment plan.[33] Seven years later, after Maharao

[30] The global conditions fanning British anxieties of empire in the nineteenth century are discussed in greater detail in my essay, 'Tod's *Rajast'han* and the Boundaries of Imperial Rule in Nineteenth-Century India', *Modern Asian Studies* 30 (1996): 185–220. See also C. A. Bayly's *Imperial Meridian: The British Empire and the World, 1788–1830* (London: Longman, 1989).

[31] James Tod, *Annals and Antiquities or, the Central and Western Rajpoot States of India*, Volume 1 (London, 1829), pp. 406 and 438.

[32] Stewart N. Gordon, 'The Slow Conquest: Administrative Integration of Malwa into the Maratha Empire, 1720–1760', *Modern Asian Studies* 11 (1977): 1–40, pp. 15–16.

[33] This tribute was initially divided between four of the Peshwa's generals – Ranoji Shinde, Malhar Rao Holkar, Yashwant Rao Pawar, and Tukoji Rao Pawar – and then became heritable by their heirs. In addition, from time to time, other Maratha leaders, such as the Peshwa, received a share. As the amount of the Maratha tribute grew the Maratha administrative apparatus for collecting it in Kota also grew in size and complexity. See Sardar Anandrao Bhao Phalke, *Shindeshahi itihasanchi sadhanen*, Volume 1 (Laskar,

Durjan Sal of Kota joined an abortive confederacy of Rajput polities that attempted to push the Marathas out of Rajasthan, the amount of khandani was raised to 400,001 rupees (the 'untidy', extra rupee apparently rendered the figure somewhat more auspicious). At the same time, the Marathas also imposed a staggering punitive fine of 1.6 million rupees, to be paid over a period of years. Then in 1756, an investiture fee (*nazranna*) of four million rupees was imposed on Maharao Ajit Singh (r. 1756–58) when he ascended the gaddi after the death of Durjan Sal.[34] In addition to these enormous financial obligations, Maratha armies were almost constantly passing through Kota after about 1740 due to the fact that Kota commanded the two principal passes through the Mukandara range separating Malwa from Rajasthan, Agra, and Delhi.

Yet despite the financial debts to the Marathas and the ubiquitous presence of their armies during the second half of the eighteenth and early nineteenth centuries, Kota was an extremely prosperous place when Tod first visited it in 1820. On his arrival, he wrote that 'the appearance of Kotah is very imposing, and impresses the mind with a more lively notion of wealth and activity than most cities in India'.[35] Moreover, in the surrounding countryside, agriculture flourished to such an extent that Tod made the following startling admission: '[Kota possesses] one of the richest and most productive soils in India, and *better cultivated than any spot even of British India*.'[36] As this confession indicates, Tod himself recognized that Kota's economic prosperity was not merely the colonial by-product of its recent incorporation into the British sphere of influence, but had earlier, eighteenth-century roots. As discussed in the previous chapter, Kota was already home to several important urban centres at the beginning of the eighteenth century. If anything, these qasbas grew in size and number during the century as they attracted merchants from elsewhere in Rajasthan and beyond. One of the most famous of these immigrants was Bahadur Mal, after whom Kota's Bahadur Bazaar is reputedly named, who moved his headquarters of his business

Gwalior: G. T. Mangaumkar Aligat Darbar Press, 1929), no. 20 and Sharma, *Kota rajya*, pp. 486 and 524–529.

[34] Apparently the nazranna was imposed because Durjan Sal died without male heir and Ajit Singh was adopted by the late maharao's principal widow without first seeking the Peshwa's approval.

[35] Tod, *Annals and Antiquities*, Volume 2, p. 662. William Hunter had much the same impression of Kota when he passed through in 1793. See William Hunter, 'Narrative of a Journey from Agra to Oujein', *Asiatick Researches* 6 (1801): 64.

[36] Tod, *Annals and Antiquities*, Volume 1, p. 14, emphasis added. Bishop Reginald Heber, who passed through Rajasthan five years later, hallowed Kota as 'a sort of Eden amid the surrounding misery'. See his *Narrative of a Journey Through the Upper Provinces of India from Calcutta to Bombay, 1824–1825, (with Notes upon Ceylon), an Account of a Journey to Madras and the Southern Provinces, 1826, and Letters Written in India* (London: John Murray, 1828), Volume 2, p. 39.

empire from Jaisalmer to Kota in 1757.[37] With this economic vitality, the size of Kota's walled city expanded more than threefold during the century prior to the British presence, and much of the expansion was undertaken to accommodate the new emporia, such as the Bahadur Bazaar, the Rampura Bazaar, and the Ladpura Bazaar, all of which stretch along the banks of the Chambal River north of the inner city from the Patan Pol gate.[38]

Agriculture also throve in the Kota region during the late eighteenth century at the height of Maratha influence. In 1776, the Comte de Modave specifically contrasted the intensive and prosperous agriculture of Kota's southern districts (that is, those territories most vulnerable to Tod's 'Maratha depredations') with the declining farming conditions that he had observed around Delhi and Agra.[39] This economic vitality also stimulated great *cultural* dynamism. It was during this period, for instance, that the royally patronized Kota school of painting achieved its greatest volume of output and many of its most stunning artistic successes. Similarly, the bold elaborations of Kota's royally sponsored public pageant-plays, such as the *Ramlila*, also date to the eighteenth century.

Despite the historically poor reputation that the Marathas have endured most everywhere in India (outside of Maharashtra, that is), recent Maratha historiography concerning the regions immediately south of Rajasthan has indicated that the 'deleterious' effect of the Marathas was not felt universally across space and time. Although the Marathas initially may have made their presence known in this region through hit-and-run plundering that greatly disrupted agricultural production, their 'slow conquest' later settled down to less violent modes of revenue extraction

[37] This information is based on a family-history interview with Seth Budh Singh Baphna on 14 October 1987. See also below the history of the Gulgule family, who established themselves in Kota in 1738.

[38] In 1695 the walls of qasba Kota enclosed only about 160 acres. This initial, inner fortification had three gates (all still standing): Patan Pol to the north, Kethuni Pol to the east, and Bhilwari Pol to the south (now also known as Kishorpura Pol). The western side of the city was (and is) flanked by the Chambal River. By 1723, new fortifications were constructed east and north of the inner city to bring an additional 244 acres under protection. Two new gates were established then: Suraj Pol to the east and Rampura Pol to the north. At the close of the eighteenth century, the walls were again extended northward to include a further 160 acres. This addition had yet another northern gate, Ladpura Pol. For more on the growth of the city, see N. L. Mishra, *Geography Behind Political History: A Study of Harauti Region* (Jaipur: R.B.S.A. Publishers, 1987), pp. 113–115. Other fortified cities such as Gagron, Shergarh, and Shahabad seem to have undergone similar expansions during this period. See Sharma, *Kota rajya*, pp. 539–540.

[39] Modave, *Voyage en Inde*, pp. 467–486. For similar observations by Charles Metcalfe in 1802, see John William Kaye, *The Life and Correspondence of Charles Lord Metcalfe* (London, 1858 [1854]), Volume 1, p. 56.

that increased tax receipts by fostering agricultural production, particularly as the region became better integrated into the Maratha sphere of influence. By the late eighteenth century, for example, the Peshwa collected regularized revenues in eastern Malwa at nearly the same levels as collected by the Mughals at the height of their rule.[40]

Rajasthan, however, remained on the fringes of the Maratha Empire throughout the later eighteenth and early nineteenth centuries and was never fully integrated into the Peshwa's domain in the same way as eastern Malwa. Instead Rajasthan fell under the spheres of influence of several of the Peshwa's generals, notably Shinde, Holkar, and (at least initially) the Pawars. In part, because of internal rivalries among these Maratha generals and, in part, because their attentions were continually diverted towards far richer prizes at Delhi and Agra, the Marathas never domesticated Rajasthan quite to the same extent that they did Malwa, and local polities were never superseded to the extent that they were further south.[41] The impact of the Maratha intrusion into Rajasthan, moreover, was not uniform but witnessed wide local variations. Along with producing several well-known 'losers', such as Mewar, the expansion of Maratha power produced some notable 'winners'. Kota was one of the localities that generally benefited from its association with the Marathas, especially as the century wore on.

Although Maratha demands for tribute from Kota at times placed a heavy stress on Kota's treasury, the Maratha presence facilitated Kota's political and economic development in other respects. Under Maratha supremacy, Kota became something of a strategic 'central place' from which Maratha policy elsewhere in Rajasthan was directed and administered. Kota's centrality was influenced by its geographic position on the northern side of the Ghatoli and Dara gaps breaching the Mukandara Range separating Rajasthan from Malwa and the Deccan. Kota thus developed into an important staging town on the caravan routes that linked Ujjain in the south with the rest of Rajasthan, Agra, and Delhi further north. The Maratha armies that passed along this route tended not to 'plunder' the countryside because they depended upon the settled

[40] Stewart N. Gordon, 'The Slow Conquest', p. 31; Stewart N. Gordon, *The New Cambridge History of India*, Volume II.4: *The Marathas, 1600–1818* (Cambridge: Cambridge University Press, 1993), pp. 139–144; and André Wink, *Land and Sovereignty in India: Agrarian Society and Politics under the Eighteenth-Century Maratha Svarajya* (Cambridge: Cambridge University Press, 1986).

[41] Although Kota's initial reaction to the Marathas may have been hostile, as witnessed in Durjan Sal's periodic attempts to push them out of Rajasthan during the 1730s and 1740s, from the 1760s a much cozier relationship developed.

agricultural population to supply abundant and dependable provisions.[42] Instead, they purchased their supplies from Kota's burgeoning markets. Tod reported that during the single year of 1803/04 Zalim Singh *sold* 'these roving hordes' grain worth in excess of '*one crore of rupees*',[43] and Maratha newswriters kept careful track of the price of foodstuffs and other commodities in Kota's markets, which were then reported back to the Peshwa.[44] When Maratha troops did run amok in Kota, Zalim Singh quickly sent his agents along with a local Maratha representative to assess the damage and make restitution to the affected peasants, the cost of which (known as *paimali*) was then deducted from the Maratha tribute.[45]

The trade stimulated by the Marathas boosted Kota's revenues in two ways. First, as discussed in the previous chapter, revenue was derived from the direct sale of state-owned grain in the marketplace. While we do not yet have entirely reliable statistics on the growth of these revenues, 'qualitative' evidence of the type quoted by Tod above suggests that it was considerable. Second, increased trade indirectly boosted the kingdom's revenues from customs tolls and transit dues (*zakat*). These levies were collected not only on goods entering the kingdom from abroad but also on goods passing through the main gates of each market town within the kingdom. In order to maximize this potentiality, Zalim Singh trebled the number of customs posts throughout the kingdom and increased the number of goods that were liable for taxation. As a result of these efforts, customs receipts that had amounted to a modest 82,000 rupees in 1780 increased five-fold to over 462,000 rupees in 1804.[46]

[42] When the Comte de Modave travelled from Agra to Hyderabad in 1776, he went via Kota, Mukandara, and Ujjain. Along the route (as far as Ujjain at least), he found caravanserai and thriving bazaars where he could outfit his company, hire guides, and buy camels and horses. At the end of the eighteenth century Kota remained the principal transit point between Agra and Ujjain. William Hunter travelled this route via Kota in March 1793 as did Charles Metcalfe in March/April 1802. See Modave, *Voyage en Inde*, pp. 327 and 459–496; William Hunter, 'Narrative of a Journey', pp. 47–67; and Kaye, *Lord Metcalfe*, Volume 1, pp. 55–56.

[43] Tod, *Annals and Antiquities*, Volume 2, p. 543. The figure, of course, must be taken with some circumspection. What is significant is the claim that the grain was sold rather than simply appropriated.

[44] For one such published example, see M. Nazim, ed., *Selections from the Peshwas' Daftar (Persian)*, Volume 46; *Miscellaneous Papers* (Bombay: Government Central Press, 1933), no. 445.

[45] See Sardar Anandrao Bhao Phalke, *Shindeshahi itihasanchi sadhanen*, Volume 2 (Laskar, Gwalior: G. T. Mangaumkar Aligat Darbar Press, 1930), nos 76 and 77. These letters date to 1769. For an example of the Marathas agreeing to a 10,000 rupee reduction in Kota's khandani for the same year, possibly in response to the above cited letters, see R. B. Ganesh Chimnaji Vad, comp., *Selections from the Satara Rajas' and the Peshwas' Diaries*, Volume 9; *Peshwa Madhavrao I*, Volume 1, ed. Kashinath Narayan Sane (Poona: The Deccan Vernaular Translation Society, 1911), no. 304.

[46] Shastri, *Zalim Singh*, pp. 326–328.

Kota's geographic centrality ultimately found political expression when Lalaji Ballal Gulgule, who succeeded as the Maratha revenue collector in Kota in 1760, was also given charge at various times of the assistant collectors (*naib-kamavisdars*) stationed at the courts of Bundi, Mewar, Rajgarh, Sheopur, and Indragarh as well as in parganas directly under Maratha administration such as Keshorai Patan and Kapren.[47] Through his personal money-lending operations, Lalaji Ballal temporarily redirected some of the inflows of tribute that passed through his hands to support the projects and agendas of local leaders in Kota, not the least of whom was Zalim Singh. In the end, Lalaji Ballal's personal fortune became so bound up with Kota that after the establishment of the Pax Britannica, when the British forced most Marathas out of Rajasthan, he resisted 'repatriation' and contrived to remain behind, fearing that if he left Kota he would never recover his debts.[48]

Zalim Singh's colonization of the 'inner frontiers' of the kingdom

Encouraged by demand stimulated by the Marathas, Zalim Singh sought to boost agricultural output in Kota by resettling abandoned villages, rehabilitating wastelands, and colonizing previously uninhabited forest tracts along the 'inner frontiers' of the kingdom. During this period, land was still relatively abundant in Kota (as elsewhere in many parts of India). Zalim Singh boasted to Tod that, when he first rose to power, two-thirds of Kota's superficial area lay unproductive but that, by 1820, this same proportion of land was under the plough.[49] If suitable land was plentiful in the eighteenth century, what was in short supply was the labour to work it. Zalim Singh therefore made liberal use of a type of land tenure in which concessionary rates of revenue assessment were granted to farmers who agreed to settle and rehabilitate unproductive land. Typically, these concessions operated on four-to-ten year terms. During the first half of the term, the cultivator paid only a nominal assessment, which was progressively raised each year thereafter so that by the end of the cycle the assessment reached its target rate.

Zalim Singh's (re)settlement scheme was also supported with various 'agricultural development programs' including the building of numerous

[47] Sinh, *Malwa in Transition*, p. 324. Sharma, *Kota rajya*, pp. 527–528. Lalaji Ballal succeeded his father, Balaji Yashvant Gulgule, who had been first appointed to the post by Ranoji Shinde in 1738.

[48] In 1738, Maharao Durjan Sal granted Balaji Yashwant Gulgule a small estate in the village Birakhedi, pargana Urmal. Thirty-three years later Lalaji Ballal Gulgule was hypothecated the lucrative Sarola estate in southeastern Kota as a surety against a debt owed him by the maharao.

[49] Tod, *Annals and Antiquities*, Volume 2, p. 543.

small-scale, tank-based irrigation systems—many of which are still in use today—as well as experimentation with different seed stocks, grafting techniques, breeds of oxen and new plough designs for the varied soil conditions of the kingdom. One of Zalim Singh's innovations—the introduction of the Konkani, a double-yoked plough which was capable of coping with much heavier soils than the traditional Rajasthani plough—enabled the cultivation of vast new tracts of land that previously had been too difficult to work. The knowledge that Zalim Singh gained from his trials was then disseminated through a series of agricultural fairs that he sponsored at various locations across the kingdom.[50]

Zalim Singh's policies to attract agricultural labour were further abetted by the political disruptions resulting from the push of the Marathas outwards from Kota into the rest of Rajasthan, particularly into Mewar. Zalim Singh himself participated with the Marathas in many of these campaigns during the last quarter of the eighteenth century. For example, he led troops into Mewar in 1774, 1776, 1778, then almost every year between 1782 and 1791, and then again in 1799, 1800, 1801, 1803, and 1805. These campaigns had the short-term effect of dislocating considerable amounts of agricultural labour which left Mewar in search of more settled conditions elsewhere. As Kota remained relatively tranquil, many farmers relocated there. During Thomas Broughton's march through southeastern Rajasthan in 1809, for instance, he encountered on the road numerous farmers with their families immigrating to Kota.[51]

As a result of the large amount of newly profitable lands brought under cultivation along Kota's 'inner frontiers', Zalim Singh conducted a kingdom-wide land survey (*mapya*) in 1792, the first universal reckoning in Kota since Maharao Bhim Singh had undertaken a similar exercise in 1717.[52] Using heavy jute ropes of a standardized length (approximately 20 metres long), known as *doris*, Zalim Singh's agents visited nearly every village in the kingdom measuring the habitation area (*abadi*), each cultivated field (*hakkat*), uncultivated land (*padat*), and uncultivatable wasteland (*nalayak*). In addition, the survey also noted the actual land revenue generated from each field for each crop (*upti*) and, where the information was available, a notation about the highest land revenue in cash terms (*hakkati dharti ka rupaya*) that had ever been generated from the fields

[50] James Tod to Charles Metcalfe, OIOC, BPC, 17/22 April 1820.

[51] Broughton, *Letters Written in a Mahratta Camp*, p. 39. For similar observations, see Tod, *Annals and Antiquities*, Volume 2, p. 540.

[52] Many smaller scale surveys of single parganas or even individual villages had been conducted from time to time between 1717 and 1792.

and the year that this sum was achieved.[53] With these figures Zalim Singh was able to determine more accurately the amount of his actual revenues as well as what potential revenues he might expect to receive under optimal circumstances.

This survey was followed in 1805 by a sweeping reform of the administration responsible for the collection of land revenue, in which Zalim Singh instituted what became known as the '*patel* system'. Zalim Singh abandoned the largely Mughal, multi-tiered system of revenue administration which was based on a hierarchy of parganas (districts), *tappa*s (subdistricts), *mauza*s (townships) and *gaon*s (villages) and, following Maratha precedent, he opted for a considerably 'flatter' structure that eliminated many administrative levels. Under the new regime village-based patels (local headmen) became directly responsible to Zalim Singh and a council of four senior patels. In addition to bypassing many entrenched intermediary elements of the administrative hierarchy, this reform elevated to social and political prominence a new class of rich peasants and local businessmen (*mahajan*s) who owed their enhanced status to the rajrana.[54] In 1807, soon after these reforms, Zalim Singh engaged in yet another land survey. This survey was conducted, in part, to account for the new lands that had been brought under cultivation since the previous survey and, perhaps more importantly, Zalim Singh utilized the information gathered to convert the vast majority of agricultural land in the kingdom to the *kuntai* regime of revenue assessment. Although other factors may have contributed, total land revenue receipts rose some 12 percent from 29 lakhs to 33 lakhs in the following year.[55]

Opium, royal revenue, and the penumbra of empire

During the last years of the eighteenth century and continuing through the first two decades of the nineteenth, the positive dynamic fuelling Kota's economic expansion was intensified by the growing traffic in opium. Although opium had long been traded in central and western India and traditionally found markets all along the Arabian Gulf, demand

[53] Masanori Sato, 'The Growth of Towns (Qasbas) of South-eastern Rajasthan under the Mughals – A Case Study of Jhalrapatan', in *Economy and Polity of Rajasthan: Study of Kota and Marwar, 17th through 19th Centuries*, eds Masanori Sato and B. L. Bhadani (Jaipur: Publication Scheme, 1997), pp. 31–56.

[54] Reflecting their elevated status, Masanori Sato notes that the patels were granted many of the same sartorial privileges as Rajputs (such as permission to ride on horses and to wear certain types of ornaments) along with the tax-free land or *inam* that they were granted for their services. See Masanori Sato, 'The Patels and the Structure of their Landholding in South-eastern Rajasthan, A.D. 1750–1850', in *Memoirs of the Research Department of the Toyo Bunko*, no. 55 (Tokyo: The Toyo Bunko, 1997), pp. 61–62.

[55] Shastri, *Zalim Singh*, p. 315.

for it rose markedly from the later 1770s indirectly stimulated, in large measure, by British interest in the commodity which itself was a by-product of the East India Company's trade for Chinese tea, silk, and porcelain.[56] Because the demand for European manufactures in China was low, commerce with China during the first half of the eighteenth century was sustained by the export of large quantities of silver causing a drain on European reserves. The one thing for which the Chinese did seem to have an appetite and which they did not produce for themselves in any great quantity was opium. The East India Company seized upon this demand in order to relieve the pressure on European specie, becoming, in the process, perhaps the world's first international drug cartel.

This strategy appeared particularly promising after Clive's victory at the Battle of Plassey in 1757 and the Treaty of Allahabad in 1765 with which the East India Company became *de facto* rulers of Bengal, Bihar, and Orissa. These provinces, particularly Bihar, were admirably suited to poppy cultivation. As the company consolidated its political position in eastern India, it instituted a monopoly, formalized in 1773, on the production and trade of opium. Under the terms of the monopoly, the company released at auction in Calcutta a steady but restricted supply of 'Bengal opium' for shipment to Canton. By keeping the supply of opium relatively stable at around 4,800 chests per annum in what was a rapidly growing market, the price per chest rose an astounding 333.5 percent between the years 1798–99 and 1816–17.[57]

This tidy state of affairs, however, was short-lived as the windfall profits enjoyed by British traders stimulated the production and trade of opium from portions of north India not under British control. Central India had long produced its own opium, and by the turn of the nineteenth century, the so-called 'Malwa opium' produced in the 'native

[56] My main sources on the general policies of the East India Company concerning Bengal opium and its implication in the China trade are David Edward Owen, *British Opium Policy in India and China* (New Haven: Yale University Press, 1934); B. Chaudhuri, 'Regional Economy (1757–1857): Eastern India II', in *The Cambridge Economic History of India*, ed. Dharma Kumar (Cambridge: Cambridge University Press, 1983), Volume 2, pp. 295–332; Narayan Prasad Singh, *The East India Company's Monopoly Industries in Bihar with Particular Reference to Opium and Saltpetre* (Muzaffarpur, Bihar: Sarvodaya Vangmaya, 1980); and K. N. Chaudhuri, 'Foreign Trade and Balance of Payments (1757–1947)', in *The Cambridge Economic History of India*, ed. Dharma Kumar, Volume 2, pp. 804–877. The best printed source on early British policy concerning Malwa opium with considerable discussion of the situation in Kota appears in *Parliamentary Papers, Third Report from the Select Committee on the Affairs of the East India Company*, Appendix IV, 'Abstracts on Malwa Opium' (1831), hereafter referred to as *Third Report*. See also Amar Farooqui, 'Opium Enterprise and Colonial Intervention in Malwa and Western India, 1800–1824', *Indian Economic and Social History Review* 32 (1995): 447–473.

[57] Owen, *British Opium*, p. 86; B. Chaudhuri, 'Regional Economy', p. 313. The Calcutta opium chest weighed 160 pounds.

states' of this region competed with company-controlled 'Bengal opium' on the Chinese market. The Malwa opium was hauled overland to ports on the Arabian Sea and from there transhipped to China. The Portuguese, who not only had coastal colonies at Goa, Daman, and Diu but also outer anchorages on East Timor and a terminus in Macao, were eager competitors with the British. It also appears that considerable quantities of opium were shipped from indigenously controlled ports (particularly Karachi, prior to 1843) on American, Dutch, and non-European, 'country' ships. The governor-general first became aware of the foreign trade of 'illicit' Malwa opium in 1803, and between 1814 and 1819, the growing market share of Malwa opium began to be reflected by a softening, and then decline, in the company's opium revenues.[58] The exact quantities of 'illicit' opium shipped to China are unknown and much debated by scholars. However, the House of Commons was informed that between 9,000 and 10,000 chests of Malwa opium exited 'Demaun and other places' each year.[59] Much of this opium was shipped to the Gulf, but perhaps half was intended for Java, the Eastern Archipelago, and China with about 900 chests per year reaching the latter destination alone.[60] These figures would suggest that Malwa opium had captured as much as a fifth of the Chinese market.

For his part, Zalim Singh became a major player in the opium trade at the end of the eighteenth century. Although Kota initially was not an important producer of the commodity, its southern frontier was at the edge of the Malwa opium-growing region, and vast quantities of the commodity passed through Kota on its way to the Portuguese port of Daman. The trade in opium, which was duly taxed, appears to have been one of the major reasons why Zalim Singh ordered the construction of the new city of Jhalrapatan, in the extreme south of the kingdom, in 1796. Jhalrapatan quickly established itself as an important wholesale centre in the trade—a sort of Medellin without the lawlessness—where the opium was initially collected, processed, and stockpiled, and where agents were posted to monitor its quality, make purchases, and place future orders. Then early in the nineteenth century, the rajrana gained valuable leaseholds (*muqata*s) to opium-growing lands in the heart of Malwa. In 1803 Zalim Singh first obtained from Jaswant Rao Holkar the lease of four parganas—known as the Chaumahal—that extended southward

58 Owen, *British Opium*, pp. 82–85; N. P. Singh, *East India Company's Monopoly Industries*, pp. 144–145.

59 *Third Report*, Appendix IV, p. 52. Farooqui more conservatively estimates Malwa opium production at 4,000–5,000 chests per annum during the years around 1820. Though a smaller sum than that of the *Third Report*, it is still comparable to the entire Bengal production. See Farooqui, 'Opium Enterprise in Malwa', p. 468.

60 *Third Report*, Appendix IV, p. 52; Farooqui, 'Opium Enterprise in Malwa', p. 452.

from Jhalrapatan.[61] Six years later Daulat Rao Shinde granted him leasehold of seven additional abutting parganas—the Satmahal.[62] With the acquisition of these eleven parganas, Zalim Singh became such a large player in the opium market that he was one of the few Indian growers mentioned by name in the parliamentary report on the 'illicit' Malwa opium trade, and was credited with the ability to manipulate the price of the commodity by releasing or withholding supplies from his vast stockpiles.[63]

The new foundations of military power under Zalim Singh

Benefiting from these growing economic conditions, Zalim Singh put the military foundations of the kingdom on a new footing that increasingly was articulated by control over the flow of cash, rather than the redistribution of landed estates. This shift took place in two stages. At first, Zalim Singh lessened his dependence upon jagirdars by contracting 'itinerant-brigades-for-hire' in the north Indian, military labour market. Perhaps the earliest military contingent of this type employed by Zalim Singh was the *jinsi* (a corps of artillery with supporting infantry) of a European 'gone native' whom we only know by the *nom de guerre* of Firangi Musakalpi. Musakalpi and his 'park of artillery' first appeared on the scene in Kota in 1776 when he was hired to help bring the siege of Aton to its conclusion. Musakalpi and his artillery then remained in Kota for at least five years during which time he was paid a salary of 20,000 rupees per year.[64] Other commanders in search of work soon followed Musakalpi's path to Kota. By 1782, for example, he was joined by another brigade led by a European officer whose *nom de guerre,* Firangi Badelbeg or Master of Thunder, suggests that he also commanded artillery. And it was not just European-led troops that were 'accreted' to Kota's army in this way. Brigades of Dadhu Panthi Naga ascetics, Marathas, and especially Pathans also found good employment in Kota.

As Dirk Kolff has documented, these 'itinerant-brigades-for-hire' had been a prominent feature of the north Indian, military labour market from at least the fifteenth century.[65] However, the activities of the British

[61] The Chaumahal were Awar, Dag, Gangdhar, and Pachpahar.

[62] The Satmahal were Susner, Nalkhera, Soyet, Kawad, Piplon, Barod and Ghusai Basai. Zalim Singh initially paid Shinde a fee of 319,308 rupees per year for these districts.

[63] *Third Report,* Appendix IV, pp. 52ff.; and Tod, *Annals and Antiquities,* Volume 2, p. 545.

[64] Sharma, *Kota rajya,* pp. 538–539. To put this figure in some perspective, a sepoy earned something on the order of 5 or 6 rupees a month at this time. For more on military pay scales in Kota, see Shastri, *Zalim Singh,* p. 290.

[65] D. H. A. Kolff, *Naukar, Rajput and Sepoy: The Ethnohistory of the Military Labour Market in Hindustan, 1450–1850* (Cambridge: Cambridge University Press, 1990).

further to the east in the upper Gangetic plain in the late eighteenth century increasingly stimulated it and gave it some of its specific character, particularly with regard to the Pathans. During the late eighteenth century there was an influx of many Pathan troops to Rajasthan in general, and Kota in particular. Many of the Pathans who migrated into central and western India had been in the service of the Rohillas who, after the decline of the Mughal Empire in the eighteenth century, dominated the upper portions of the Gangetic Plain in the vicinity of Rampur. But after British troops helped the Nawab of Oudh defeat the Rohillas in 1774 and compelled the demilitarization of that region, a large segment of the Pathan military labour-pool migrated west of the Ganges.[66] Here they sought the patronage of other native powers, and Zalim Singh only too happily employed these soldiers who had no previous footing in Kota.

Perhaps the most famous commander of this type to frequent Kota was the Pathan leader Mir Khan (later Nawab Amir Khan of Tonk) whose history is typical of the type of military 'big man' operating in the region.[67] Mir Khan's grandfather had been in the military service of Muhammad Ali, the remarkable Rohilla leader who, in the years after 1740, seized large tracts of land in Rohilkhand—including the districts of Moradabad, Barielly, and Shahjahanpur. Muhammad Ali assigned Mir Khan's grandfather several villages in Moradabad district where his father became a mullah. Mir Khan was born here at Sambhal in 1767. By 1787, however, he had left Rohilkhand and was selling his military services and that of ten followers to various Maratha leaders in Ahirwada and Malwa. During the next thirty years he remained constantly on the move, finding employment with the Nawab of Bhopal, the ex-chiefs of Raghogarh, Jaswant Rao Holkar, the Maharajas of Jaipur and Jodhpur and, from time to time, Zalim Singh.[68] At each turn, Mir Khan increased the size of his military following so that by 1814, Henry Princep reported that 'he had a force of at least 30,000 horse and foot, furnished with an artillery well manned and served'.[69]

Although these new forces in Kota were 'standing' and waged, the army was not yet a modern 'professional' army in the sense that it had a

66 Bayly, *Rulers, Townsmen, and Bazaars*, p. 121.

67 For more on the biography of Mir Khan, see Busawan Lal, *Memoirs of the Puthan Soldier of Fortune, the Nuwab Ameer-ood-Doulah, Mohummad Ameer Khan, Chief of Seronj, Tonk, Rampoora, Neemahera, and Other Places in Hindoostan*, trans. H. T. Princep (Calcutta: G. H. Huttman, Military Orphan Press, 1832), and Sir John Malcolm, *A Memoir of Central India Including Malwa, and Adjoining Provinces, with the History, and Copious Illustrations, of the Past and Present Condition of that Country* (London: Parbury, Allen, and Co., 1832 [1824]), Volume 1, pp. 325–348.

68 Busawan Lal, *Memoirs of the Puthan Soldier*, p. 271.

69 Henry T. Princep, *A Narrative of the Political and Military Transactions of British India under the Administration of the Marquess of Hastings, 1813–1818* (London: John Murray, 1820), pp. 31–32.

unified structure of graded ranks with linear chains of command whose officers and troopers were interchangeable. Links between officers and common soldiers continued to be highly personalized as these officers often recruited, provisioned, and paid their own followers, and the 'brigades' typically maintained significant degrees of internal autonomy and segmented loyalties. Among the Dadhu Panthi Nagas, for example, the contingents remained under the leadership of religious gurus and recruitment was attached to specific forms of discipleship and devotional practice that, among other things, preserved their distinct identity.[70]

Towards the end of the eighteenth century, however, Zalim Singh instituted a number of military reforms that brought the organization of Kota's army, on the face of it, much more in line with modern European norms. Indeed, military contacts between Zalim Singh and French officers in the employ of the Marathas may have stimulated these reforms. The infantry, for example, was organized into fourteen battalions (*paltan*s; that is, 'platoons') that, in turn, were subdivided into squadrons (*nishan*s) in which officers, subalterns, troopers, and support staff were all given standardized ranks. Soldiers, moreover, were outfitted from central stores, had set pay scales that were pegged to their rank, and enjoyed codified benefits (for travel, disability, or death) whose payments were centrally disbursed.[71] Yet even then, it would be misleading to push the comparison with European armies too far. Many of these new battalions were formed by co-opting existing 'itinerant-brigades-for-hire'. As a result, the battalions varied greatly in size and their names, such as Hussaini Paltan, Nazeem Paltan, Jafari Paltan or Narayan Paltan, continued to index the centrality of their leaders.[72] This latter fact shows that personal loyalties and the ethic of service binding common troopers and their immediate leaders remained strong.

Yet, significantly, the Maharao of Kota was largely tangential to this system of loyalties, completely removed as he was from any direct involvement in the military apparatus of the kingdom. Unlike many of his predecessors who had died while leading troops in battle (recall Bhim Singh at Pandhar as well as Mukund Singh and his brothers at Dharmat), Umed Singh never personally commanded troops nor led the army in the field.[73] Concerning the primary loyalties of Kota's troops during this period, Tod noted that the:

70 Shastri, *Zalim Singh*, p. 291.

71 These reforms did not extend to the jagirdari contributions to the army, which remained unchanged.

72 Ibid., pp. 290 and 297.

73 Indeed the last Maharao of Kota for whom there is evidence of actively leading an army into battle is Shatru Shal (r. 1758–64).

men [were] entertained, raised, and fed by Zalim Singh [and] knew of Omed Singh only by name and as far as Zalim Singh chose. The commandants of the battalions, artillery, and the head of the paega horse were men who had been fostered by [Zalim Singh's] kindness and raised from private soldiers to rank: troops whom [Zalim Singh] had formed and thro' whose means he had preserved the state thro' all the storms of Mahratta turmoil and spoilation; their officers of twenty and thirty years standing were treated like his children.[74]

Thus as Tod noted, the web of loyalties in the new military was ultimately articulated by Zalim Singh and he cultivated an almost familial attitude of personal devotion from his troops during the many military campaigns that he personally led.[75]

Zalim Singh and the construction of new coordinates of political value

While Zalim Singh benefited from a period of tremendous economic expansion in Kota during the latter half of the eighteenth century which allowed him to raise a larger standing army that he used to marginalize the power of the jagirdars and separate the maharao from the kingdom's military foundations, it is also evident that the maharao's place of detention was very much a 'gilded cage' in which, as Tod revealingly admitted, 'there was no appearance of constraint'.[76] Zalim Singh spent lavishly on the upkeep of Umed Singh and that of his immediate family, thereby earning the court the reputation, according to Modave, of being 'one of the most magnificent in all of Hindustan'.[77] Not only did Zalim Singh cater to the maharao's passion for the chase by organizing numerous elaborate hunting parties, which were then recorded in opulent paintings, but he sanctioned truly Rabelaisian celebrations—involving feasting, merriment, and the presentation of expensive gifts—to mark all the major annual and life cycle events of the maharao and his family. Similarly, whenever the rajrana entertained the maharao at his estate of Nandta, he laid on munificent hospitality. The official record of one such visit in 1772 describes the persistent determination of Zalim Singh's magnanimity. On the maharao's arrival at Nandta,

[74] James Tod to George Swinton, OIOC, BPC, 11/16 April 1822.

[75] In this regard it is significant that Zalim Singh forsook his palace in Kota after about 1800 in order to live among his soldiers in their military cantonments (*chaoni*s) that were established around the kingdom. Even when he visited the capital, he stayed at the chaoni of Gumanpura two kilometres east of the city.

[76] Tod, *Annals and Antiquities*, Volume 2, p. 553.

[77] Modave, *Voyage en Inde*, p. 480. Modave himself did not concur with this estimation when he finally reached Kota. But it is significant that this was its reputation at the time.

Mamaji [that is, Zalim Singh] presented [the maharao] one gold mohar as a nazar.[78] Zalim Singh's wife also performed Nyochhawar[79] with Rs. 10/-. All the ladies of Zalim Singh's family offered nazars. Zalim Singh's mother performed Nyochhawar with one gold mohar. Zalim Singh's aunt also did the same. The other relations of Zalim Singh also offered nazars.

The maharao then briefly interrupted this embarrassment of riches by giving Zalim Singh a pair of diamond-set bracelets that had belonged to his father, Guman Singh, and he also presented Zalim Singh's mother two gold mohars. But not to be outdone, when the maharao prepared to return to his palace, Zalim Singh presented him with a beautiful horse.[80]

As sometimes happens in relationships lasting fifty years or more, there were occasions when Umed Singh harboured misgivings towards Zalim Singh. But when tensions became manifest, they tended to arise out of fears that were more diffuse than tangible. The most well-known instance of this occurred in 1791 when Umed Singh accused Zalim Singh of placing a mortal hex (*maran mantra*) on him. The maharao made his suspicions known in a letter to the rajrana, in which he wrote:

I have come to know that some tantrik Brahmans are performing 'maran mantra' against me by your order. This is highly improper of you. You were not expected to do such things secretly against me. I have always considered you my elder. It does not, therefore, behoove you to behave like this against me. Now I have a keen desire to go on a pilgrimage to Nathdwara. Therefore, please arrange for my journey to that place. If my being ruler stands in the way of my undertaking a pilgrimage, I am prepared even to abdicate.[81]

We do not know for certain how Umed Singh came to know (or believe) that Zalim Singh had engaged tantrik specialists to perform the maran mantra against him. But Umed Singh's suspicions clearly abated (especially the longer he lived on) and he did not carry through with his threat to abdicate.

More generally, however, correspondence between the two indicates that Umed Singh generally felt his personal well-being and that of the kingdom depended on Zalim Singh. In 1805, for instance, while Zalim Singh was campaigning in Mewar with Daulat Rao Shinde, Umed Singh wrote the following, almost desperate, plea to the rajrana for him to return to Kota in order to look after affairs there.

[78] *Nazar* is an offering, or gift, to a superior.

[79] An offering of cash in which the money is first waved around the head of the recipient.

[80] Cited in Shastri, *Zalim Singh*, pp. 77–78.

[81] Ibid., p. 80. That abdication was the maharao's only recourse to stop the alleged actions of the rajrana (rather than, say, replacing him outright) is a further indication of the extent to which he did not control the executive apparatus of the kingdom.

What is the reason of your long stay in Udaipur [Mewar]?... Just find a good excuse and take leave of Daulat Raoji Sindhia and return here.... You wrote to me that after satisfying Sindhia you will soon return to Kota but you have not yet come. Now please return immediately and manage the affairs of Kota. Having gone to Mewar, you have busied yourself too much with the matters there. If our state survives, it will help us all. I, therefore, propose to come to Mewar and secure permission for you to return here. Our administration is suffering and you are busy in Mewar. Please see that our state survives; only then we can be saved. Sindhia is powerful, greedy and selfish. If you stay on with him and there will be nobody here to look after the administration, it is likely that somebody may invade the state.[82]

It was the prevalence of these latter sentiments, rather than the former, that accounts for why Umed Singh never joined in the several coup attempts that were directed against his prime minister. Indeed, as indicated earlier in this chapter, the threats entailed by these revolts were directed, more often than not, as much against the maharao as against the rajrana.

Whatever misgivings Umed Singh may have felt on occasion towards Zalim Singh were tempered by the clear benefits his service brought. Under Zalim Singh's guidance the kingdom underwent its largest territorial expansion since the reign of Maharao Bhim Singh. I have already mentioned the Battle of Bhatwada in 1761, which brought the Kotriat Thikanas on Kota's northern frontier within its influence. This was followed in 1779 by Zalim Singh's conquest from one of Mahadji Shinde's clients of the pargana of Shahabad on Kota's extreme eastern frontier. Then the first decade of the nineteenth century saw Zalim Singh extend Kota's influence over fourteen additional parganas through muqata leaseholds. In 1803, Zalim Singh arranged for the muqata of three parganas in Mewar to Kota's west.[83] And, as we saw above, during this same year he negotiated the leasehold for the Chaumahal followed, in 1806, the leasehold for the Satmahal which extended Kota's influence further south.[84] In each of these three latter cases, the leases were made out formally in the name of the maharao, and Zalim Singh explicitly eschewed any augmentation to his own personal territorial possessions. Similarly, when Umed Singh offered to add pargana of Shahabad to Zalim Singh's jagir after his conquest of it, the rajrana likewise refused.[85] This persistent

82 Ibid., pp. 80–81. Similarly Umed Singh often wrote cover letters for Zalim Singh's official correspondence affirming the maharao's support of rajrana's work.

83 Jahazpur, Sanganer, and Itoda.

84 In addition, Zalim Singh was constantly 'nibbling away' at the frontiers of the kingdom, seizing from his neighbours three villages here, four villages there.

85 Lakshmandan, *Vansha prashasti*, p. 63.

reluctance to accept personal gain became one of the hallmarks of Zalim Singh's regency and, as we shall see in the next section, holds the key to understanding his authority insofar as it came to be associated with the 'disinterested' service of Yashoda to the infant Krishna.[86]

Chakri and seva in late precolonial Kota

To his dying day in 1824, Zalim Singh continued to profess his loyalty to the Maharao of Kota within the well-established terms of his duty to serve (*chakri kar*). At the same time, however, it is also clear that Zalim Singh's idea of service became infused with significant new meanings deriving from Vallabha doctrine. Service was no longer perceived as a way of establishing a relationship with an unambiguously superordinate being through whom subordinates came to participate with a distant, overawing, and transcendent power. Instead Zalim Singh's conception of chakri increasingly played upon Vallabha notions of seva (service), particularly as experienced through the emotive state of vatsalya bhav, the 'disinterested' maternal love of the foster parents, Nanda and (especially) Yashoda, for their foster child, Krishna. As discused in chapter 3, vatsalya bhav was the favoured emotional mode/mood governing devotional practice among the Pushtimargis in western India. This mode/mood took its inspiration from circumstances and events surrounding Krishna's birth and early life as recounted in numerous religious texts that were widely circulated in the area during the period.[87]

According to these legends, Krishna, Vishnu's eighth avatar, was born in Braj in order to defeat the evil king Kamsa who had seized the throne of the Yadavas at Mathura. But before the birth of Krishna, Kamsa is warned of the god's impending manifestation and learns that his very own cousin, Devaki, is destined to bear the child-god. The fearful Kamsa therefore imprisons Devaki and her devoted husband, Vasudeva, at Mathura and then proceeds to kill each of the children born to the unfortunate couple. Krishna is the eighth child to be born, but on the night

86 Zalim Singh did hold one of the largest jagirs in Kota consisting of 29 villages valued with an annual income of 64,000 rupees. Although very large, it did not differ on an order of magnitude from other large jagirs in Kota at the time. For the sizes of larger jagirs in Kota during the later nineteenth century, see Sharma, *Kota rajya*, pp. 549–550. For British observations about Zalim Singh's reluctance to increase unduly the size of his jagir, see Ochterlony to Swinton, 21 September 1824, OIOC, BPC, 23/15 October 1824.

87 Classical texts, such as the *Harivamsha*, the *Vishnu Purana*, and the *Bhagavata Purana*, each of which existed in a profusion of editions in Kota's Saraswati Bhandar Library, all contain versions of the myths of Krishna's birth and youth as do vernacular texts too numerous to mention here.

of his birth a spell descends upon Braj causing the soldiers guarding Devaki and Vasudeva to fall into a deep sleep and the prison doors are miraculously thrown open. Under the cover of darkness, Vasudeva takes the newborn Krishna from Mathura across the river to Gokul where the child is given to the cowherders, Nanda and Yashoda. Fleeing the armies of Kamsa who search the countryside for the infant Krishna, Nanda and Yashoda then take the child-god to the forest of Brindavan where they raise him. Krishna spends his childhood and adolescence in sylvan safety of Brindavan before eventually returning to Mathura in order to slay Kamsa.

The relationship that developed between Krishna and his foster parents during his youth became an important focus of Vallabha devotional practice for it defined a slightly altered relationship between devotee and god than existed in many other bhakti traditions. The form of service that was detailed in this relationship was *not* the devotion of servant to his master, a modality of devotion known as *dasya bhav*, in which the devotee experiences, as Richard Barz explains, 'a wide gulf between himself and his god [and] emphasizes the glory and the power of the deity at the same time as he belittles and humbles himself... [as in] the relationship between a mighty king and an ordinary subject'.[88] Instead, the modality of vatsalya bhav was premised on the much more mundanely intimate and hierarchically paradoxical sense of mutual interdependence existing between a helpless child-god and a protective parent-devotee.[89]

For our present purposes, this relationship had one important consequence and one crucial precondition. The consequence was that if the devotee is able to perfect his devotional practice, then 'Krishna, the omnipotent, the being within which all exists, will place himself in that *bhakta*'s [devotee's] control' just as Krishna placed himself in the control of Yashoda, becoming himself powerless in the process.[90] Krishna's utter vulnerability and his reliance upon Yashoda's supervision and guidance is perhaps best illustrated in the verse of Surdas, one of the greatest and most beloved Pushtimargi poets. Let me quote just two of Surdas's poems that use the event of the young Krishna's learning to walk in order to develop these themes.

[88] Richard Barz, *The Bhakti Sect Vallabhacarya* (Faridabad, Haryana: Thomson Press, 1976), p. 88.

[89] The ironic contrast, or what Bryant has called 'an epiphany', at the heart of this attitude is well represented in the verse of Surdas, one of the greatest and best-loved Pushtimargi poets.

[90] Barz, *Bhakti Sect*, p. 89. See also Kenneth E. Bryant, *Poems to the Child-God: Structures and Strategies in the Poetry of Surdas* (Berkeley: University of California Press, 1978), pp. 109–111.

Yashoda delights in watching him walk.
Clumping along on faltering feet,
    showing off when he sees his mother,
He walks as far as the doorstep,
    but returns again and again;
Stumbles and falls, but can't quite cross –
    and the gods are made to wonder:
For he makes in a second a million worlds,
    and destroys in a second a million more;
Yet he sits in the lap of a cowherd's wife
    as she teaches him to play,
And she leads him by the hand
    across that doorstep
        step by step by step.
The sight of the Lord of Sur
    stuns the minds of gods and men.[91]

What happened to that strength of yours, God?
The strength by which you plunged as the Fish into the sea,
    took back the Vedas, and slew the ancient demon;
The strength by which you took the mountain
    on your Tortoise-back,
        and thus contrived to churn the sea;
The strength by which you took upon your Boar's-tusks
    the Earth as if it were a flower;
The strength by which you split Hiranyakasipu's breast,
    and bestowed a wealth of kindness on your devotee;
The strength by which you once trapped Bali,
    and measured the Earth in just three steps;
The strength by which you took form
    to place upon the Brahmin the *tilak* of your protection;
The strength by which you cut off Ravana's heads,
    and made Vibhisana king at last;
The strength by which you broke the pride of Jambavat;
    the strength by which you heard the plea of the Earth.
Surdas says: Now you can't even cross the threshhold
    of your house!
        You just stand there; Lord, you don't *know*![92]

The precondition to achieving this exalted state of exercising control over Krishna, however, was that one's service to Krishna must be truly disinterested in the way that Yashoda's service to the infant Krishna was supremely unselfish. It could not be motivated by the hope of personal gain, on the one hand, or coercion, on the other. Instead it must be given

[91] Translated by Bryant, *Poems to the Child-God*, p. 161.
[92] Ibid., pp. 161–162.

freely and selflessly. Recall from chapter 3, it was precisely this attitude of selflessness by which Pushtimargis distinguished their understanding of service (seva) from other forms of worship (puja).

This same soteriology, with its attendant devotional practices, also informed Zalim Singh's unstinting service to the maharao in which his indulgent guardianship of the powerless (that is, infantalized) king was assimilated with the maternal affection of Yashoda for the infant Krishna. The foster parent-child relationship suggested itself, of course, in actual fact during the minority of Umed Singh when Zalim Singh was his guardian. During this time Zalim Singh assumed the appropriate parental roles: such as, encouraging the young maharao in his passion for the hunt, directing him in his religious practices, finding him a bride and arranging his wedding, and protecting him from dangerous enemies. Zalim Singh's maternal kinship with the maharao, which was foregrounded in his very title of 'mamaji', also enjoyed a special resonance with Yashoda's disinterested devotion insofar as, within the virilocal/patrilocal household of most north Indian upper castes, maternal kinship relations were generally perceived to be less burdened with self-interested agendas and, hence, freer and more genuinely affectionate.

The sense of 'protective guardianship' that was fostered during these formative years continued into Umed Singh's adulthood. It seems to have been personally felt by Umed Singh as revealed in the above-quoted letter of 1805 (when the maharao was fully 36 years old) in which he pleaded to Zalim Singh to return to Kota from Mewar and save the kingdom from feared invasion. But more importantly, the maharao's dependency on his prime minister was also reflected in numerous official representations of their relationship. This is most strikingly reflected in miniature paintings from Umed Singh's reign that stress, rather than hide, the maharao's utter reliance upon Zalim Singh. The maharao was rarely portrayed separately from Zalim Singh; rather, the overwhelming majority of portraits show him in the ubiquitous company of his prime minister who is always just behind, opposite, or to one side of the maharao.[93] This is very different from earlier royal portraiture in Kota where rulers often appeared alone or with a supporting cast(e) of characters that changed at bewildering speed as to render them individually anonymous.

Thus in some respects, Tod was not completely inaccurate when, shortly after the death of the maharao, he wrote that 'at the age of threescore and ten, Omed Sing found himself as much a minor as when his

[93] See, for example, Stuart Cary Welch, ed., *Gods, Kings, and Tigers: The Art of Kotah* (Munich: Prestel-Verlag, 1997), cat. nos 45, 46, 48, 49, 50, and (probably) 30.

dying father "placed him in the lap" of the Protector Zalim Sing'.[94] In adopting the language of guardianship, Tod quite likely was reflecting important aspects of the devotional language used by his informants to describe the relationship. However, Tod clearly did go awry in his interpretation of this root metaphor, especially as it informed his conclusion that, once the prime minister's guardianship extended beyond its natural term, his exercise of power became a wholly illegitimate usurpation. Instead we can now see that the graphic displays of the maharao's dependency upon his prime minister as exhibited in portraiture along with other similar public displays mentioned in the introduction to this chapter (his opulent villa within the very precincts of the maharao's palace, his mounted escort which was four times the size of the maharao's cavalcade, and so on) also resonated with important aspects of Vallabha doctrine in ways that upheld the prime minister's moral standing and established his legitimacy. These displays not only attested to Zalim Singh's spiritual attainment (insofar as the maharao had placed himself in his prime minister's complete control), but it also served as proof of Zalim Singh's unselfish concern with personal gain (insofar as he steadfastly refused to seize the throne for himself even though he clearly had the power to do so). Therefore, though most of Zalim Singh's colonial critics felt that he maintained the maharao on the gaddi as a charade of legitimate rule in order to cloak his *self-interested* (that is, illegitimate) exercise of power behind the scenes, Zalim Singh's actions were predicated upon the *explicit* foregrounding of the maharao's weakness, for it was precisely in this weakness that the rajrana's exercise of power could be shown to be truly *disinterested*.

[94] Tod, *Annals and Antiquities*, Volume 2, p. 552.

6 An incidental history of a supplementary article: Hindu kin(g)ship and early colonial rule

This chapter explores the breakdown, under early colonial rule, of the asymmetric, yet to some extent symbiotic, relationship that had developed during the previous fifty years between Maharao Umed Singh of Kota and his prime minister, Rajrana Zalim Singh. It shall suggest that the increasing tensions between the maharao and rajrana during the early years of colonial 'indirect rule' were clearly shaped by the way in which the British misconceived their relationship and enshrined that misconception in the treaty that brought Kota under British influence. But this chapter shall also argue that specific details of the conflict between maharao and rajrana also influenced the agenda of other local actors who initially helped fashion at least one critical aspect of the treaty and then creatively used it to suit their own projects and agenda, many of which went beyond the formal concerns of the treaty. The disturbances of the early years of colonial indirect rule, therefore, were not simply the consequence of the well-oiled machinery of the 'traditional' state breaking down under European (mis)management. Rather, ongoing political tensions and the contending aspirations of local leaders were projected onto new domains of action and political circumstances and contributed much to the shape and texture of these conflicts.

Prologue

On 26 December 1817, Maharaja Sheodan Singh, Sahukar Jivan Ram, and Lala Hool Chand signed a treaty on behalf of Maharao Umed Singh of Kota and Rajrana Zalim Singh with Charles Theophilus Metcalfe, then Resident at Delhi, that brought Kota under colonial 'indirect rule' and defined the terms of Kota's subordinate alliance with the British.[1] In

[1] C. U. Aitchison, *A Collection of Treaties, Engagements, and Sunnuds Relating to India and Neighboring Countries*, Volume III: *The Treaties, &c., Relating to the States in Rajpootana, Central India, and the Mediatized Chiefs in Central India and Malwa* (Calcutta: Foreign Office Press, 1876), no. 40, pp. 149–153. All citations from the treaty below are from this source.

April of the following year, Kota was grouped with the neighbouring states of Mewar and Bundi, signatories of similar treaties, to form the 'Mewar and Hadauti Political Agency' under the charge of James Tod, one of the early architects of British policy in the region and author of the *Annals and Antiquities of Rajast'han*.[2] Over the next fourteen years, these states in turn were incorporated, via several intermediate administrative configurations, into the 'Rajputana Agency' that initially included seventeen native states and covered, with the exception of Ajmer which fell under direct British administration, the entire area of contemporary Rajasthan.[3]

In bringing the kingdoms of Rajasthan under British protection, the treaties theoretically guaranteed the native rulers continued self-determination in domestic matters while imposing their absolute subordination to the British in foreign affairs. Thus although the tenth article of Kota's treaty stipulated that 'The Maha Rao, and his heirs and successors, shall remain absolute rulers of their country, and the civil and criminal jurisdiction of the British Government shall not be introduced into that principality',[4] most of the remaining articles specified the conditions of Kota's foreign relations with other native states.[5] In short, there were to be none, apart from those sanctioned by the British. Article Four: 'The Maha Rao... will always act in subordinate co-operation with the British Government, and acknowledge its supremacy, and will not henceforth have any connection with the chiefs and states with which the state of Kotah has been heretofore connected'. Article Five: 'The Maha Rao... will not enter into any negotiations with any state without the sanction of the British Government'. Article Six: 'The Maha Rao... will not commit aggressions on any one; and if any dispute accidentally arise with any one, proceeding either from acts of the Maha Rao, or acts of the other party, the adjustment of such disputes shall be submitted to the arbitration of the British Government'. And so on.

Although the treaties signed by each of the rulers of the Rajputana States bear remarkable similarities, each treaty also contained significant

[2] Although Tod's official headquarters were at Mewar's capital, Udaipur, the events related in this chapter caused him to spend most of 1820 and 1821 in Kota where his assistant (and cousin) Patrick Waugh was also stationed.

[3] For a step by step chronology of the formation of the Rajputana Agency, see Vijay Kumar Vashishtha, *Rajputana Agency, 1832–1858: A Study of British Relations with the States of Rajputana During the Period with Special Emphasis on the Role of Rajputana Agency* (Jaipur: Aalekh Publishers, 1978).

[4] By the late nineteenth century, this stipulation and similar provisions with other native states was largely a charade as attested in the six volumes and 2,600 pages of J. M. Macpherson's *British Enactments in Force in Native States* (Calcutta: Superintendent Government Printing, 1914 [1895]).

[5] Two additional articles specified the schedule of tribute to be paid by Kota to the British and the terms under which troops were to be furnished to the British.

provisions that were unique to it and that reflected the local political conditions within each of these states.[6] The treaties varied in terms of the obligations of the native rulers to their new British overlords in such matters, for example, as the amount and schedules of tribute payable to the colonial government or in the number of troops they were required to supply to the British and the conditions under which they were to be furnished.[7] They also varied in terms of the return obligations of the British concerning such matters as helping suppress recalcitrant jagirdars and settling other internal and external disputes. One area where Kota's treaty was unusual lay in its attention to the office of the prime minister. The Pax Britannica caught Kota at an 'anomalous' moment insofar as in addition to the hereditary ruler, Umed Singh, Kota had an enormously influential and powerful prime minister in Zalim Singh. A few weeks after agents of both governments had signed the treaty – but before the treaty had been formally ratified by the executives of either side – Zalim Singh, apparently at the urging of his eldest son Madho Singh, requested that a supplementary article be appended to the treaty.[8] This article, which initially was kept secret from the maharao, stipulated two things. First, it specified that Kishor Singh would succeed his father as maharao and, second, it guaranteed 'that the entire administration of the affairs of the principality shall be vested in Raj Rana Zalim Sing, and after him his eldest son, Koowar Madhoo Sing and his heirs, in regular succession and perpetuity'.

The East India Company had encountered this vexing phenomenon of powerful regents and puppet-kings in other parts of late eighteenth- and early nineteenth-century India and generally was loath to perpetuate the relationship, which it held to be inherently adversarial and, thereby, unstable.[9] In Mewar, for example, the Rawats of Salumber had a hereditary hold over the administration of that kingdom, but the company chose not to formally recognize their authority in treaties despite submissions to do so from the rawat.[10] Instead the company endeavoured to

[6] For a more detailed discussion of the differences amongst the various treaties, see Sukumar Bhattacharya, *The Rajput States and the East India Company from the Close of the Eighteenth Century to 1820* (New Delhi: Munshiram Manoharlal, 1972), pp. 229–235.

[7] Kota's tribute was initially fixed at about 290,000 rupees per year. Other states, such as Jaipur, were subjected to much higher tributes. Others were exempted altogether.

[8] For the suggestion that it was Madho Singh, rather than Zalim Singh, who sought the supplementary article, see James Tod, *Annals and Antiquities of Rajast'han*, Volume 2 (London), p. 565.

[9] For a representative statement of British attitudes concerning the stability of this relationship, see Charles Metcalfe, Secretary to the Government in the Political Department, to Captain James Tod, Political Agent to the Governor General in the Western Rajputana States, 6 October 1821, OIOC, BPC, 31/6 October 1821.

[10] Anil Chandra Banerjee, *The Rajput States and British Paramountcy* (New Delhi: Rajesh Publications, 1980), pp. 191–192.

consolidate power in the hands of those whom it saw as 'legitimate' sovereigns.[11]

With this end in mind, the company initially attempted to draw Zalim Singh away from Kota altogether by offering the prime minister sovereignty over some territory of his own in return for relinquishing his position in that state. As part of an opening gambit in January 1818, Tod offered Zalim Singh sovereignty over the four parganas of the Chaumahal that the British had acquired from Jaswant Rao Holkar in the Treaty of Mandisor.[12] Zalim Singh was well acquainted with these parganas as he had been farming them on muqata from Holkar since 1803 and they contained some of the richest opium gardens in all of western India, yeilding an annual revenue of about 310,000 rupees.[13] However, in a grand gesture of 'disinterested magnanimity', Zalim Singh confounded the British by insisting that these four parganas be united with the rest of Kota in the name of Maharao Umed Singh.[14] Of course, this humble generosity of spirit also ensured that Zalim Singh would keep his hands firmly on the far richer prize of Kota itself.

At about the same time that Zalim Singh turned down the offer of the Chaumahal, he put forward, at his son's behest, the request for the supplementary article to the treaty. The impetus impelling the British to accede in this instance to the rajrana's request was to secure his help in controlling the 'Pindaris', the pejorative of the time meaning 'freebooter',

[11] This policy in Rajasthan reflected a desire to (re)establish strong centrally controlled buffer states on what was, at that time, the company's long frontier with the large and still threateningly independent kingdom of Ranjit Singh. One of the rare cases where the company chose to maintain a 'titular' ruler in his state of relative powerlessness was at the Mughal Court in Delhi where the emperor previously had been under the effective control of Shinde. But in this case the company itself assumed the role of *maire-du-palais*. The company's maintenance of the puppet emperor may have reflected a desire to deflect local resistance to British rule by masking it in the cloak tradition. However, it is equally likely that it sprung from a desire to assuage that vocal segment of public opinion in England that was hostile to the company's expanding land empire in India. Similarly, within what had been the Maratha Empire, the British 'freed' the Raja of Satara from the 'thralldom' of his hereditary prime minister, the Peshwa. In this case, however, the restoration of the Raja to a small domain in western India was intended to divert public attention from the larger grab of land that the company had confiscated from the Peshwa which not only opened colonial Bombay up to the hinterland but it also struck at the economic heartland of one of the greatest indigenous rivals of the British of the time.

[12] Tod to Adam, 29 January 1818, OIOC, BC 1098/29690, 'Affairs of Kotah'.

[13] For the revenues of the Chaumahal, see Major James Caulfield, Political Agent in Harouti, to Major General David Ochterlony, Bart., Resident in Malwa and Rajputana, 15 June 1823, OIOC, BPC, 19/21 July 1823. Holkar had actually resumed these parganas from Zalim Singh some nine months earlier in 1817 when Zalim Singh supported the British during their operations against Holkar. Thus Zalim Singh should have been doubly pleased to recover them. See Tod to Swinton, OIOC, BSC, 20 February 1818.

[14] Tod to Metcalfe, 12 March 1820, 'Kotah Affairs', NAI, FDPC, 15/22 April 1820.

applied to irregular contingents of demobilized native troops that continued to raid British territories north of the Jamuna River from safe havens in Rajasthan and Malwa in the wake of the Third Anglo-Maratha War of 1816 to 1818.[15] At this time, European arms did not yet enjoy absolute command over every field of battle in South Asia (or at least, the British were not yet confident that they did). Thus the company's territorial expansion rested on a divide-and-rule strategy that, to a significant degree, made the co-optation of key native powers a major concomitant of conquest. Although the positive contribution of Kota's army to the Pindari campaign is still a matter of some dispute, [16] it was nevertheless important to the company that Kota's roughly 22,000-man strong army, at least, did not lend its support to the Pindaris. Moreover, it is also clear that Kota had strategic geographical and logistical consequence insofar as the kingdom was at the epicentre of these operations and was the region's principal breadbasket.[17] As Zalim Singh controlled the largest stake in Kota's lucrative grain market, his allegiance was absolutely vital to the provisioning of British-led troops in the field.

For his part, Zalim Singh had a somewhat more ambivalent attitude toward the Pindaris than the British. On the one hand, Pindari troops occasionally destroyed (or appropriated) standing crops as they moved through Kota's territory. On the other, Zalim Singh himself employed Pindaris as military auxiliaries in his own army. Use of these troops was crucial to Zalim Singh's rise to power in Kota, and he continued to employ them throughout his career. In addition to their military labour, Zalim Singh also welcomed the influx of cash and cattle that they brought from their raids to Kota's established markets at such places as Baran and Shergarh.[18] The British were therefore keen to make sure that Zalim Singh did not forge a common cause with these forces.[19] In order to keep the Rajrana firmly allied to their cause, the British agreed to the

[15] For a concise statement of the company's aims in engaging in these treaties with Kota see, Francis, Marquis of Hastings, Governor General, to Court of Directors, 19 May 1818 and 1 March 1820, OIOC, BC 1098/29690, 'Affairs of Kotah'.

[16] John Sutherland reported that, during the operations against the Pindaris, Kota placed only 500 cavalry, 1,000 infantry, and four guns at James Tod's disposal, and 'it does not appear they rendered any service of importance'. Tod, on the other hand, gave a much more generous appraisal of Zalim Singh's contributions. See John Sutherland, *Sketches of the Relations Subsisting between the British Government in India and Different Native States* (Jaipur: Publication Scheme, 1988 [1837]), p. 81.

[17] Tod, *Annals and Antiquities*, Volume 2, pp. 555–556 and 564–565.

[18] C. A. Bayly, *Rulers, Townsmen, and Bazaars: North Indian Society in the Age of British Expansion, 1770–1870* (Cambridge: Cambridge University Press, 1983), pp. 28–30.

[19] See Tod to John Adam, Secretary to Government in the Political Department, 29 January 1818, OIOC, BC 1098/29690, 'Affairs of Kotah', for British fears concerning a potential alliance between Zalim Singh and Daulat Rao Shinde that would be hostile to the British.

supplementary article. Thus from the very outset, the treaty between Kota and the company was a negotiated document and, although the relative strengths of the contracting parties were by no means equal, it is nonetheless clear that the impetus behind the most distinctive feature of the treaty was provided as much by Zalim Singh as by the British.

A brief history of a small war

For nearly two years after the treaty was signed, the situation in Kota remained remarkably quiescent. Umed Singh was isolated as before and initial intelligence concerning his eldest son and presumed heir, Kishor Singh, indicated that he too preferred to lead a secluded life well removed from the affairs of state.[20] But then in November 1819 Maharao Umed Singh fell ill and after a few days 'Lord Rama called' (*ram kaho*; that is, 'death knocked'), and Kishor Singh mounted the gaddi. This was followed, a few months later, by the venerable Zalim Singh suffering a stroke. Although he made a substantial recovery from his 'bout of palsy' and lived for a further four years, relations between maharao and rajrana quickly deteriorated. A series of confrontations between the two broke out over control of the kingdom's military, judicial, and revenue apparatuses and, before long, Kishor Singh found himself in the unusual position of engaging in acts of 'civil disobediance' that eventually culminated in an armed 'insurrection' against his own prime minister.

The unrest, which lasted about eighteen months in total, fell into two broad phases of about nine months. During the first phase, Kishor Singh made repeated attempts to 'interfere' in the administration of the kingdom. In particular, the maharao contested the prime minister's right to make appointments to key ministerial 'portfolios' without his full consent, and he repeatedly complained to James Tod on this account. Tod, however, referring to the provisions of the treaty, steadfastly backed the prime minister's prerogative to make these specific appointments and to exercise control over the executive more generally.

By June 1820, the maharao was completely frustrated, and he and several hundred (mostly) Hada Rajput supporters blockaded themselves in the city palace, refusing the prime minister entry (the rajrana's own haveli and many 'government offices' were inside the city palace complex). Zalim Singh cut off supplies to the palace and after a week the maharao was forced out for lack of food and fodder. When James Tod promised to guarantee Kishor Singh's 'dignity, comforts, and happiness'

[20] Sukumar Bhattacharya, *The Rajput States and the East India Company from the Close of the Eighteenth Century to 1820* (New Delhi: Munshiram Manoharlal, 1972), p. 255.

while making it clear that he could do nothing to change the rajrana'a administrative power, the maharao seemed satisfied and a short-lived reconciliation with the rajrana was effected. But by late December, Kishor Singh had once again blockaded himself in the city palace with about 500 followers (and considerably more provisions). Again a stand-off ensued, during which time the maharao attempted to foment 'rebellion' among the regular, standing army. Although Kishor Singh was only able to convince part of one of Kota's fourteen infantry battalions to join his cause, Zalim Singh nevertheless became alarmed by these moves, and he ordered his artillery to direct intimidating fire *over* the palace hoping to frighten the maharao, flush him out, and separate him from his supporters. However, in the dead of the night of 26 December 1820, the maharao and a couple of hundred Hada Rajputs slipped out of the palace, eluded the rajrana sentries and fled to neighbouring Bundi.

For the next nine months, Kishor Singh remained in exile, seeking to rally support for his cause outside the kingdom. But during his absence, Zalim Singh continued to profess his loyalty to Kishor Singh, blaming the maharao's belligerency and flight on the influence of evil advisors and, in an act recalling Bharat's loyalty to Ram during his fourteen-year-exile in the *Ramayan*, placed a pair of the maharao's sandals on the vacant gaddi, declaring that he would receive the wisdom to rule from them.[21] The rajrana's actions appear to have had some effect as Patrick Waugh noted that the maharao's absence from Kota was greeted calmly by the city's residents. In a report sent to Tod just one month after the maharao's flight, Waugh wrote:

> Kotah continues in the most perfect tranquillity. No feeling of popular attachment or sympathy toward the Maha Rao is manifest by any class of its inhabitants. Indeed the perfect security of person and property which under the long and equitable administration of the Raj Rana they have enjoyed, and which has only been interrupted by the threatened excesses of those inimical to his authority, renders the existence of such a feeling extremely improbable.[22]

During his exile Kishor Singh first called on several fellow native rulers in eastern Rajasthan (notably Bundi, Karauli, and Bharatpur). Although they were generous with their *ziyafat* (hospitality), they offered little in terms of material support (probbly as a result of stern warnings by Tod

[21] Suryamalla Mishran, *Vamshabhaskar* (Jodhpur, 1899), p. 4100. Kaviraja Lakshmandan, '*Maharao Shatru Shalji Bahadur ki vamsa prashasti*'. Unpublished manuscript belonging to Kaviraja Mahipat Singh of Kotri, Kota. Typescript copy, under the title of '*Kota rajya ke hastalikhita itihas ki pratilipi*', in the Brijraj Bhawan Palace Library, Kota; p. 75.

[22] Captain Patrick Waugh, Assistant in Kota, to Tod, 29 January 1821, OIOC, BPC, 7/1 March 1821.

not to assist the maharao).[23] But Kishor Singh pinned his principal hopes on swaying opinion in Delhi and, aiming to 'go over Tod's head', he travelled there in May to plead his case directly with the British Resident, David Ochterlony, who had recently replaced Metcalfe. At the same time Kishor Singh sent a vakil, Mirza Muhammad Ali, to Calcutta to make presentations to the then Governor-General, the Marquis of Hastings. In the early summer both Ochterlony and the Marquis of Hastings received petitions from Kishor Singh to redress his situation and grant him full control over the kingdom's administration in preference to Zalim Singh.[24] However, both the Resident and the Governor General refused to consider the maharao's petitions and both men ordered the maharao to return to Kota where, if he had any complaints, they could be lodged with James Tod in accordance with the East India Company chain of command.[25] Despite these rebuffs, Kishor Singh remained in Delhi throughout the monsoon months during which time he secured a number of loans from various local bankers (including several from the Residency's own native treasurer!), as a result of which he began to attract a substantial following from the large pool of recently demobilized troops still roaming the region. During the summer, the maharao's camp expanded from a few hundred followers to 2,000, and in mid-September Kishor Singh decided to leave Delhi for Kota, attracting even greater numbers of supporters along the way.

Finally, on 1 October 1821 Kishor Singh and his army crossed the frontier into Kota and the rebellion culminated with a pitched battle near the pargana headquarters of Mangrol, some 80 kilometres northeast of the capital. Here Kishor Singh and his following, which by then numbered some 8,000 troops, were decisively defeated by Zalim Singh's army, which was further fortified by two battalions of British-led infantry and six squadrons of British-led cavalry.[26] The battle claimed the life of

[23] See, for example, 'Intellegence received from Captain Tod's Akbur Nuvees at Boondi', tr., 24 and 29 January 1821, enclosure in Waugh to Tod, 29 January 1821, OIOC, BPC, 7/1 March 1821 and 'Reports from the Raj Rana's Hiccarras', enclosure in Waugh to Tod, 5 March 1821, OIOC, BC 1100/29693, 'Affairs of Kotah'.

[24] For example, see Kishor Singh to Ochterlony, tr., letter received 7 May 1821, OIOC, BPC, 9/9 June 1821 and three letters from Kishor Singh (via Mirza Muhammad Ali) to the Governor General: 1) letter received 4 May 1821, OIOC, BPC, 12/9 June 1821; 2) letter received 17 May 1821, OIOC, BPC, 10/9 June 1821; and 3) letter received 19 May 1821, OIOC, BPC, 11/9 June 1821.

[25] H. T. Prinsep to Mirza Muhammad Ali, 9 June 1821, OIOC, BPC, 13/9 June 1821.

[26] For this estimate of the size of Kishor Singh's army, see Kaviraja Lakshmandan, '*Maharao Shatru Shalji Bahadur ki vamsha prashasti*'. Uncatalogued manuscript in the Thikana Kotri *daftar,* Kota. Uncatalogued typescript copy, under the title of '*Kota rajya ke hastalikhita itihas ki pratilipi*', in the Brijraj Bhawan Palace Library, Kota; p. 74. For other estimates, see Tod to George Swinton, Esq., Secretary to Government in the Political Department, 2 October 1821, OIOC, BC 1101/29694, 'Affairs of Kotah,' as well as Southerland, *Sketches*, p. 82. In all, British-led troops comprised about a third of

the maharao's youngest brother, Prithvi Singh, but the maharao himself survived and retreated from Mangrol across the Parbati River into territory controlled by Shinde. Much grieved by the loss of his brother, Kishor Singh dismissed his remaining troops before seeking sanctuary with some 150 servants and followers at Nathadwara in Mewar.[27]

After the battle the British contemplated deposing the maharao for sedition. But when James Tod broached the idea with Zalim Singh, the rajrana pleaded that the maharao should be allowed to return to Kota's gaddi. In showing clemency to Kishor Singh, the rajrana argued, 'the fame of [the British] sirkar will be exalted… and my own reputation consulted'.[28] Thus despite the recent events, Zalim Singh continued to see himself (and wanted himself seen) as a guardian of the maharao rather than as his vanquisher. The British were perplexed by Zalim Singh's request but heeded it and, by year's end, the maharao was permitted to return to Kota where once again he was seated on the gaddi.[29] This gesture, however, did not restore Kota to tranquillity. Tensions between the maharao and the rajrana became increasingly uncontrollable over the next eighteen years during which time Kota was to become in England one of the most high profile of India's 'indirectly ruled' Native States. It became a *cause célèbre* in the ongoing debate concerning the company's evolving status as a land-based ruling power in India. As a result thousands of pages of documents were transferred to London for closer scrutiny by the Board of Control. Nevertheless, ill-will periodically unsettled the remainder of Kishor Singh's reign and the first eleven years of the reign of his nephew and successor Maharao Ram Singh (r. 1827–66) as well as the administrations of three rajranas – Zalim Singh (d. 1824), his son Madho Singh (d. 1834), and grandson Madan Singh. Despite the tensions it was not until 1838 that the British successfully segregated the contending parties by creating a separate Princely State – named Jhalawar after the rajrana's clan – for Madan Singh and his heirs by taking some seventeen parganas from Kota's southern and eastern territories.

Colonial contradictions

It is clear that the conditions of the treaty, although intended by the British to stabilize the relationship between the maharao and rajrana by

the force arrayed against Kishor Singh. Zalim Singh himself commanded 8 battalions of infantry and 14 *paigas* (squadrons) of cavalry.

27 M. L. Sharma, *Kota rajya ka itihas* (Kota: Kota Printing Press, 1939) pp. 574–575.

28 Tod to Swinton, 31 October 1821, OIOC, BPC, 36/24 November 1821.

29 The maharao's reinstallation took place on 31 December 1821.

standardizing and regularizing it, in fact had the opposite effect. Whereas previously the relationship between ruler and prime minister combined elements of separation and 'incommensurability' within certain domains of action with forms of symbiosis in others, the treaty increasingly forced the maharao and rajrana into a more highly competitive and directly confrontational environment. The principal effect of the treaty was to end the traditional latitude that existed within the open-ended political system(s) of the precolonial era whereby multiple and overlapping sovereignties permitted individuals to establish their authority simultaneously in several different, non-congruent locations. Instead the colonial treaties fashioned spatially discrete, territorially defined state-formations with unitary hierarchies of command whose foreshortened political horizons increasingly brought the maharao and the rajrana into more direct, head-to-head forms of competition.

Two aspects of the treaty in particular conspired to create these new, spatially limited 'unitary states' in Rajasthan. First, as indicated in the introduction to this chapter, the treaty explicitly prohibited formal political relations between indigenous powers excepting those that were *sanctioned and articulated* by the British. The principal goal of this provision was to sever all vertical linkages between 'little kingdoms', such as Kota, and larger indigenous political formations, such as the Maratha Empire. The seventh and eighth articles of Kota's treaty with the British respectively stipulated that 'The tribute heretofore paid by the principality of Kotah to the Mahratta chiefs, for instance, the Peshwa, Sindia, Holkar, and Pawar, shall be paid at Dihlee to the British Government…' and that 'No other power shall have any claim to tribute from the principality of Kotah…' In ending Kota's subordination to the Marathas the British also negated an important basis for larger collective forms of political identification and mass mobilization within the region.

Second, in order to more effectively break the political bonds linking various indigenous powers, the British simultaneously oversaw the transfer of significant amounts of territory among these leaders in order to separate out the interlocking and layered rights to the land often held by different leaders. Again the principal targets of these land transfers were the Marathas who in addition to their claims to tribute from the Rajput kingdoms also ceded control over most of the territories they had a hand in directly administering in Rajasthan. Malhar Rao Holkar was put under a formal obligation by the Treaty of Mandisor, signed in January 1818, to relinquish to the British all his Rajasthani possessions. Similar, but more informal, pressures were applied to Daulat Rao Shinde to do likewise. The most important directly administered territory that Holkar relinquished was Ajmer (which he ceded to the British), but he also relinquished control over a large number of other land holdings to various

Rajasthani rulers including the Nawab of Tonk, the Rao Raja of Bundi, and the Maharana of Udaipur. Initially, Kota was also a beneficiary of these transfers. The Chaumahal, for example, was transferred from Holkar to Umed Singh of Kota in early 1818. Soon thereafter Holkar also ceded to the British eight additional villages within Kota which likewise were transferred to Kota's authority.[30] However, Kota was also on the losing end of this effort to tidy the political map of Rajasthan. For instance, Tod forced Kota to relinquish to the Maharana of Udaipur the *muqata* of three particularly large and prosperous *parganas* that the rajrana held in Mewar. One of these *parganas* – Jahazpur – yielded an annual income in excess of 100,000 rupees.

It is hard to determine the net financial implications of these land transfers for Kota, but what is clear is that new types of states were generated in the process. Within a short time, more or less unitary, but relatively limited, states had been fashioned in southern Rajasthan out of the pre-existing, interlaced and overlapping sovereignties that loosely linked large tracts of territory and large numbers of people. The rajrana's sphere of operations became increasingly restricted to Kota – no longer could he aspire to establish his authority at a more general level encompassing several locations within a larger political arena. As Kota became the common ground of political action for the 'administrative' and 'titular' authorities, competition between them became more acute.

Along with these transformations at the institutional level, the treaty also worked a vital epistemological change that helped cut the conceptual relationship previously binding the rajrana's authority to the maharao insofar as the British became guarantors of the rajrana's authority. This move facilitated the unyoking of the rajrana's authority from his attitude of 'maternal devotion' towards the maharao, enabling him to establish his authority in an idiom that was increasingly self-constituting without any reference to the Hada dynasty. Curiously, however, even after the imposition of colonial indirect rule, Zalim Singh himself seems to have been disinclined to change what had become a lifelong habit of expressing his authority in terms of his 'maternal devotion' towards the maharao. One witnesses the rajrana's continuity of attitude in this regard in such acts as placing Kishor Singh's sandals on the gaddi during the maharao's flight from Kota and interceding with James Tod to have the maharao reinstated to the gaddi after the Battle of Mangrol. These actions suggest that the colonial epistemological shift was more 'enabling' than 'over-determining'. But Zalim Singh's eldest son, Madho Singh, who most probably authored the supplementary article in the first place, quickly seized upon

[30] Tod to Adam, 19 January 1821, OIOC, BC 1098/29690, 'Affairs of Kotah'.

the possibilities in it in order to redefine his relationship with the kingdom's 'titular sovereign'. This redefinition first became apparent in Madho Singh's deteriorating relationship with the maharao's eldest son and heir Kishor Singh. During the last years of Maharao Umed Singh's life, Tod noted mounting tensions between Madho Singh and Kishor Singh.

> Placed very early by the Regent [Zalim Singh] in a situation of great control, the command of all the forces of the state, he [Madho Singh] had funds at his disposal with which he fulfilled all he had a desire for. His gardens, his horses, his boats were all in a style to *excite envy of the sons of his sovereign* who had none of these conveyances.[31]

This rivalry became even more overt after Umed Singh died. Symptomatic of these strained relations were a series of disputes between Madho Singh and the new Maharao Kishor Singh over the display of royal regalia and the performance of other ritual acts associated with the royal court. British intelligence reported, for instance, that Madho Singh attempted to restrict Kishor Singh's use of the *mahi-o-maratib* to those occasions when Madho Singh was also present, thereby creating an ambiguity as to whom the regalia appertained.[32] Moreover, unlike his father, Madho Singh began to stay away from important royal ceremonies at which he was normally expected to engage in acts of ritual submission to the maharao, such as at Dasahra when he 'served' the maharao by carrying his sword and shield.[33]

Yet if the civil unrest in Kota during the early years of colonial 'indirect rule' ultimately manifested itself as a dispute between the ruler and his prime minister in which the stipulations of the treaty with the British were to play a major role, it is equally clear that the strife was not limited to this axis of confrontation. Nor did it even initially manifest itself as that. Folded into this dispute were several other conflicts about which the British were only dimly aware (if at all) and whose origins lay elsewhere, but which provided much of the drive and impetus for the rebellion. It is to these local agendas that we now turn our attention.

Other actors, other agendas

In his reflections on the rebellion in the *Annals and Antiquities of Rajast'han*, James Tod concluded that Kishor Singh's revolt was a broadly

[31] Tod to Metcalfe, 28 March 1820, 'Kotah Affairs', NAI, FDPC, 16/22 April 1820 (emphasis added).

[32] Major General David Ochterlony, Bart., Resident in Malwa and Rajputana, to Swinton, 3 October 1822, OIOC, BSC, 1/7 December 1822.

[33] Major James Caulfield, Political Agent in Harouti, to Ochterlony, 1 November 1822, OIOC, BSC, 2/7 December 1822.

based, popular uprising in support of a legitimate and aggrieved sovereign against his usurping and despotic prime minister. He described the maharao's cause as enjoying 'general sympathy, amounting to enthusiasm,... not only from chief and peasant within the bounds of Harouti, and the foreign mercenary army raised and maintained by the Regent, but from the neighbouring princes and nobles'.[34] The final advance of the maharao and his army towards Kota in the early autumn of 1821 was portrayed in almost millenarian terms.

> As [Kishor Singh] proceeded, this force increased, and he reached the Chumbul, toward the end of the monsoon 1821, with about three thousand men. Having crossed the river, he issued his summons in a language neither to be misunderstood nor disobeyed by a Rajpoot; he conjured them by their allegiance to join his cause... and the call was obeyed by every Hara of the country. His conduct afforded the most powerful illustration of the Rajpoot's theory of fidelity, for even those closely connected by ties of blood and by every species of benefit, withdrew from the Regent, to whom they owed everything, in order to join their hereditary and lawful prince, whom some had never seen, and of whom they knew nothing.[35]

Although Tod rooted Kishor Singh's support in deep-seeded, long-held notions of 'fidelity' between king and subject, it is curious that this support did not manifest itself earlier. Tod himself noted that 'previous thereto, no voice was raised against [Zalim Singh's] usurpation and crime' which had been long 'looked upon... in silence'.[36] Tod went on to attribute, rather superciliously, the sudden change in popular attitudes towards the rajrana's regime to the regeneration of the country's 'moral aspect' that British rule had brought about!

If Tod concluded that Kota's civil disturbances stemmed first and foremost from popular outrage over a deeply agonistic relationship between an aggrieved sovereign and a usurping prime minister (a relationship that had been enshrined unwittingly within a flawed treaty with the British), his own careful descriptions of events reveal that the disturbances were largely fuelled, at least during the early stages, by yet other fault-lines of political discord that did not initially pit the maharao against the rajrana. In other words, if the conditions of the treaty were a 'necessary' cause predisposing conflict between the maharao and rajrana, they cannot be seen as a 'sufficient' cause. This situation is most graphically made in the diverging attitudes of Zalim Singh and Madho Singh towards Kishor Singh (as discussed above, Zalim Singh continued to express his 'maternal devotion' toward the maharao while Madho Singh found this increasingly hard to do). Similarly, Kishor Singh betrayed a considerably ambivalent

[34] Tod, *Annals and Antiquities*, Volume 2, p. 563.
[35] Ibid., p. 573.
[36] Ibid., p. 563.

attitude towards Zalim Singh. Tod's own writing often depicts Kishor Singh as a reluctant and hesitant leader of the rebellion. Throughout the entire course of the disturbances, the maharao remained loath to ever fully demonize the rajrana. For instance, Kishor Singh's condemnations of the way Zalim Singh had gained control over the apparatus of state were tempered by expressions of his 'every confidence in Nanajee Zalim Singh', and until a few days before the climactic Battle of Mangrol, Kishor Singh continued to propose various formulae of reconciliation with the rajrana.[37] This ambivalence perplexed (and enraged) Tod who could not understand why Kishor Singh would not be more decisive in his opposition to his prime minister.

It appears that Kishor Singh's belligerence towards Zalim Singh was driven, at least at first, by two other individuals – Prithvi Singh (Kishor Singh's youngest brother) and, especially, Gordhan Das (Zalim Singh's own younger son). In fact, Tod himself identified these two men as Kishor Singh's chief counsellors who were constantly in his company 'moulding the new Maharao to their will'.[38] Both of these individuals had their own agendas which fell beyond the parameters of the treaty and which they attempted to channel through the maharao.

Prithvi Singh's immediate ambition apparently concerned the acquisition of a jagir, his lack of which he held the rajrana directly responsible for. As a younger son of Maharao Umed Singh, Prithvi Singh would have expected to receive, as per established custom, an estate sometime during the lifetime of his father or at his death. Indeed Bishan Singh, Umed Singh's second son, had been granted the jagir of Anta, initially worth 25,000 rupees. But Prithvi Singh did not receive a similar grant, and he lived on the largess of his eldest brother.[39] Exactly why Prithvi Singh was not granted an estate is still somewhat unclear. In all likelihood, it reflects the hand of Zalim Singh who not only was reluctant to see additional lands alienated from the royal fisc,[40] but who also probably wanted to fan discord among the three royal brothers. Kishor Singh certainly complained of this sort of jealousy and, unsurprisingly, Bishan Singh did not

[37] Kishor Singh to James Tod, tr., 16 September 1821, OIOC, BPC, 12/6 October 1821.

[38] Tod, *Annals and Antiquities*, Volume 2, p. 562. It was not just James Tod who saw Prithvi Singh as the instigator behind Kishor Singh's actions. Chand Khan, Tod's agent in Kishor Singh's camp during the period immediately prior to the Battle of Mangrol, for example, also described Prithvi Singh as 'the chief disturber'. See Chand Khan, *vakil*, to James Tod, tr., 10 September 1821, letter attached to James Tod to George Swinton, 18 February 1822, OIOC, BPC, 12/16 April 1822.

[39] Lakshmandan, '*Vamsha prashasti*', p. 73. Tod claimed that both Bishan Singh and Prithvi Singh had received estates valued at 25,000 rupees from their father, but this assertion is apparently incorrect. See Tod, *Annals and Antiquities*, Volume 2, p. 560.

[40] As it was, Bishan Singh's jagir of 25,000 rupees was relatively small. Traditionally younger brothers to the heir to the throne were granted jagirs worth four times that amount.

join his brothers during the rebellion.[41] Instead, he remained with Zalim Singh hoping, perhaps, that events would ultimately place him on the gaddi in preference to his elder brother.

Whatever the case, Prithvi Singh's frustration over his 'estateless-ness' gave him a common cause with a number of the old regime whose jagirs had been resumed by Zalim Singh during the previous fifty years. Prithvi Singh rallied a group of these jagirdars, numbering 500 or 600, behind the maharao and they pressed him to take an ever more confrontational attitude towards the prime minister. Ironically, Tod noted that the core of these jagirdari supporters was the group of Rajputs who had participated in the Conspiracy of Mohsian some twenty years earlier.[42] In other words, these jagirdars had long-standing grievances against Zalim Singh going back two decades (and more) before the formal onset of colonial rule.

Of potentially greater concern, owing to his connections to Kota's large standing army, however, was the support of Gordhan Das for Kishor Singh. Gordhan Das was Zalim Singh's younger son by a Muslim concubine (*khawas*) and was by all accounts a capable and ambitious leader.[43] Earlier in his career, his father had appointed him to several important military and administrative posts. As a young man, for example, he had been sent for military instruction with French generals in the employ of the Marathas and, upon completing this training, he took an active role in his father's reorganization of Kota's army. In the process, he became particularly closely associated with the elite Tilanga Paltan, which he personally drilled and commanded.[44] By 1820, he also held the administrative post of *pradhan*, the ministerial 'portfolio' which, in Kota, oversaw the kingdom's lucrative grain and cattle departments.

Gordhan Das's advocacy of Kishor Singh's cause was clearly informed by a looming succession dispute with his older half-brother. In fact, Tod's very first reports of troops being mobilized for the purposes of civil unrest in Kota did not involve Kishor Singh at all, but focused on the rajrana's two sons, both of whom were amassing supporters in spring of 1820 shortly after Zalim Singh's debilitating stroke. In a dispatch of April of that year, Tod warned Charles Metcalfe of the brewing troubles:

> With the security of the times the Raj Rana at various periods within these few months disbanded several thousand men – the whole had been re-entertained in secret by his son Madhoo Sing and corresponding preparations had been made

[41] Regarding the bad blood between Kishor Singh and Bishan Singh, see Kishor Singh to David Ochterlony, tr., OIOC, BPC, 16/24 February 1821 and Kishor Singh to Marquis of Hastings, tr., letter received 4 May 1821, OIOC, BPC, 12/9 June 1821.

[42] Tod to Metcalfe, 18 March 1820, 'Kotah Affairs', NAI, FDPC, 17/22 April 1820.

[43] Tod, *Annals and Antiquities*, Volume 2, p. 562.

[44] Shastri, *Zalim Singh*, p. 292.

by Gordhun Das, who had taken advantage of a situation he holds of the whole grain Department of the State, to purchase horses and military equipment to a considerable amount for the occasion so that he has at his disposal a considerable party.[45]

In anticipation of his father's final demise, Madho Singh also had begun to remove from office many powerful individuals who had risen to prominence under his father's administration but whose loyalties to him (as opposed to his half-brother) were uncertain. In a letter to David Ochterlony, Kishor Singh himself detailed precisely the way in which Madho Singh methodically gained control over all the most important departments and administrative offices in the kingdom during the last years of Umed Singh's reign.

In the time of Maha Rao Sahib Ommeid Sing, [Zalim Singh] submitted his request to the Maha Rao that he would be pleased to confer the office of Purdhan (or Vizeer) upon his younger son Gordhun Doss. The control of the forces and arsenal, etc. was then possessed by Duleel Khan; Girdhur Lal had the business of the Revenue collections while Kaloo Ram and his son Sheo Buksh had charge of the public records and the judicial functions were performed under Zalim Singh's control by his elder son Madhoo Singh. During this period, Girdhur Lal died and Madhoo Singh represented … that the office of Purdhan having been bestowed on Gordhun Doss, if the appointment of Juhseel [revenue minister] should be given to another he would get nothing by remaining in the country. So after strenuous applications, the Maha Rao conferred on [Madho Singh] the Juhseeldaree. Duleel Khan afterwards died also and … upon this Madhoo Singh … forwarded a representation to the Raj Rana Zalim Singh, saying … that … the Rao must give him control of the troops also, which was afterwards granted to Madhoo Singh. As Kaloo Ram and his son remained in charge of the public records he first confined them and pretended imputations of sorcery and then deprived them of life. With Gordhun Doss even, the younger son, who had but a single appointment of Purdhan he raised dissension.[46]

Significantly, it was precisely the prospect of this dispute between brothers (and Madho Singh's concomitant desire to root out potential supporters of his brother within the administration) that appears to have been at the root of Madho Singh's request for the supplementary article in the first instance. Although Tod and other British commentators saw this clause as an attempt to regulate the relationship between the offices of maharao and rajrana, the available evidence suggests that Madho Singh wanted this article more to secure his position vis-à-vis his younger brother than to secure his position vis-à-vis the maharao. Recall from

[45] James Tod to Charles Metcalfe, 12 March 1820, 'Kotah Affairs', NAI, FDPC, 15/22 April 1820.

[46] Kishor Singh to Ochterlony, tr., 4 May 1821, OIOC, BPC, 12/9 June 1821.

chapter 2 that although notions of primogenitural succession to office certainly existed in Rajasthan, they were never firmly fixed as a primary principle of practice. And although Tod made much of Gordhan Das's 'illegitimate, half-caste' birth in order to further discount his right to his father's office, his status did not necessarily bar him from holding the prime ministership within indigenous practice. Kota's history is replete with many people of similar status holding this post, and some of them even achieved 'full-blooded' Rajput status as a result of their service in similar capacities.[47]

This ongoing dispute between the rajrana's sons explains two curious features about the supplementary article to the treaty. The first is that the request for the supplementary article originated with Madho Singh rather than Zalim Singh. As Tod himself pointed out Zalim Singh felt sufficiently secure in his relationship with the maharao that he felt no need to have his office guaranteed by the treaty.[48] Madho Singh, on the other hand, did have a history of conflict with his half-brother and the treaty was intended principally to make sure that he succeeded to his father's office. Thus, the one feature about which the supplementary article is absolutely unambiguous is the order of succession to office. Unlike the main body of the treaty in which succession is exhorted to be 'regular' but without specifying what constitutes 'regular', the supplementary article specifically mentions that Madho Singh is to succeed his father just as Kishor Singh was to succeed his.[49] In other words, Madho Singh's supplementary article was principally designed to establish the principle of primogeniture in the succession to office.

Second, and by way of contrast with its clarity concerning succession, the supplementary article is highly ambiguous with regard to the relative spheres of competence of the offices of maharao and musahib-i-ala. It merely assigns sovereignty to the maharao and administrative authority to the rajrana. The relative status and hierarchical relationship between sovereignty and administrative authority are nowhere explicitly spelled out and, as we shall see shortly, the supplementary article was certainly capable of several interpretations including, contrary to the British view,

[47] The most famous example of this change in status is Rao Ram Singh of Kota's youngest brother. In some chronicles this brother appears as Santok Singh Khawas while in others he appears as the 'full-blooded' Rajput, Arjun Singh. At this point it is still unclear what service Santok Singh did to merit his 'elevation', but one may conjecture it was connected to his support of Ram Singh during his succession dispute with their eldest brother Bishan Singh (see figure 1).

[48] Tod, *Annals and Antiquities*, Volume 2, p. 559.

[49] The supplementary article was unusual insofar as it identified the heirs by name. Although the British may have assumed that primogeniture was the governing norm concerning the succession to high office, the treaties of subsidiary alliance with other rulers in Rajasthan, including the Maharao of Kota, did not specify the heirs nominally.

that administrative authority should be subordinate to sovereignty. In any case, the reason for this ambiguity lies with the fact that the supplementary article was not meant to address this issue in the first place (indeed it was never intended to be seen by the maharao). Rather it was meant to address the problem of succession. From Madho Singh's perspective, then, the supplementary article was initially designed to serve a purpose different from that understood by the British. Moreover, the article served that purpose well for in June 1820, three months into the unrest, Tod got fed up with Gordhan Das's 'influence' over Kishor Singh and had him exiled to Delhi thereby (unwittingly) removing from the scene Madho Singh's greatest rival to office and assuring his succession. This coup on behalf of Madho Singh was effected through Tod's intervention but without him ever being fully aware of the range of rivalries and issues that were involved.

Thus, in prospect, the treaty was more prejudicial towards Gordhan Das than it was towards Kishor Singh and, according to Tod, it was Gordhan Das who first brought the supplementary article to Kishor Singh's attention and who pushed Kishor Singh to demand its abrogation or, at least, reinterpretation. This course of action appeared to be Gordhan Das's best hope to hold onto the *pradhani*, if not eventually succeed to the office of prime minister. However, once the treaty became known to Kishor Singh, he and his supporters breathed new life into it by putting it to new uses, to which we now turn our attention.

Lost and found in the translation

Curiously, once Gordhan Das made Kishor Singh aware of the supplementary article to the treaty the maharao demanded the abrogation neither of the treaty as a whole nor of the supplementary article in itself. He certainly had grounds for doing so: that the treaty was concluded by illegitimate means insofar as Maharao Umed Singh was never informed of the supplementary article and, in all likelihood, he never even knew of the original treaty itself. Several months before the Battle of Mangrol, for example, Kishor Singh stated in a letter to Mirza Muhammad Ali, his agent in Calcutta, that 'my father knew nothing of the treaty and never signed it nor sealed it, his seal having been with Zalim Sing' and he later added that he himself did not learn of the treaty's existence until well after the fact.[50]

Instead of contesting the treaty's overall validity, Kishor Singh decided to accept it but aimed to reinterpret its provisions to suit his own ends. This tactic had two prongs or dimensions. The first was to argue for a

[50] Kishor Singh to Mirza Muhammad Ali, tr., n.d., OIOC, BPC, 61/9 February 1822

reinterpretation of the treaty that would align British power firmly behind him. For Kishor Singh, the terms of the treaty, even including the disputed supplementary article, did not guarantee the prime minister with absolute control over the apparatus of governance. Nor did it prohibit the maharao from being involved in the active administration of the kingdom. What was rendered in English as a separation of 'titular sovereignty' and 'administrative authority' was rendered in the Hindi translation of the treaty by the distinction between *raj*, which was assigned to Umed Singh and his heirs, and *muktiari*, which was assigned to Zalim Singh and his heirs. For Kishor Singh, the difference between these two terms did not involve a distinction between its 'symbolic' and the 'substantive' dimensions, but rather one of hierarchy as expressed through the well established trope of service as entailed in the master/servant (*swami/malik*) relationship. Shortly before Mangrol, Kishor Singh objected to James Tod about his exclusion from active involvement in the fiscal and military matters of the kingdom.

> [Zalim Singh] administers the duties of the government but he was not appointed by the British Government.... The treaty made at Dehlee you ought to consider well – there will be seen who is the master and who is the servant. If therein you find the sovereignty guaranteed to him, give it him; but if it is directly said to be mine, put me in possession.[51]

In a slightly earlier letter Kishor Singh laid out what he thought were the treaty's significant terms:

> In the treaty it is written that the administration of affairs [*muktiari*] is with [Zalim Singh],[52] and to me is the Raj, or state, but nowhere is it written the Raj is to be with him... Formerly from the time of Maha Rao Bheem Sing [and] Durjan Sal to the reign of Chattersal there were officers of Government in every Department but [Zalim Singh], having given... satisfaction to Omcid Sing, has made himself Chief over all.[53]

Kishor Singh wrote in similar terms to Mirza Muhammad Ali in Calcutta: 'Even in the treaty... it is not written that the Servant is to oppress his Master.'[54] Thus according to Kishor Singh's reading of the treaty, Zalim Singh was to be subservient to the maharao, and although the maharao was prepared to concede that Zalim Singh had a strong hereditary claim

51 Kishor Singh to Tod, tr., 24 September 1821, OIOC, BPC, 24/31 October 1821.

52 Although Tod did not provide the Hindi gloss for 'administration' in this passage, elsewhere he renders this term as *muktiari*. See, for example, Kishor Singh to Tod, tr., 29 September 1821, OIOC, BPC, 24/31 October 1821.

53 Kishor Singh to Tod, tr., 3 September 1821, OIOC, BPC, 23/6 October 1821.

54 Kishor Singh to Mirza Muhammad Ali, tr., n.d., OIOC, BPC, 61/9 February 1822.

to the position, that claim was contingent upon the satisfactory performance of duties by him and his heirs. These arguments, with respect to Zalim Singh, at least, fell on deaf ears. The colonial administration argued that, irrespective of the actual wording of the treaty, its intent was to uphold the primacy of the rajrana's authority.[55]

These arguments, however, did have a much greater impact in how James Tod came to understand political relations more generally in Kota and indeed throughout Rajasthan, particularly as they informed his understanding of political relations between local rulers and the jagirdars. It has often been pointed out that Tod's conception of political relations in Rajasthan bear the heavy imprint of Henry Hallam's formulation of European feudalism, and this is true enough. When confronted with the segmented nature of political power in Rajathan and the bonds of personal loyalty through which this political structure was articulated, Tod found in European feudalism an apt model. However, within the broad contours of this model there were many particulars concerning Rajasthan that remained to be worked out. One of these concerned whose rights and prerogatives in the dyadic relationship between patron and client were to be considered primary. Kishor Singh, and many of his fellow rulers, conceived of the relationship between king and client within a devotional framework that was informed by notions of *dasya bhav*, that is the devotion of a slave to his master in which there is considered to be a wide, awe-inspiring gulf between ruler and client. It was precisely this relationship that Kishor Singh was trying to instantiate through his repeated assertions to Tod that the swami/malik relationship must be the basis for proper political relations. While Tod, no doubt, did not fully appreciate the devotional aspects of this relationship, he did understand the clear form of hierarchy that it entailed.

At the same time, however, numerous jagirdars, whose notions of kingship were informed by the ethic of *bhaibhant* ('sharing among brothers'), were making petitions to Tod urging him to understand that the king was but *primus-inter-pares* and that sovereignty was collectively held by the ruler with his jagirdars. Tod himself translated and reproduced one of these petitions from a group of jagirdars in Marwar (Jodhpur), who were explaining their status vis-à-vis Maharaja Man Singh of Marwar, which in his use of emphasis betrays the extent to which he understood their position.

> [Man Singh's] forefathers have ruled for generations; our forefathers were their ministers and advisors, and whatever was performed was performed by the collective wisdom of the council of our chiefs... *When our services* [to the

[55] Tod, *Annals and Antiquities*, Volume 2, p. 499.

Maharaja of Marwar] *are acceptable, then he is our lord; when not, we are again his kindred, claimants and laying claim to the land.*[56]

Significantly, Tod was sympathetic to these petitions precisely because he saw them linked to larger debates on the role of the landed aristocracy in providing a 'natural bulwark' against the 'despotic' tendencies of the monarchy. Incidentally this was a debate that Tod saw as applicable to Britian and Europe as much as to India.[57] Yet in the end, Kishor Singh's arguments carried the day with Tod, if not with respect to Zalim Singh, then at least with respect to the jagirdars.

Indeed, Tod saw the millenarian aspects of the final advance on Mangrol by Kishor Singh's forces as a prime example of the literally 'blind loyalty' that jagirdars owed their ruler, rather than as a corporate action that was brought about by contingent alignment of diverse interests. Kishor Singh never did enjoy the fruits of his success in shaping Tod's understanding of the relationship between Hindu king and political client. After his defeat at Mangrol and his later reinstallation on the gaddi he remained largely excluded from any executive control over the kingdom. Elsewhere in Rajasthan, however, Tod became a strong supporter of native rulers in their disputes with their nobility, and one witnesses a distinct shift in the balance of power within most Rajput states away from the landed aristocracy in favour of the rulers. Moreover, when Kota was finally split into two kingdoms in 1838 in order to physically separate maharao and rajrana, Kishor Singh's successor, Ram Singh, enjoyed a degree of authority over his jagirdars of which his ancestors could have only dreamed.

56 Tod, *Annals and Antiquities*, Volume 1, pp. 149–150.

57 See my 'Tod's *Rajast'han*' for related aspects of this line of reasoning in Tod's writings. See also James Tod, 'letter to T. Hyde Villiers, Esq', *Parliamentary Papers, 1831–32, Report from the Select Committee on the Affairs of the East India Company*, Volume XIV, Appendix VI, No. 13, pp. 122–38.

7 Conclusion: Beyond orientalism

The findings of this study indicate that, during the eighteenth and early nineteenth centuries, the ways in which political legitimacy was linked to kingship in Kota was informed by several competing principles, each of which defined slightly different relations of political power and social hierarchy. Although these various principles inflected one another in important ways, they also mapped cultural orientations, social spaces, and personal agenda that did not fully overlap and, therefore, were not fully reducible one to another. The fissures and discontinuities between these 'multiple orders of reality' established fertile grounds in which competitive local politics were waged and where rival agendas could be advanced, defended, mediated, and transformed. As mentioned in the introduction to this book, most recent ethnohistorical studies of precolonial societies have tended to minimize or downplay these disjunctures in favour of more internally consistant, integrated, and consensual models of social organization that substantially homogenized the diversity of values and orientations present in local societies, thereby 'sanitizing' accounts of local politics.[1] In the context of South Asian studies, this ironically has been a failure not only of Dumontian structuralism but also of much of what Jonathan Parry has called the 'neo-Hocartian' critique of Dumont.[2]

This 'romanticized' view of the precolonial also has had unfortunate knock-on effects for studies of the early colonial encounter.[3] Against the backdrop of monolithic cultural unity and political equilibrium, any detectable form of social change has been viewed as a marker of cultural

[1] In using the term 'sanitizing', I am following Sherry Ortner's use of the term in her article 'Resistance and the Problem of Ethnographic Refusal', *Comparative Studies in Society and History* 37 (1995): 173–193.

[2] Jonathan P. Parry, 'Mauss, Dumont, and the Distinction Between Status and Power', in *Marcel Mauss: A Centenary Tribute*, eds Wendy James and N. J. Allen (Oxford: Berghahn Books, 1998), pp. 151–172.

[3] In calling this view 'romanticized', I am obviously extending into the field of 'colonial studies' a critique similar to that raised by Lila Abu-Lughod with respect to early subaltern studies. See Lila Abu-Lughod, 'The Romance of Resistance: Tracing Transformations of Power through Bedouin Women', *American Ethnologist* 17 (1990): 41–55.

inauthenticity and therefore has been stigmatized as being wholly exogenous (that is, western) in origin rather than having important links to local, ongoing processes of change as well. Yet the dominant discourses of European colonialism were never created *in toto* from whole cloth. Instead they emerged out of social fields that included processes of social contest and social change that had at least some roots in the political tensions and disjunctures of the precolonial era. In appreciating this fact, one begins to see that early colonial transformations often had a different, more hybridized, ontological status. Native agenda and actions (which hitherto have been ignored as inconsequential to colonial history) thereby find greater importance, and 'the colonial' becomes somewhat less European and more fully the product of an encounter (however asymmetrical) between European and non-European societies. It is precisely this dynamic that helps explain the significant differences among the colonial experiences in, say, early eighteenth-century India, mid-twentieth-century sub-Saharan Africa, and sixteenth-century Latin America. Indeed it calls into question the analytic usefulness of the blanket term of 'colonialism', rendered in the singular, and suggests that we need to be thinking about many colonialisms.

These conclusions have two further important implications for how we understand the nature of historical transformation and social change more generally. First they help remind us that colonialism, just as whatever went on before it, has a history in which political relations and forms of domination shifted over time in, often, contingent and unanticipated ways. If, as I have argued earlier, ethnohistorians have tended to treat the precolonial polity in a largely ahistorical fashion, most scholars of the colonial period have tended to treat the transformations of the period under European rule in an overdetermined fashion. Change is viewed as being governed in a relatively straightforward manner by the operations of a specific 'colonial' (that is, western) discourse. But part of the truth-effect of these studies, of which Said's and Inden's are paradigmatic, is achieved by a methodological sleight of hand. As al-ᶜAzm has argued with respect to Said and as I have previously suggested with respect to Inden,[4] these critiques of colonial discourse generally take a particularly 'mature' moment in its history as their starting point and then 'read back' their resulting conclusions onto earlier epochs (sometimes quite anachronistically). This methodological conceit of retrospective projection has rendered colonial discourse unduly unified and stable over time, and the

4 Sadik Jalal al-ᶜAzm, 'Orientalism and Orientalism in Reverse', *Kamsin: Journal of Revolutionary Socialists of the Middle East* 8 (1981): 5–26, and Norbert Peabody, 'Tod's Rajast'han and the Boundaries of Imperial Rule in Nineteenth-Century India', *Modern Asian Studies* 30 (1996): 185–220.

resulting history of the colonial encounter has become excessively reductionist, unilinear, and teleological. In a sense, this remains a very Whiggish reading of history, only without the epiphany.

This book, on the other hand, has advocated a much more open-ended, multi-potentialled, and conditional sense of history. It has suggested that particular discursive forms that had one use at one historical moment often embodied a range of possibilities for alternative uses at other historical moments or in other contexts. But nothing inherent to the earlier forms fully preordained their transformation into later forms. In order to understand why a particular vector of change took place one must also look to the situational conjuncture of other contingent factors, including the agenda of local agents, that favoured one possible *bricolage* over others. This multi-agentive, multi-potentialled view of historical change makes it much more difficult to read history as some sort of moral parable in which one can blithely assign blame and innocence for the very real social injustices that history (colonial and otherwise) has thrown up. It however does open up more subtle and sophisticated understandings of how these iniquities emerged.

Finally, let me draw one additional general implication of this discursive heteroglossia for our understanding of the nature and limits of individual agency. Under the conditions of hermeneutical indeterminacy described here, social actors are never able to define the terms of political power and social hierarchy entirely to suit their own requisites. Because a dominant discourse is not created *ex nihilo* but always with reference to other discourses, it is always incumbent on those who aspire to positions of power and authority to domesticate competing discourses by incorporating aspects of them into derivative locations within their own creeds. In other words, social and political hierarchies are always negotiated dialogically between dominant groups and those whom dominant groups need to co-opt into political alliance, yet whose own agendas may be construed on different terms. This social fact is what prevents dominant constructions from ever becoming completely malleable in the hands of powerful actors. The dialogic conditions under which a discourse is produced, then, is what lends the culture that it encodes a discernable rigidity which shapes the actions of entrepreneurial agents. It is this negotiated aspect of discourse that inhibits indvidual actors from freely shaping and reshaping their social worlds at will. In other words, if there is any sense in which one can say a shared culture exists, it is less as a corpus of common understandings and collective beliefs than as the tension-filled space between conflicting ones.

Glossary

annadan: the gift of food and wealth
annakut: 'the mountain of food' festival
ashrama: one of the four Hindu stages of life
avatar: incarnation

batai: a revenue assessment based on a division of the crop at the time of threshing after the harvest
bhaiband: brotherhood, fraternity, 'the bond of brothers'
bhog: enjoyment, pleasure in food; gratification
bhakta: devotee
bhakti: devotion
biradari: brotherhood, fraternity, kin, community

chakri: service; also a grant of land for service

darbar: the royal court or assembly
darikhana: lit. 'a room of carpets'; a darbar in Kota
darshan: sight or vision, especially of a respected or divine being
dasya bhav: the devotion of a servant to his master
dhabhai: foster-brother
dharamaraja: a righteous king
divan: prime minister
doab: the land between two rivers

farman: a Mughal edict, decree; a royal letter, charter
faujdar: military commander, general
fitna: rebellion, sedition, drawing away from allegiance

gaddi: a cushion; a throne, a royal seat
ganj: local market
goswami: a sectarian hierarch within the Vallabha Sampraday

haveli: temple or villa
hundi: a bill or letter of credit

ijara: land let out on a revenue, or tax, farming basis
inam: land given to a client on a tax-free basis
ishtadevata: personal or chosen deity
jagir(dar): (holder of) an estate
jinsi: a brigade of infantry with supporting mobile artillery

kamavisdar: a Maratha revenue official
khalsa: government or crown land
khandani: a tribute payable to the Maratha Empire
khyat: a Rajasthani historical account
kos: a Mughal unit of distance of about 2 miles (3 kilometres)
kuntai: a revenue assessment determined by the average yield for each specific crop within a specific field over a number of preceding years

latai: a revenue assessment reckoned in cash terms based on the yield of a crop estimated while still standing

mafi(dar): (holder of) a rent free estate
mahajan: 'great person'; merchant or trader
maharao: great king
mahi-o-maratib: the fish and dignities standard
mahotsav: great festival
mamaji: maternal uncle
mandi: small grain market
manorath: heartfelt desire
mansab(dar): (holder of) a non-hereditary estate
maya: illusion
mayavad: the philosophical system of Shankaracharya whereby the world is regarded as illusion
mleccha: barbarian
moksha: liberation from the karmic cycle of rebirths
muqata(dar): (one who holds) a revenue farm
murti: religious image, especially a statue
musahab-i-ala: prime-minister, 'chief companion'

nakkar: large ceremonial kettle drum
naukar(i): (service of) a retainer or client
navnidhi: 'the nine treasures'; the nine most esteemed images of the Vallabha Sampradaya
nazar: a ceremonial gift from an inferior to a superior
nidhi-svarup: a religious statue of the Vallabha Sampraday that was found fully formed; that is, it was not made by human manufacture

pagri badal bhai: brother(s) through the exchange of turban(s)
pargana: a fiscal district, a territorial division
parwana: a royal command or edict
patrani: senior ranking queen

patel: village headman
prasad: a transvalued substance; a eucharistic leaving of the gods
prashasti: a panegyric
punya: moral or spiritual merit; virtue; virtuous act
pushti: divine grace
pushti-svarup: an image that has been 'consecrated' by a descendant of Vallabhacharya
Pushtimargi: 'a follower of the path of divine grace'; a follower of Vallabhacharya

qasba: a market town

rakhiband: a right of protection performed between brothers and sisters

sagai: betrothal, marriage, or alliance through marriage
sampraday: sect, community, tradition
seth: a merchant or money-lender
seva: service, worship
sevak: one who does seva, a devotee
sevya-svarup: an image that had been worshipped personally by Vallabhacharya
siropav: a robe of honour that covers the recipient 'from head to toe'
shuddhadvaita: Vallabhacharya's philosophy of 'pure non-dualism'
svarup: a religious image of the Vallabha Sampraday
svarajya: lit. 'self-rule'; name of the Maratha Empire

thakur: lord

utsav: religious festival within the Vallabha Sampraday

vakil: an agent
vamsha: lineage
varta: an account, hagiography or (hi)story, especially in the Vallabha Sampraday
vat: Rajasthani tale or account
vatan(dar): (holder of) a hereditary estate
vatsalya bhav: the maternal, familial, or disinterested love (especially of Yashoda for her foster-child Krishna)

zakat: customs duty or transit dues
zamindar: landlord

Bibliography

Abu-Lughod, Lila. 1990. The Romance of Resistance: Tracing Transformations of Power through Bedouin Women. *American Ethnologist* 17: 41–55.

Ahmad, Aijaz. 1991. Between Orientalism and Historicism: Anthropological Knowledge of India, *Studies in History* 7: 135–163.

Aitchison, C. U. 1876. *A Collection of Treaties, Engagements, and Sunnuds Relating to India and Neighboring Countries*. Volume III: *The Treaties, &c., Relating to the States in Rajpootana, Central India, and the Mediatized Chiefs in Central India and Malwa*. Calcutta: Foreign Office Press.

Alam, Muzaffar. 1986. *The Crisis of Empire in Mughal North India: Awadh and the Punjab, 1707–48*. Delhi: Oxford University Press.

al-ᶜAzm, Sadik Jalal. 1981. Orientalism and Orientalism in Reverse. *Khamsin: Journal of Revolutionary Socialists of the Middle East* 8: 5–26.

Alberuni. 1888. *Alberuni's India: An Account of the Religion, Philosophy, Literature, Geography, Chronology, Astronomy, Customs, Laws, and Astrology of India About A.D. 1030* (2 volumes), Edward Sachau, trans. London: Trübner.

Ali, M. Athar. 1997 [1966]. *The Mughal Nobility under Aurangzeb*, revised edn. Delhi: Oxford University Press.

Amatiya, Ramachandrapat. 1929. The Ajnapatra or Royal Edict Relating to the Principles of Maratha State Policy, trans. S.V. Puntambekar. *Journal of Indian History* 8: 81–105, 207–233.

Ambalal, Amit. 1987. *Krishna as Shrinathji*. Ahmedabad: Mapin.

Anderson, Benedict. 1991 [1983]. *Imagined Communities: Origins and Spread of Nationalism*, 2nd edn. London: Verso.

Appadurai, Arjun. 1982. *Worship and Conflict under Colonial Rule: A South Indian Case*. Cambridge: Cambridge University Press.

——1993. Number in the Colonial Imagination. In *Orientalism and the Postcolonial Predicament: Perspectives on South Asia*, eds Carol A. Breckenridge and Peter van der Veer, pp. 314–339. Philadelphia: University of Pennsylvania Press.

Archer, W. G. 1959. *Indian Painting in Bundi and Kotah*. London: Her Majesty's Stationery Office.

Arnold, David. 1986. Cholera and Colonialism. *Past and Present* 113: 118–151.

——1993. *Colonizing the Body: State Medicine and Epidemic Disease in Nineteenth-Century India*. Berkeley: University of California Press.

Bahura, Gopal Narayan and Chandramani Singh. 1988. *Catalogue of Historical Documents in Kapad Dwara, Jaipur*. Amber-Jaipur: Jaigarh Public Charitable Trust.

Bajekal, Madhavi. 1988. The State and the Rural Grain Market in Eighteenth Century Eastern Rajasthan. *Indian Economic and Social History Review* 25: 443–473.

Bakhtin, Mikhail M. 1981 [1934–35]. Discourse in the Novel. In *The Dialogic Imagination: Four Essays by M. M. Bakhtin*, ed. and trans. Michael Holquist. Austin: University of Texas Press.

Banerjee, Anil Chandra. 1980. *The Rajput States and British Paramountcy.* New Delhi: Rajesh Publications.

——1983. *Aspects of Rajput State and Society*. New Delhi: Rajesh Publications.

Barz, R. K. 1976. *The Bhakti Sect of Vallabhacarya*. Faridabad, Haryana: Thomson Press.

Bautze, Joachim K. 1992. Victory and Death of Maharao Bhim Singh of Kota. In *South Asian Archaeology 1989. Papers from the Tenth International Conference of South Asian Archaeologists in Western Europe*, Musée National des Arts Asiatique–Guimet, Paris, France, ed. Catherine Jarrige, pp. 309–316. Madison, WI: Prehistory Press.

——1994. Jhala Zalim Singh of Kotah: A Great Patron of Rajput Painting. In *Festschrift Klaus Bruhn*, eds Nalini Balbir and Joachim K. Bautze, pp. 105–125. Reinbek: Inge Wezler.

——1997. The History of Kotah in an Art-Historical Context. *Gods, Kings, and Tigers: The Art of Kotah*, ed. Stuart Cary Welch, pp. 39–60. Munich: Prestel-Verlag.

Bayly, C. A. 1983. *Rulers, Townsmen, and Bazaars: North Indian Society in the Age of British Expansion, 1770–1870*. Cambridge: Cambridge University Press.

——1989. *Imperial Meridian: The British Empire and the World, 1788–1830*. London: Longman.

Bennett, Peter J. 1983. Temple Organization and Worship among the Pustimargiya-Vaisnavas of Ujjain. PhD thesis, School of Oriental and African Studies, University of London.

——1990. In Nanda Baba's House: The Devotional Experience in Pushti Marg Temples. In *Divine Passions: the Social Construction of Emotion in India*, ed. O. M. Lynch, pp. 182–211. Berkeley: University of California Press.

Bhatnagar, V. S. 1974. *Life and Times of Sawai Jai Singh, 1688–1743*. Delhi: Impex India.

Bhattacharya, Sukumar. 1972. *The Rajput States and the East India Company from the Close of the Eighteenth Century to 1820*. New Delhi: Munshiram Manoharlal.

Bloch, Marc. 1989 [1962]. *Feudal Society*, trans. L. A. Manyon. London: Routledge.

Bohannan, Paul. 1955. Some Principles of Exchange and Investment among the Tiv. *American Anthropologist* 57: 60–70.

——1959. The Impact of Money on an African Subsistence Economy. *Journal of Economic History* 19: 491–503.

Bourdieu, Pierre. 1977. *Outline of a Theory of Practice*, trans. R. Nice. Cambridge: Cambridge University Press.

Brajbushan. 1956. *Shri Dvarkadhis ki prakatya varta*. Kankroli: Vidya Vibhag.

Breckenridge, Carol A. and Peter van der Veer, eds. 1993. *Orientalism and the Postcolonial Predicament: Perspectives on South Asia*. Philadelphia: University of Pennsylvania Press.

Broughton, Thomas Duer. 1817 [1813]. *Letters Written in a Mahratta Camp during the Year 1809 Descriptive of the Character, Manners, Domestic Habits, and Religious Ceremonies of the Mahrattas*. London: Archibald Constable and Company.

Burghart, Richard. 1978. Hierarchical Models of the Hindu Social System. *Man* (N.S.) 13: 519–536.

Busawan Lal. 1832. *Memoirs of the Puthan Soldier of Fortune, the Nuwab Ameer-ood-Doulah, Mohummad Ameer Khan, Chief of Seronj, Tonk, Rampoora, Neemahera, and Other Places in Hindoostan*, trans. H. T. Prinsep. Calcutta: G. H. Huttman, Military Orphan Press.

Carstairs. G. M. 1975. *The Twice-Born: A Study of a Community of High-Caste Hindus*. Bloomington: Indiana University Press.

Chakravarti, Anand. 1975. *Contradiction and Change: Emerging Patterns of Authority in a Rajasthan Village*. Delhi: Oxford University Press.

Chandra, Satish. 1959. *Parties and Politics at the Mughal Court (1707–1740)*. Aligarh: Aligarh Muslim University Publications.

Chandra, Satish, Raghubir Sinh, and G. D. Sharma, eds. 1976. *Jodhpur hukumat ri bahi: Marwar under Jaswant Singh, 1658–1678*. Meerut: Meenakshi Prakashan.

Chaudhuri, B. 1983. Regional Economy (1757–1857): Eastern India II. In *The Cambridge Economic History of India*. Volume I: *c. 1757 – c. 1970*, ed. D. Kumar, pp. 295–332. Cambridge: Cambridge University Press.

Chaudhuri, K. N. 1982. European Trade with India. In *The Cambridge Economic History of India*. Volume I: *c. 1200 – c. 1757*, eds Tapan Raychaudhuri and Irfan Habib, pp. 382–407. Cambridge: Cambridge University Press.

——1983. Foreign Trade and Balance of Payments (1757–1947). In *The Cambridge Economic History of India*. Volume II: *c. 1757 – c. 1970*, ed. D. Kumar, pp. 804–877. Cambridge: Cambridge University Press.

Cohn, Bernard S. 1962. Political Systems in Eighteenth Century India: The Banares Region. *Journal of the American Oriental Society* 83: 312–320.

——1984. The Census, Social Structure and Objectification in South Asia. *Folk* 26: 25–49.

Cooper, Randolph G. S. 1989. Wellington and the Marathas in 1803. *International History Review* 11: 31–38.

Cooper, R. G. S. and N. K. Wagle. 1995. Maratha Artillery: From Dabhoi to Assaye. *Journal of the Ordnance Society* 7: 58–78.

Dalmia, Vasudha. 1994. The Establishment of the Sixth *Gaddi* of the Vallabha Sampraday: Narrative Structure and the Use of Authority in a *Varta* of the Nineteenth Century. In *Studies in South Asian Devotional Literature*, eds Alan W. Entwistle and Françoise Mallison, pp. 94–117. New Delhi: Manohar.

Daniel, E. Valentine. 1984. *Fluid Signs: Being a Person the Tamil Way*. Berkeley: University of California Press.

Daniel, Sheryl B. 1983. The Tool Box Approach of the Tamils to the Issues of Moral Responsibility and Human Destiny. In *Karma: An Anthropological Inquiry*, eds Charles F. Keyes and E. Valentine Daniel, pp. 27–62. Berkeley: University of California Press.

Das, Chaube Raghunath. 1896. *Report on the Administration of the Kotah State for the Year 1894–95 (Sambat 1951)*. Ajmer: Rajputana Mission Press.

Dirks, Nicholas B. 1987. *The Hollow Crown: Ethnohistory of a South Indian Kingdom*. Cambridge: Cambridge University Press.

Dossal, Marriam. 1991. *Imperial Designs and Indian Realities: The Planning of Bombay City, 1845–1875*. Delhi: Oxford University Press.

Dumont, Louis. 1980 [1966]. *Homo Hierarchicus: The Caste System and Its Implications*, M. Sainsbury, L. Dumont, and B. Gulati, trans. Chicago: University of Chicago Press.

Eck, Diana L. 1985 [1981]. *Darsan: Seeing the Divine Image in India*. Chambersberg, PA: Anima Books.

Edney, Matthew H. 1990. *Mapping an Empire: The Geographical Construction of British India, 1765–1845*. Chicago: University of Chicago Press.

Entwistle, A.W. 1987. *Braj: Centre of Krishna Pilgrimage*. Groningen: E. Forsten.

Errington, Shelly. 1979. Some Comments on Style in the Meaning of the Past. *Journal of Asian Studies* 38: 231–244.

Farooqui, Amar. 1995. Opium Enterprise and Colonial Intervention in Malwa and Western India, 1800–1824. *Indian Economic and Social History Review* 32: 447–473.

Fisher, Michael H. 1990. The Resident in Court Ritual, 1764–1858. *Modern Asian Studies* 24: 419–458.

Fox, Richard G. 1971. *Kin, Clan, Raja and Rule: State–Hinterland Relations in Preindustrial India*. Berkeley: University of California Press.

Frykenberg, Robert Eric. 1963. Traditional Processes of Power in South India: An Historical Analysis of Local Influence. *Indian Economic and Social History Review* 1: 122–142.

Fuller, C.J. 1989. Misconceiving the Grain Heap: A Critique of the Concept of the Indian Jajmani System. In *Money and Morality of Exchange*, eds J. Parry and M. Bloch, pp. 33–63. Cambridge: Cambridge University Press.

Geertz, Clifford. 1973 [1959]. Ritual and Social Change: a Javanese Example. In *The Interpretation of Cultures: Selected Essays*, pp. 142–169. New York: Basic Books.

——1980. *Negara: The Theatre-State in Nineteenth Century Bali*. Princeton: Princeton University Press.

Gordon, Stewart N. 1977. The Slow Conquest: Administrative Integration of Malwa into the Maratha Empire, 1720–1760. *Modern Asian Studies* 11: 1–40.

——1993. *The New Cambridge History of India*, Volume II.4: *The Marathas, 1600–1818*. Cambridge: Cambridge University Press.

Gottlieb, Alma. 1986. Dog: Ally or Traitor? Mythology, Cosmology and Society among the Beng of Ivory Coast. *American Ethnologist* 13: 477–488.

—— 1989. Hyenas and Heteroglossia: Myth and Ritual among the Beng of Côte d'Ivoire. *American Ethnologist* 16: 487–501.

Gupta, B. L. 1987. *Trade and Commerce in Rajasthan during the Eighteenth Century*. Jaipur: Jaipur Publishing House.

Gupta, Beni. 1979. *Maratha Penetration into Rajasthan through the Mukandara Pass*. New Delhi: Research Publications in the Social Sciences.

Gupta, K. S. 1971. *Mewar and the Maratha Relations (1735–1818 A.D.)*. New Delhi: S. Chand & Co.

Gupta, Mata Prasad. 1962. *Raso sahitya vimarsh*. Ilahabad: Sahitya Bhavan.

Gupta, Satya Prakash. 1974. The Jagir System during the Evolution of Jaipur State (c. 1650–1750). *Proceedings of the Indian History Congress* 35: 171–179.

——1986. *The Agrarian System of Eastern Rajasthan (c. 1650 – c. 1750)*. Delhi: Manohar.

Habib, Irfan. 1963. *The Agrarian System of Mughal India (1556–1707)*. London: Asia Publishing House.

Hariray. 1986. *Shrinathji ki prakatya varta*. Nathadvara: Vidyavibhag Mandir Mandal.

——1992. *Chaurasi vaishnavan ki varta*. Indore: Vaishnav Mitr Mandal.

——1992. *Do sau bavan vaishnavan ki varta* (3 volumes). Indore: Vaishnav Mitr Mandal.

Heber, Right Rev. Reginald. 1828. *Narrative of a Journey Through the Upper Provinces of India from Calcutta to Bombay, 1824–1825, (with Notes upon Ceylon), an Account of a Journey to Madras and the Southern Provinces, 1826, and Letters Written in India* (2 volumes). London: John Murray.

Henige, David P. 1974. *The Chronology of Oral Tradition: Quest for a Chimera*. Oxford: Clarendon Press.

Hiltebeitel, Alf. 1976. *The Ritual of Battle: Krishna in the* Mahabharata. Ithaca: Cornell University Press.

Horstmann, Monika. 1994. Govinddevji of Vrindaban and Jaipur and its Kachvaha Patrons from the Mid-Seventeenth to the Mid-Eighteenth Century. In *Studies in South Asian Devotional Literature*, eds Alan W. Entwistle and Francoise Mallison, pp. 82–93. New Delhi: Manohar.

Humphrey, Caroline and James Laidlaw. 1994. *The Archetypal Actions of Ritual: A Theory of Ritual Illustrated by the Jain Rite of Worship*. Oxford: Clarendon Press.

Hunter, William. 1801. Narrative of a Journey from Agra to Oujein. *Asiatick Researches* 6: 47–67.

Inden, Ronald. 1978. Ritual, Authority and Cyclic Time in Hindu Kingship. In *Kingship and Authority in South Asia*, ed. J. F. Richards, pp. 28–73. Madison: University of Wisconsin South Asia Publication Series, No. 3.

——1990. *Imagining India*. Oxford: Basil Blackwell.

Irvine, William. 1922. *Later Mughals*, Volume II, *1719–1739*, ed. Jadunath Sarkar. Calcutta: M. C. Sarkar & Sons.

Ishwaran, K. 1980. Bhakti Tradition and Modernization: The Case of Lingayatism. *Journal of Asian and African Studies* 15: 72–83.

Jhala, Jayasinhji. 1991. Marriage, Hierarchy, and Identity in Ideology and Practice: An Anthropological Study of Jhala Rajput Society in Western India against a Historical Background (A.D. 1090–1990) (2 volumes). PhD Thesis, Department of Anthropology, Harvard University.

Jindel, Rajendra. 1976. *Culture of a Sacred Town*. Bombay: Popular Prakashan.

Joshi, Varsha. 1995. *Polygamy and Purdah: Women and Society among Rajputs*. Jaipur: Rawat Publications.

Kane, P. V. 1974. *History of Dharmasastra*. Poona: Bhandarkar Oriental Research Institute, Volume 2, Part 2.

Kaplan, Martha and John D. Kelly. 1994. Rethinking Resistance: Dialogics of 'Disaffection' in Colonial Fiji. *American Ethnologist* 21: 123–151.

Kaye, John William. 1858 [1854]. *The Life and Correspondence of Charles Lord Metcalfe* (2 volumes). London.

Khafi Khan. 1874. *Muntakhab al-lubab*, Volume II. Calcutta, n.p.

Kolenda, Pauline. 1967. Toward a Model of the Hindu Jajmani System. In *Tribal and Peasant Economies*, ed. G. Dalton. Garden City, NY: American Museum of Natural History.

Kolff, D. H. A. 1990. *Naukar, Rajput and Sepoy: The Ethnohistory of the Military Labour Market in Hindustan, 1450–1850*. Cambridge: Cambridge University Press.

Kopytoff, Igor. 1986. The Cultural Biography of Things: Commoditization as Process. In *The Social Life of Things*, ed. Arjun Appadurai, pp. 64–91. Cambridge: Cambridge University Press.

Krishnadatta. 1983. *Pratap prakash*, ed. and annotated Gopalnarayan Bahura Jaipur: Maharaja Sawai Man Singh II Museum Trust.

Laknawi, Shiv Das. 1980. *Shahnama Munawwar Kalam*, trans. Syed Hasan Askari. Patna: Janaki Prakashan.

Lakshmandan. n.d. [ca. 1868]. *Maharao Shatru Shalji Bahadur ki vamsha prashasti*. Unpublished manuscript in the Thikana Kotri *daftar*, Kota. Typescript copy, under the title of '*Kota rajya ke hastalikhita itihas ki pratilipi*', in the Brijraj Bhawan Palace Library, Kota.

Lynch, Owen M. 1988. Pilgrimage with Krishna, Sovereign of the Emotions. *Contributions to Indian Sociology* (N.S.) 22: 171–194.

Macpherson, J. M. 1914 [1895]. *British Enactments in Force in Native States*. Calcutta: Superintendent Government Printing.

Madan, T. N. 1987. *Non-Renunciation*. Delhi: Oxford University Press.

Magier, David. 1992. The Language of the Bard. In *A Carnival of Parting*, by A. Gold, pp. 335–350. Berkeley: University of California Press.

Malamoud, Charles. 1981. On the Rhetoric and Semantics of Purusartha. *Contributions to Indian Sociology* (N.S.) 15: 33–54.

Malcolm, Sir John. 1832 [1824]. *A Memoir of Central India Including Malwa, and Adjoining Provinces, with the History, and Copious Illustrations, of the Past and Present Condition of that Country* (2 Volumes). London: Parbury, Allen, and Co.

Mani, Lata. 1998. *Contentious Traditions: The Debate on* Sati *in Colonial India*. Berkeley: University of California Press.

Marriott, McKim. 1976. Hindu Transactions: Diversity without Dualism. In *Transactions and Meaning: Directions in the Anthropology of Exchange and*

Symbolic Behavior, ed. B. Kapferer, pp. 109–142. Philadelphia: Institute for the Study of Human Issues.

Mathur, R. S. 1986. *Relations of Hadas with Mughal Emperors (1568–1720 A.D.)*. Delhi: Deputy Publications.

McGregor, R. S. 1984. *Hindi Literature from Its Beginnings to the Nineteenth Century*. Wiesbaden: Otto Harrassowitz.

McGregor, R. S., ed. 1993. *The Oxford Hindi-English Dictionary*. Oxford: Oxford University Press.

Mehta, Judge U. C. 1972. *State of Rajasthan* v. *Goswami Ranchodlalji Maharaj Sri*. Unpublished judgment, Kota District Sessions Court.

Metcalf, Thomas. 1994. *The New Cambridge History of India*, Volume III.4: *Ideologies of the Raj*. Cambridge, UK: Cambridge University Press.

Mishra, N.L. 1986. *Geography Behind Political History: A Study of Harauti Region*. Jaipur: R.B.S.A. Publishers.

Mishran, Suryamalla. 1899. *Vamshabhaskar* (8 volumes). Jodhpur, n.p.

Mital, Prabhudayal. 1968. *Braj ke dharam-sampradayom ka itihas*. Delhi: National Publishing House.

Modave, le Comte de (Louis Laurent de Federbe). 1971. *Voyage en Inde du Comte de Modave*, ed. J. Deloche. Paris: Ecole Française d'Extrême-Orient.

Moore, Sally Falk. 1986. *Social Facts and Fabrication: 'Customary' Law on Kilimanjaro, 1880–1980*. Cambridge: Cambridge University Press.

Mukhia, Harbans. 1981. Was There Feudalism in Indian History? *Journal of Peasant Studies* 8: 273–310.

[Mulji, K.] 1865. *History of the Sect of Maharajas, or Vallabhacharyas, in Western India*. London: Trubner.

Nainsi, Munhata. 1960, 1962, 1964, & 1967. *Munhata Nainsiri khyat*, ed. Badriprasad Sakariya (4 volumes). Jodhpur: Rajasthan Prachyavidya Pratishtan.

——1968, 1969, & 1974. *Marvar ra parganan ri vigat*, ed. Narayansinh Bhati (3 volumes). Jodhpur: Rajasthan Prachyavidya Pratishtan.

Narayana Rao, Velcheru, David Shulman, and Sanjay Subrahmanyam. 1992. *Symbols of Substance: Court and State in Nayaka Period Tamilnadu*. Delhi: Oxford University Press.

Nazim, M. ed., 1933. *Selections from the Peshwas' Daftar (Persian)*, Volume 46; *Miscellaneous Papers*. Bombay: Government Central Press.

O'Flaherty, Wendy Doniger. 1980. Karma and Rebirth in the Vedas and Puranas. In *Karma and Rebirth in Classical Indian Traditions*. ed. Wendy Doniger O'Flaherty, pp. 3–37. Berkeley: University of California Press.

O'Hanlon, Rosiland. 1988. Recovering the Subject: Subaltern Studies and Histories of Resistance in Colonial South Asia. *Modern Asian Studies* 22: 189–224.

Ojha, Gaurishankar Harichand. 1925. *Rajputane ka itihas*, Volume 1. Ajmer: Vedik Yantralya.

Oldenberg, Veena Talwar. 1984. *The Making of Colonial Lucknow, 1756–1877*. Princeton: Princeton University Press.

Ortner, Sherry B. 1995. Resistance and the Problem of Ethnographic Refusal. *Comparative Studies in Society and History* 37: 173–193.

Owen, David Edward. 1934. *British Opium Policy in India and China*. New Haven: Yale University Press.

Padmanabha. 1953. *Kanhadade prabandha*, ed. Kantilal Baldevram Vyas. Jaipur: Rajasthan Puratattva Mandir.

Parliamentary Papers. 1831. *Third Report from the Select Committee on the Affairs of the East India Company*, Appendix IV, Abstracts on Malwa Opium.

Parry, Jonathan P. 1998. Mauss, Dumont, and the Distinction Between Status and Power, In *Marcel Mauss: A Centenary Tribute*, eds Wendy James and N. J. Allen, pp. 151–172. Oxford: Berghahn Books.

Peabody, Norbert. 1991. *Kota Mahajagat*, or the Great Universe of Kota: Sovereignty and Territory in Eighteenth-Century Rajasthan. *Contributions to Indian Sociology* (N.S.) 25: 29–56.

——1995. Review of *The New Cambridge History of India*, Volume III.4: *Ideologies of the Raj* by Thomas R. Metcalf. *American Ethnologist* 22: 1045–1046.

——1996. Tod's *Rajast'han* and the Boundaries of Imperial Rule in Nineteenth-Century India. *Modern Asian Studies* 30:185–220.

Phalke, Sardar Anandrao Bhao. 1929, 1930, & 1937. *Sindeshahi itihasanchin sadhanen* (3 volumes). Laskar, Gwalior: G. T. Mangaumkar Aligat Darbar Press.

Pocock. David. F. 1973. *Mind, Body and Wealth*. Oxford: Basil Blackwell.

Pollock, Sheldon I. 1993. Ramayana and The Political Imagination in India. *Journal of Asian Studies* 52: 261–297.

Prakash, Gyan, ed. 1995. *After Colonialism: Imperial Histories and Postcolonial Displacements*. Princeton: Princeton University Press.

Price, Pamela G. 1996. *Kingship and Political Practice in Colonial India*. Cambridge: Cambridge University Press.

Princep, Henry T. 1820. *A Narrative of the Political and Military Transactions of British India under the Administration of the Marquess of Hastings, 1813–1818*. London: John Murray.

Pritchett, Francis W. 1980. Prithviraj Raso: A Look at the Poem Itself. *Indian Literature* 23, 5: 56–75.

Raheja, Gloria Goodwin. 1989. Centrality, Mutuality, and Hierarchy: Shifting Aspects of Inter-caste Relationships in North India. *Contributions to Indian Sociology* (N.S.) 23: 79–101.

Richards, John F. 1993. *The New Cambridge History of India*, Volume I:5, *The Mughal Empire*. Cambridge: Cambridge University Press.

Richardson, Edwin A. 1979. Mughal and Rajput Patronage of the Bhakti Sect of the Maharajas, the Vallabha Sampradaya, 1640–1760 A.D. PhD thesis, Department of Oriental Studies, University of Arizona.

Rocher, Rosane. 1993. British Orientalism in the Eighteenth Century: The Dialectics of Knowledge and Government. In *Orientalism and the Postcolonial Predicament: Perspectives on South Asia*, eds Carol A. Breckenridge and Peter van der Veer, pp. 215–249. Philadelphia: University of Pennsylvania Press.

Rudolph, Lloyd I. and Susanne H. Rudolph. 1984 [1966]. Rajputana under British Paramountcy: The Failure of Indirect Rule. In *Essays on Rajputana: Reflections on History, Culture, and Administration*, pp. 3–37. New Delhi: Concept Publishing Company.

Sahlins, Marshall. 1972 (1965). On the Sociology of Primitive Exchange. In *Stone Age Economics*, pp. 185–275. New York: Aldine de Gruyter.

——1985. *Islands of History*. Chicago: University of Chicago Press.

Said, Edward. 1978. *Orientalism*. New York: Routledge & Kegan Paul.

Saran, Richard D. 1978. Conquest and Colonization: Rajputs and Vasis in Middle Period Marvar. PhD thesis, Department of History, University of Michigan.

Sardesai, G. S. ed. 1933. *Selections from the Peshwas' Daftar*, Volume 29, *Peshwa Madhavrao I, 1761–1772*. Bombay: Government Central Press.

Sarkar, Jadunath, 1984. *A History of Jaipur, c. 1503–1938*, ed. Raghubir Sinh. Hyderabad: Orient Longman.

Sato, Masanori. 1997. The Growth of Towns (Qasbas) of South-Eastern Rajasthan under the Mughals – A Case Study of Jhalrapatan. In *Economy and Polity of Rajasthan: Study of Kota and Marwar, 17th through 19th Centuries*, eds Masanori Sato and B. L. Bhadani, pp. 31–56. Jaipur: Publication Scheme.

——1997. The Formative Process of Towns and Market Town/Villages in South-Eastern Rajasthan, 1650–1850 A. D. In *Economy and Polity in Rajasthan: Study of Kota and Marwar, 17th through 19th Centuries*, eds Masanori Sato and B. L. Bhadani, pp. 57–86. Jaipur: Publication Scheme.

——1997. The Chamars of South-Eastern Rajasthan, A.D. 1650–1800. In *Caste System, Untouchability and the Depressed*, ed. H. Kotani, pp. 31–53. Delhi: Manohar.

——1997. The Patels and the Structure of their Landholding in South-Eastern Rajasthan, A.D. 1750–1850. In *Memoirs of the Research Department of the Toyo Bunko*, No. 55, pp. 61–79. Tokyo: The Toyo Bunko.

Sharma, G. D. 1986. *Vakil Reports Maharajgan (1693–1712 A.D.)*. New Delhi: Radha Krishna.

Sharma, Kashiram and Raghuvir Sinh, eds. 1982. *Ratan raso*, Volume 1, *bhumika*. Jodhpur: Rajasthan Prachyavidya Pratishtan.

Sharma, M. L. 1939. *Kota rajya ka itihas* (2 volumes). Kota: The Kota Printing Press.

Shastri, Kanthamani. 1939. *Kankroli ka itihas*. Kankroli: Shrividya-Vibhag.

Shastri, R. P. 1971. *Jhala Zalim Singh*. Jaipur: Raj Printing Works.

Shyamaldas. 1986 [1886]. *Virvinod* (2 volumes, Volume 2 in 3 Parts). Delhi: Motilal Banarasidas.

Siegal, James T. 1979. *Shadow and Sound: The Historical Thought of a Sumatran People*. Chicago: University of Chicago Press.

Singer, Milton. 1972. *When a Great Tradition Modernizes*. New York: Praeger.

Singh, Dilbagh. 1990. *The State, Landlords and Peasants: Rajasthan in the 18th Century*. Columbia, MO: South Asia Publications.

Singh, Narayan Prasad. 1980. *The East India Company's Monopoly Industries in Bihar with Particular Reference to Opium and Saltpetre*. Muzaffarpur, Bihar: Sarvodaya Vangmaya.

Sinh, Raghubir. 1936. *Malwa in Transition, or a Century of Anarchy: The First Phase 1698–1765*. Bombay: D. B. Taraporevala.

Skelton, Robert. 1973. *Rajasthani Temple Hangings of the Krishna Cult*. New York: American Federation of the Arts.

Smith, John D. 1991. *The Epic of Pabuji: A Study, Transcription and Translation*. Cambridge: Cambridge University Press.

Solanki, Acharya Parameshvar. 1960. *Kavivar Krisnadatta vircit 'prasad panc vimsati'*. *Shodh Patrika* 12, 2: 53–63.

Southall, Aidan. 1953. *Alur Society: A Study in Processes and Types of Domination*. Cambridge: W. Heffer.

——1988. The Segmentary State in Africa and Asia. *Comparative Studies in Society and History* 30: 52–82.

Spodek, Howard. 1974. Rulers, Merchants and Other Groups in the City-States of Saurashtra, India, around 1800. *Comparative Studies in Society and History* 16: 448–470.

Stein, Burton. 1977. The Segmentary State in South Indian History. In *Realm and Region in Traditional India*, ed. R. G. Fox, pp 3–51. Durham: Duke University Program in Comparative Studies on Southern Asia, Monograph and Occasional Paper Series, No. 14.

——1980. *Peasant State and Society in Medieval South India*. Delhi: Oxford University Press.

——1989. *The New Cambridge History of India*, Volume I:2, *Vijayanagara*. Cambridge: Cambridge University Press.

——1991. The Segmentary State: Interim Reflections. *Purusartha* 13: 217–238.

Stokes, Eric. 1978. *The Peasant and the Raj: Studies in Agrarian Society and Peasant Rebellion in Colonial India*. Cambridge: Cambridge University Press.

Subrahmanyam, Sanjay. 1999. Friday's Child: Or How Tej Singh Became Tecinkurajan, *Indian Economic and Social History Review* 36: 69–113.

Subramanian, Laksmi. 1996. *Indigenous Capital and Imperial Expansion*. Delhi: Oxford University Press.

Sutherland, John. 1988 [1837]. *Sketches of the Relations Subsisting between the British Government in India and Different Native States*. Jaipur: Publication Scheme.

Talbot, Cynthia. 1999. The *Prithviraj Raso* in the Making of Tod's *Annals*. A paper presented at the Annual Meeting on South Asia, University of Wisconsin at Madison, 15 October 1999.

Tambiah, S.J. 1976. *World Conqueror and World Renouncer: A Study of Buddhism and Polity in Thailand against a Historical Background*. Cambridge: Cambridge University Press.

——1985 [1977]. The Galactic Polity in Southeast Asia. In *Culture, Thought and Social Action: An Anthropological Perspective*, pp. 252–286. Cambridge, MA: Harvard University Press.

——1985. A Reformulation of Geertz's Conception of the Theatre State. In *Culture, Thought and Social Action: An Anthropological Perspective*, pp. 316–338. Cambridge, MA: Harvard University Press.

Taylor, Woodman. 1997. Picture Practice: Painting Programs, Manuscript Production, and Liturgical Performances at the Kotah Royal Palace. In *Gods, Kings, and Tigers: The Art of Kotah*, ed. Stuart Cary Welch, pp. 61–72. Munich: Prestel-Verlag.

——1997. Visual Culture in Performative Practice: The Aesthetics, Politics and Poetics of Visuality in Liturgical Practices of the Vallabha Sampradaya Hindu Community at Kota. PhD thesis, Department of Art, University of Chicago.

Tod, Lt. Col. James. 1829. *Annals and Antiquities of Rajast'han or, the Central and Western Rajpoot States of India*, Volume I. London.

——1832. *Annals and Antiquities of Rajast'han or, the Central and Western Rajpoot States of India*, Volume II. London.

Toomey, Paul M. 1990. Krishna's Consuming Passions: Food as Metaphor and Metonym for Emotion at Mount Govardhan. In *Divine Passions: The Social Construction of Emotion in India*, ed. O. M. Lynch, pp. 157–181. Berkeley: University of California Press.

Tripathi, G.C. 1978. *Navakalevara*: The Unique Ceremony of the 'Birth' and 'Death' of the 'Lord of the World'. In *The Cult of Jagannath and the Regional Tradition of Orissa*, eds A. Eschmann, H. Kulke, and G. C. Tripathi, pp. 223–264. Delhi: Manohar.

Vad, R. B. Ganesh Chimnaji, comp. 1911. *Selections from the Satara Rajas' and the Peshwas' Diaries*, Volume IX; *Peshwa Madhavrao I*, Volume I, ed. Kashinath Narayan Sane. Poona: The Deccan Vernacular Translation Society.

Vashishtha, Vijay Kumar. 1978. *Rajputana Agency, 1832–1858: A Study of British Relations with the States of Rajputana during the Period with Special Emphasis on the Role of Rajputana Agency*. Jaipur: Aalekh Publishers.

Vaudeville, Charlotte. 1980. The Govardhan Myth in Northern India. *Indo-Iranian Journal* 22: 1–45.

van der Veer, Peter. 1987. Taming the Ascetic: Devotionalism in a Hindu Monastic Order. *Man* (N.S.) 22: 680–695.

Viroli, Maurizio. 1995. *For Love of Country: An Essay on Patriotism and Nationalism*. Oxford: Oxford University Press.

Vishwanatha. 1996. *Shatrushalyacharitmahakavya*, ed. Bholashankar Vyas. Jodhpur: Rajasthan Prachyavidya Pratisthan.

Viswanathan, Gauri. 1990 [1989]. *Masks of Conquest: Literary Study and British Rule in India*. London: Faber and Faber.

Washbrook, David. 1990. South Asia, the World System, and World Capitalism. *Journal of Asian Studies* 49: 479–508.

Weber, Max. 1963. *The Sociology of Religion*. trans. Ephraim Fiscoff. Boston: Beacon Press.

Welch, Stuart Cary, ed. 1997. *Gods, Kings, and Tigers: The Art of Kotah*. Munich: Prestel-Verlag.

——1997. Kotah's Lively Patrons and Artists. In *Gods, Kings, and Tigers: the Art of Kotah*, ed. Stuart Cary Welch, pp. 15–38. Munich: Prestel-Verlag.

White, Hayden. 1973. *Metahistory: The Historical Imagination of Nineteenth Century Europe*. Baltimore: Johns Hopkins University Press.

Wink, André. 1986. *Land and Sovereignty in India: Agrarian Society and Politics under the Eighteenth-Century Maratha Svarajya*. Cambridge: Cambridge University Press.

Ziegler, Norman P. 1973. Action, Power and Service in Rajasthani Culture: A Social History of the Rajputs of Middle Period Rajasthan. PhD thesis, Department of History, University of Chicago.

——1976. The Seventeenth Century Chronicles of Marvar: A Study of the Evolution and Use of Oral Tradition in Western India. *History in Africa: A Journal of Method* 3: 127–153.

——1976. Marvari Historical Chronicles: Sources for the Social and Cultural History of Rajasthan. *Indian Economic and Social History Review* 13: 219–250.

——1978. Some Notes on Rajput Loyalties During the Mughal Period. In *Kingship and Authority in South Asia*, ed. J. F. Richards, pp. 215–251. Madison: University of Wisconsin South Asia Publication Series, No. 3.

Index

OTHER TITLES IN SERIES

1 C. A. Bayly, *Empire and Information: Intelligence Gathering and Social Communication in India, 1780–1880*
2 Ian Copland, *The Princes of India in the Endgame of Empire, 1917–1947*
3 Samita Sen, *Women and Labour in Late Colonial India: The Bengal Jute Industry*
4 Sumit Guha, *Environment and Ethnicity in India from the Thirteenth to the Twentieth Century*
5 Tirthankar Roy, *Traditional Industry in the Economy of Colonial India*
6 Claude Markovits, *The Global World of Indian Merchants, 1750–1947: Traders of Sind from Bukhara to Panama*
7 Prasannan Parthasarathi, *The Transition to a Colonial Economy in South India: Industry and Commerce in the Eighteenth-Century*
8 Nandini Gooptu, *The Politics of the Urban Poor in Early Twentieth-Century India*